Love Scopes

Hay House Titles of Related Interest

YOU CAN HEAL YOUR LIFE, *the movie,* starring Louise L. Hay & Friends
(available as a 1-DVD program and an expanded 2-DVD set)
Watch the trailer at: **www.LouiseHayMovie.com**

THE SHIFT, *the movie,*
starring Dr. Wayne W. Dyer
(available as a 1-DVD program and an expanded 2-DVD set)
Watch the trailer at: **www.DyerMovie.com**

♡

ASTROLOGY THROUGH A PSYCHIC'S EYES, by Sylvia Browne

BORN TO BE TOGETHER: *Love, Relationships, Astrology,
and the Soul,* by Terry Lamb

COSMIC ORDERING FOR BEGINNERS: *Everything You Need to Know
to Make It Work for You,* by Barbel Mohr and Clemens Maria Mohr

EASY ASTROLOGY ORACLE CARDS: *Unlock Your Inner Guide,* by Maya White

THE ULTIMATE ASTROLOGER: *A Simple Guide to Calculating and Interpreting
Birth Charts for Effective Application in Daily Life,* by Nicholas Campion

VEDIC ASTROLOGY SIMPLY PUT: *An Illustrated Guide
to the Astrology of Ancient India,* by William R. Levacy

ZODIAC BABY NAMES: *The Complete Book of Baby Names
Defined by Star Sign,* by Russell Grant (available November 2009)

♡

All of the above are available at your local bookstore,
or may be ordered by visiting:

Hay House USA: **www.hayhouse.com®**
Hay House Australia: **www.hayhouse.com.au**
Hay House UK: **www.hayhouse.co.uk**
Hay House South Africa: **www.hayhouse.co.za**
Hay House India: **www.hayhouse.co.in**

Love Scopes

What Astrology Knows about You
and the Ones You Love

MARK S. HUSSON

HAY HOUSE, INC.
Carlsbad, California • New York City
London • Sydney • Johannesburg
Vancouver • Hong Kong • New Delhi

Published and distributed in the United States by: Hay House, Inc.: www.hayhouse.
com • *Published and distributed in Australia by:* Hay House Australia Pty. Ltd.: www.
hayhouse.com.au • *Published and distributed in the United Kingdom by:* Hay House
UK, Ltd.: www.hayhouse.co.uk • *Published and distributed in the Republic of South
Africa by:* Hay House SA (Pty), Ltd.: www.hayhouse.co.za • *Distributed in Canada by:*
Raincoast: www.raincoast.com • *Published in India by:* Hay House Publishers India:
www.hayhouse.co.in

Editorial supervision: Jill Kramer • *Design:* Tricia Breidenthal

Library of Congress Cataloging-in-Publication Data

Husson, Mark S.
  LoveScopes : what astrology knows about you and the ones you love / Mark S.
Husson. -- 1st ed.
      p. cm.
  ISBN 978-1-4019-2004-3 (tradepaper)
  1. Astrology. 2. Love--Miscellanea. I. Title.
  BF1729.L6H87 2009
  133.5'48--dc22
                                    2008054855

ISBN: 978-1-4019-2004-3

12 11 10 09   5 4 3 2
1st edition, May 2009
2nd edition, May 2009

Printed in the United States of America

*To my family of psychics at **12Listen.com**
and **12Angel.com**, without whose
magic and support this book
would not have been possible.*

Editor's note: In order to avoid awkward "he/she," "him/her" references, the plural "they" or "their" is often used to refer to singular antecedents such as "mate" or "partner" even though this construction doesn't adhere to strict grammatical rules.

Contents

Leo

Virgo

Libra

Scorpio

Introduction

There's no doubt that the moon was in Libra when I decided to tackle a relationship book based on astrology. There's just no other logical explanation why I would take on such a Herculean task. Libra does, after all, represent the quest for perfect love. Had the moon been in Capricorn, pointing me toward daunting tasks, I might have been inclined to write a more technical work on astrology. Perhaps if the moon had been in Gemini, which raises meaningless information into an art form, I would have felt the urge to pen a book on astrological tidbits that no one knew (or cared about in the first place). But luckily, it was in Libra, the sign that transforms a typical dance of relationships into a finely choreographed ballet. Since I'm a Cancer who's *ruled* by the moon, I had to obey; I had no choice!

There's certainly a market for relationship books. The most popular Websites and magazines are dedicated to those tormented by Cupid's arrow. Advice columns are filled with thousands of letters asking "Does she love me?" or "Should I leave him?" or the proverbial "Are we soul mates?" and every other variation of the same theme: *Is my love lasting? What can I do to make sure we go the distance?*

I'm not a cynic about that feeling of bliss, or about mating in general, but our obsession with matters of the heart needs illumination, and I hope to shed some light by examining not only how the different signs relate, but *why.*

♡

LoveScopes uses astrology and its mythological references to uncover the patterns of love and romance, as well as the motives, inherent in each sign. When we apply the appropriate metaphors to

our love lives, we uncover huge possibilities for relating that might otherwise end up being irreconcilable differences in a divorce court.

Let's dissect the sign of Libra as an example, since that was the moon that kicked off this adventure. Libra's story can be found in many myths, but the one that most exemplifies its motive is that of Paris and the golden apple:

> Paris was an ultra-handsome mortal whose judgment was considered impeccable, so he was ordered by Zeus to judge what could be considered the first Ms. Universe pageant.
>
> [Here we see our first Libra characteristic: *impeccable judgment.*]
>
> Paris had to stop some serious squabbling between Hera, Athena, and Aphrodite, the glamour goddesses of their day. [Here are two more Libra characteristics: *dislike of conflict* and *love of looking good.*] These formidable *femmes of fate* argued incessantly as to which one of them was the most beautiful in all of Olympus. And since there was no *People* magazine then to dub the *Sexiest Goddess Alive,* Paris got the dubious honor of deciding.
>
> Zeus ordered Paris to offer a golden apple to the goddess whom he deemed the most beautiful in the hopes that all this celestial bickering would stop. First, Paris suggested slicing the apple three ways, but Zeus would have none of that—there could be only one winner. [Libra trait number four: *fairness.*]
>
> Zeus knew that if *he* chose between the feuding femmes, he'd be tortured by the two *losers* for eternity, so he wasn't about to do it. Privately, he would tell each of the goddesses that her beauty was unparalleled and incomparable. Zeus knew that by making Paris choose, he would not only get himself off the hook, but Paris would suffer at the hands of the goddesses only for the rest of his *mortal* lifetime—a small price to pay for the bragging rights associated with helping the ruler of Olympus. [Libra trait number five: *often confronted with difficult choices regarding love.*] Paris definitely lived in rough times.

Paris's dilemma is much like our own *American Idol*—or an *Olympian Idol,* as I like to call it. [Paris would be Simon Cowell, who also happens to be a Libra, with that charming smile and an insatiable appetite for destruction every time he berates the "talent" on *American Idol.*] So, Paris had the unenviable task of choosing the most beautiful goddess among the queenly but vindictive Hera; the wise, cunning, and creative Athena; and the stunningly gorgeous Aphrodite.

Make no mistake about it: Paris knew who the hottest goddess of the day was, but if he was to die at the hands of the losers anyway, he might as well let them bribe him. So he proceeded to allow the three "contestants" to plead their cases.

Each goddess made her promise to him. Hera offered unlimited wealth and Athena offered untold power, but Paris saw those prizes as too much trouble. [Libra trait number six: *dislike of being tied to too much responsibility.*] Then Aphrodite presented him with the prize that won his heart: the hand in marriage of the most beautiful woman in all the land, Helen of Troy. For that, Aphrodite was awarded the golden apple.

Paris chose the goddess who had offered him what he wanted most, which was love. [Libra trait number seven: *deep desire for love.*] He was given that single motive, which made his decision easy. [Libra trait number eight: *indecision as a result of the inability to determine which choice serves best.*] Well, the other two goddesses trudged off arm in arm to plot his destruction, but I'll save that story for another time. [This illustrates one last Libra trait: *often caused considerable difficulty by their choices in love.*]

It's easy for others to tell you that you've made a bad choice when it comes to love, but there's nothing worse than someone pointing out a problem without an accompanying solution. Typical astrology books predict the demise of your relationship due to your particular

combination of signs, but they offer little in the way of a solution. So what should you do when you see your sign's stereotypical worst trait emerging?

The answer is simple: *observe!* By kicking in your inner observer, you begin a very important process of separation. You go from *being* the sign, to *watching* yourself being the sign. It may seem like a subtle distinction, but the latter demands an answer to the question "*Who* is watching?" The difference is much like that of an eagle's perspective versus a mouse's. Generally speaking, the mouse can look at minute details, but that can lead to overanalysis. The eagle can soar high above the earth where everything looks the same size, allowing it to keep a broader perspective. The eagle's vantage point is more helpful in this case, because it raises you above the details and lets you look at yourself as part of the whole picture. This is a very important key in allowing you to fully embrace who you are.

As you become the observer of your own life, phrases like "I have intimacy issues" rapidly become nonsensical judgments. Certainly, the way you love may be an issue for someone *else,* but chances are good that it works just fine for *you.* The observer helps you find the "So what?" in the "What's so." Astrology gives you an eagle's perspective so you can see yourself as belonging to something bigger, a part of a grander flow that functions in perfect unison with the universe.

Destination: LoveScopes

So what does astrology really have to do with *love?* And what exactly is a *LoveScope?*

If astrology can shine a little light of understanding on the people we choose to love, or help us map out the possible difficulties we may encounter in our relationships with them, then it's a worthwhile pursuit.

In fact, anything that improves your relationship with the person who shares (or hogs) your pillow is worthwhile. Astrology's wisdom is not only cheaper than years of therapy, it's faster, too. You can "LoveScope" yourself today—right *now,* in fact—and instantly find

profound truths about matters of the heart. It makes no difference if you're currently on love's lonely highway, with no one on your relationship horizon, or if you're in a committed, two-way relationship with its inevitable road bumps. Maybe you've experienced the heartbreak of a drive-by romance and wonder how you can avoid those destructive detours again. Or you might even have a heart that aches from a deeper type of loss.

Your LoveScope can shed the light you desire.

So what *is* a LoveScope? If a horoscope defines your personal characteristics based on your astrological sign, then a LoveScope does so for your relationship based on your signs in love. By taking a look at two of them from astrology's perspective, we can analyze an entire relationship, including levels of passion, friendship, lifestyle compatibility, emotional land mines, and commitment. Your LoveScope score will help you identify what's working and what *needs* work on your part and as a couple.

It's my hope that *LoveScopes* will help make your journey on the freeway of love a smooth one. Think of this book as your own portable GPS for romance!

For years I watched people come into my New Age store and run straight to the relationship book section, feverishly looking for the answer that would tell them if love was possible between their astrological sign and that of their new love. Or perhaps there was some answer yet unseen, a *key* they could pull from the pages that might unlock their currently exiled love.

As I watched them, I righteously protested that they couldn't find their answers in an astrology book because it was just too general. "To really understand someone, you need their entire birth chart," I'd insist. And that was correct; a complete and accurate assessment of their relationship could only be done with the dates, times, and places of birth of both parties. People in pain (or who are questioning) don't want to wait for the "proper protocol"; they want something to help them make the hurt or questions go away.

It's like going to the doctor with a bleeding finger only to have the nurse insist that you fill out the six-page admission form before they will treat you. What if they first staunched the wound and treated the pain and *then* let you relax and do the paperwork? It just seems like a smarter way to do it.

That's another reason why I wrote *LoveScopes:* I want to provide a quick way to stop the "bleeding" of your heart until you can collect your wits about you and apply them to your situation.

Why Astrology?

I'm an astrologer. I love the symbolic map created when we each take our first breath at birth. It's a map of planets and myths and metaphors that makes such perfect sense to me that it seems criminal that modern psychological institutions won't at least have a look at it. In fact, the psychologists who *do* look become my astrology clients, and eventually students of this field themselves.

Psychiatrist Carl Jung's embrace of astrology is well known, but has been ignored by mainstream psycho-professionals. Even so, his perspective on astrology was brilliant. Jung believed that we harbor inside us a *shadow,* or a dark judgment about ourselves, that is so difficult to see that we have to "project" it out into the world and onto the people in it, and then convince ourselves that it belongs to *them.* This shadow remains a source of great pain until we realize that it dwells *within* us.

That's a heavy chunk of words, I know, but stick with me here. Jung also believed that our quest for fulfillment depends on our ability to reclaim our shadow and actually embrace it. He was clear that, if we accept the idea of projection, we'll begin to realize that what we see outside of us belongs to *us;* our perceptions are formed based on our own personal upbringing, experiences, and beliefs. That's why no two of us will ever have exactly the same experience.

What does this have to do with love? Oh, just about everything.

The most personal access we each have to our own shadow is through our relationships. Nowhere else will there be such a mainline to it than through someone we love. Therein lie the potential answers to the mysteries of ourselves; we just haven't realized it yet. We aren't driven to the point of insanity over someone we're enamored of because we *know* we're chasing some displaced dark side of ourselves. But as we become aware of our part in our dramas, we come to a greater understanding of our relationships and how they serve us.

Let's start with the assumption that everything we encounter is invited by some part of us—one that is connected to a perfect design. It would make sense to conclude, then, that every relationship we've had or *will* have is no coincidence, but rather part of a very personal process of growth. In a way, we could look at our relationships as symbols placed before us that hold a key to our happiness. To be clear, the other person is *not* holding that key. Instead, it lies in our ability to interpret *why* we brought him or her into our life.

LoveScopes is the key that gives you the ability to interpret this "why."

Why Love?

It might be easier *not* to figure this love stuff out, but rather just sit at home and watch *Buffy* reruns. However, since true happiness can only be gained by a complete acceptance of who we are, and since *that* can only be realized by acknowledging and reclaiming the pieces of ourselves that we project onto other people, we would be doing ourselves a huge injustice not to allow ourselves the gift of relationships. And no amount of unrequited-love TV can serve as a replacement.

The only way to *really* figure all this out is to dive in and follow your heart. It will help unfold the road map to that deep internal place where your most intense emotions dwell.

I call that map your *LoveScope.*

— **Mark**

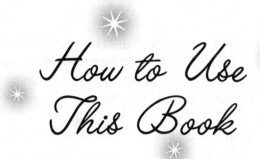

How to Use This Book

I want this book to be the metaphorical impetus that stimulates you to work within the context of your own relationship. It's not meant to be treated as the final verdict, so resist the temptation to judge and sentence yourself—or those you love.

My hope is that these pages will inspire you to fly above your current partnership and become the observer. I believe that whenever you can be a witness to your own life, it's a lot easier to view the positives and the negatives. Why? Because suddenly you're not taking everything so personally, and you become a part of the bigger order of things, allowing yourself to see your situation with humor and openness. Use this book as a general guide that can take you into complex and sometimes painful territory, but with flickers of light and splashes of humor.

LoveScopes is broken down by astrological sign. You can use the Contents pages to find your sign or your partner's. As you look over Part II, you'll notice that the Zodiac-sign combinations listed per section will get progressively shorter. The reason is that the coupling of any two signs might occur earlier on. If you're a Pisces—the last sign of the Zodiac—you'll need to find in the Contents where the combination of your sign and your mate's is first introduced. For example, Aries and Pisces will show up where Aries is listed first since that sign appears earlier in the Zodiac.

Within this book, you'll find advice, wisdom, humor, and just about everything you can imagine about each specific sign. I've mapped out why you would pick someone as a partner, how to please

that person, and even how to lose him or her. (It's not that I *want* you to lose the one you love, but it's helpful to read how it can happen.) These sections may show you that something you're doing is harming your significant other so you can then be aware of and adjust certain behaviors.

Part I is a great overview of how each sign interacts in different relationships, so it's also extremely helpful to people who are exploring potential lovers. The science of astrology requires some thought on your part; it's never just black and white. For instance, if you're a neat freak, like many Virgos, would you be most compatible with another such person—say, an Aquarius? Would you find passion . . . or just fight over who used the last of the Windex? Or are you better off with a sloppier sign (Pisces, for example)? It's hard to say. Straightening up after a Pisces would likely make a more dramatic difference and could be more rewarding, but with Aquarius, there would be way less work to do.

Your personal makeup will determine your answer.

If you're someone who longs for everlasting loyalty, you might want to be with a Taurus. If you're not so into commitment in the first place, you may be better suited for someone who is a little looser about it (Gemini, I'm calling you out!). The answer always lies in your birth chart, but if that's not available, I've got you covered here.

I've also included some fun and informational sidebars that help you delve a little deeper into different topics. I think love should also include joy and humor, so there will be plenty of smiles as I offer you direction on keeping the romance alive with that Aries, Libra, Gemini, or whomever in your life.

This book gives you a semi-comprehensive compatibility analysis for each sign as well as for the union itself.

Let's say you're an Aries dating a Cancer, or a Taurus dating a Leo. I've provided you with all the pertinent facts you'll need for an immediate evaluation. For each pairing, I'll give you an actual numeric LoveScope for these variables. Ratings are based on a 1–10 scale. They're not a measurement of success or failure, but are an easy way to see where your challenges are as a couple. If you work on the areas where you have problems, then you can significantly increase your chances of a successful relationship together.

Your LoveScope is your base number, and is like a starting point or your foundation. What you bring to the relationship can raise the number or lower it—that's ultimately up to you. The LoveScope is not meant as a final decree, but as a quick way to determine how much effort it will take for you to make it as a couple in the long run.

Let me strongly suggest that you look up some of the past loves in your life by their signs in order to gain a better understanding of why things may have ended. It doesn't serve you to dwell on what's over and done with, but reading your past LoveScopes might provide you with some long-needed closure and insight.

In the end, I don't believe that you should target "easy" relationships and thumb through the book to find the signs that are an obvious fit. My wish is that you instead find meaning in all of your relationships, even if it takes some work. Believe me, it will be worth it. The things that require effort have the most meaning, and the most reward.

The Elements and the Modalities

Before we begin, it's helpful to go through a quick astrological primer on the *motives* (also known as *elements*) and the *modes* (also known as *modalities*) of all the signs because they can help provide added wisdom that goes to the heart of each one.

The Motives

Each sign carries a desire to activate an effect on its environment: some want to inspire, others want to create safety, and so on. If you know what motivates a sign, you can relate far more deeply because you not only better understand the person who belongs to it, but your loved one feels better understood, and that makes for a closer bond. Let's look at some of the motives below, according to their element (and remember that what they want to "give" is also what they want to "feel" within themselves):

Fire signs: Aries, Leo, and Sagittarius. The motives of Fire signs are to provide inspiration, energy, leaps of faith, and spirituality.

Earth signs: Taurus, Virgo, and Capricorn. The motives of Earth signs are to provide stability, material security, and a feeling of safety (sure-footedness).

Air signs: Gemini, Libra, and Aquarius. The motives of Air signs are to provide communication, intellectual stimulation, and social connection.

Water signs: Cancer, Scorpio, and Pisces. The motives of Water signs are to provide nurturance, sensitivity, and emotional expression.

The Modes

The modes explain *how* each motive is achieved. Is the sign aggressive or pushy? Or is it stable until it's time to strike? The modes relate to the three different phases of a season: the Beginning (also known as *Cardinal*), the Middle (also known as *Fixed*), and the End (also known as *Mutable*). Let's take a closer look at how these energies work:

Cardinal: These are signs that introduce each new season, including Aries (spring), Cancer (summer), Libra (autumn), and Capricorn (winter). Their mode of expressing their elements is by *assertion of their will.*

Fixed: These signs symbolize stabilization and are represented by the middle of each season. They include Taurus, Leo, Scorpio, and Aquarius. Their mode of expressing their elements is through *persistence.*

Mutable: These are the signs that prepare the seasons for change, including Gemini, Virgo, Sagittarius, and Pisces. Their mode of expressing their elements is through *adaptability.*

PART I

The Signs

Introduction to Part I

Part I is an introduction to the signs of the Zodiac, but with a twist. It's based on the mythology that actually helped sculpt the original characteristics of each sign. For example, did you know that Leo natives *don't* have big egos? It often just looks that way because they're trying to make up for the fact that as children they didn't get approval from their fathers. It's in the myth of Perceval (Parsifal) and the Holy Grail.

This first part of this book will help clarify the motives for each sign, just before they're paired off in Part II. By reading these pages, you'll find that it will really start making sense that someone who needs approval may not do very well with someone who's a critic— or maybe that's perfect for where the person is at that point in time. This section should be a fun exploration that isn't carved in stone, and it can be used as a guide that will give you a basic understanding of each sign's behaviors in a relationship.

Aries

Motive: To inspire (Fire)
Mode: Assertion (Cardinal)
Symbol: The Ram

The Myth in 30 Seconds: Jason and the Argonauts

When he was an infant, Jason's rightful inheritance to the throne was usurped by a jealous uncle. Baby Jason was secretly smuggled out of the country, where he was raised to be a warrior. As a man, he came back to reclaim what was rightfully his, while his uncle—sensing the young warrior's ability to destroy him—pretended to be defeated so that his life would be spared. Jason's uncle told him that a curse was placed upon his kingdom that could only be removed by the retrieval of the Golden Fleece, knowing that it would almost certainly

result in his nephew's death. Jason, believing the lie, set sail to find the Fleece with the help of the Argonauts and a couple of goddesses. He retrieved it, gained a wife in the process, and ultimately, won the final battle for his throne.

Aries Overview

Aries are born with the strength and mind-set of a warrior. They're the kind of warrior of long ago: fighters who took pride in their power and willingness to defend those they loved. What Aries echo from their mythos (legend) is a sense of inadequacy—a belief they inherited from a disapproving paternal figure (like Jason's uncle in the myth). As a result, these underappreciated warriors tend to create an external "father" to challenge them. This could be a parent, a teacher, or others in authority who may or may not consciously realize that they're provoking the Aries, but nevertheless incite the Rams' need to prove themselves. Aries assume that if they can demonstrate their worth to an external authority, then they can relax and enjoy the bounty symbolized by the Golden Fleece. It's a form of "I'll be happy when . . ." The only problem is that "when" never comes. Happiness is ultimately the acceptance of what is, of what they have right now.

Aries LoveScoop

Aries bring the baggage of having to prove themselves into their relationships. It's not as if they're so weak and unsure that they need to impress you with their power; rather, they just have to know that they're perceived as strong and fit—and they'll need more than your words to internalize those feelings.

Aries must prove their worth on a daily basis, and as it is for any warrior, that's determined by battles won and lives saved. If they can't get their daily quota of challenges from the outside world, they'll begin to create them with you or whoever is closest. It could start by finding fault with you for something you didn't do, and depending on how you respond, it may escalate into a tirade about their complete disappointment in something else. Whatever form the confrontation takes, it's designed to goad you into battle.

Naturally, Aries want their partners to be strong and daring—strong enough to stand up to them and daring enough to stop them when they're charging full speed ahead. But there's a side to Aries in love that needs to measure up. In a relationship, you won't be able to stop the voice inside of them that constantly asks, "Am I worthy?"

Realize that an Aries partner is always in motion—internally and externally. Some signs might find this constant movement exciting, and others will deem it exhausting. Either way, Aries won't care because they're learning to be what they authentically are, without asking you to alter yourself. Sometimes people born under this sign appear harsh and nagging, and at other times open and accepting, but they never give you much credit for the things you do. They assume that you're doing exactly what you want to be doing—just as they are.

Aries Recap

- Must prove themselves
- Love a battle
- Tend to get help when needed
- Champion the underdog
- Must overthrow authority

What Repels an Aries

- Rules
- Appointments
- Working for someone
- Instructions
- The common cold

What Compels an Aries

- Challenges
- Freedom
- Sunshine
- Sports
- Robust debate

Taurus

Motive: To master the physical world (Earth)
Mode: Persistence (Fixed)
Symbol: The Bull

The Myth in 30 Seconds: King Minos and the Bull

King Minos persuaded Poseidon to send him a bull as a symbol of Minos's power and esteem. He promised to sacrifice it as a gesture of appreciation once everyone saw how powerful he was as a ruler. The king received the bull and got his due respect, but rather than sacrificing it, he kept it and tried to give Poseidon a weak imitation. Angered by this, the god put a spell on Minos's wife that made her have lustful feelings for the bull—whom she mated with, giving birth to an evil Minotaur. This shamed Minos for the rest of his days.

Taurus Overview

King Minos is a dramatic representation of the Taurus motive associating possessions with power. He so desperately believed that the bull would protect him by providing the security of wealth, and became so blinded by his desire to "own," that he didn't think rationally—he convinced himself that he could fool a god. Lack of thinking and a powerful desire are demonstrated throughout the life of the Taurus native.

Taureans are also born with an intense sensuality. Even as infants, they delight in hanging out in their bodies and observing the world. Most develop the reflective function much later than other people because they get all the information they need from their physical experience; they learn by doing, not by thinking. At some point, most parents grow worried that their Taurus child is developing too slowly and begin to add the element of agitation, hoping to move their son or daughter into reacting faster when in fact all they're doing is creating unnecessary anxiety.

As adults, Taureans become quite opinionated about their personal possessions. They often come to realize that *things* can make them feel secure, and the higher the quality of their stuff, the more secure they feel.

If they aren't connoisseurs in the kitchen, they'll still have strong opinions about food. Many of the finest chefs in the world are of this sign or have strong Taurus placements in their charts.

The body type of the native of this sign is usually strong, with a large bone structure and pronounced neck (think Audrey Hepburn or Cher), but every now and then you meet one who is fragile and weak. The indication is that this Bull hasn't learned to be guided by his or her body and has turned to the mind for support, which is usually a survival response from childhood. An overtalkative Taurus has learned somewhere that it's better to be active than receptive, taking a more difficult route to finding happiness.

Taurus LoveScoop

Now that you understand you're dealing with an Earth sign that admires quality objects and thrives on appreciation, there are some important things to keep in mind. No matter how close you feel to your Taurus partner or how much on the same page you seem, your Bull won't agree with you about anything without first letting it sink in.

Taureans are truly unbendable on this point because it's *not* a point to them . . . it's a way of life. This doesn't mean that they don't love you or can't agree with you, but they can only move at their own pace. If you aren't fully prepared for this, it can frustrate you. On the other hand, if you're patient, you may discover what *they* already know, which is that they have a foolproof system built right into their bodies. Give them a massage or insist that they take a long hot bath to show them that you understand their carnal needs. Your reward will be a lifelong companion who can offer security, guidance, and mounds of reciprocal appreciation that few others can match.

Taureans' Fixed mode means that they like their routines and knowing that there are no surprises (except for the occasional birthday party or new car sent over as a gift). In a fight, don't harp; let things come to a gentle conclusion, allowing your Taurus to approach you in time. Remember, they are *Fixed Earth,* and it may take a while for them to let go of their anger, but it *will* happen. On some deeper level, closer to their wound is a little child waiting for you to be disappointed in them. Trust will come in time, and when it does, you'll find that this is among the most loyal signs of the Zodiac.

Taurus Recap

- Must learn to tame the bull of desire
- Tend to be hedonistic (pleasure seeking)
- Carry a deep insecurity about being smart enough
- Say no as a way to gain more time
- Are gifted in the use of flattery and seduction

What Repels a Taurus

- Fake leather
- Fast food
- Fast talkers
- Fast sex
- Frugal friends

What Compels a Taurus

- Expensive food
- Flattery
- Foot massages
- Scarves
- Wiggle room
- Favorite chairs
- Your credit card
- Instructions
- Complete control
- Comfortable shoes

Gemini

Motive: To communicate (Air)
Mode: Adaptability (Mutable)
Symbol: The Twins

The Myth in 30 Seconds: Castor and Pollux

Twins of different fathers, Castor, a mortal, and Pollux, an immortal (son of Zeus), were close and fought many battles together. Castor was fatally wounded in the last one and lay dying. Zeus gave Pollux a choice: to spend all his time on Mount Olympus without Castor, or to divide his immortality and give half to Castor. He chose the division, enabling his brother to live with him for half of the day on Olympus and the other half in Hades. These two are the brightest stars in the Gemini constellation.

13

Gemini Overview

Within the wit and wisdom of the Gemini is the division of self. One side sees life as full of grand possibilities in the connection with others, and the other sees it as full of personal events that can't be shared.

The separation of our emotions from our thoughts is a common metaphor that exists in each of us. We usually create a distinction between our *idea* of who we are and our experience of who we *actually* are in life, and this split is clear in all Geminis. They have a part that they just love (the mental, clear, light, easy side—considered the one that came from a god), and another that they aren't so accepting of (the heavier, more distrusting, cautious, easily hurt side—said to be the one that came from a mortal). The eventual goal is to get these two separate components to spend time together so that they bring balance to their extreme world: to metaphorically bring the light into the dark and a bit of the dark to the light. If they can bring these two outlooks closer to each other, it will give more purpose to their seemingly trivial pursuits and more hope to their bouts of depression. It's a worthy goal that isn't so easy to accomplish; however, as long as Geminis understand the concept of this split and can create an inner observer, the battle is already won.

Gemini LoveScoop

There's one important fact to consider when involved with these airy essences: they absolutely abhor a cage. They're composed of Mutable (flexible) Air (thoughts), and their ideas are moving around in their heads at the speed of light. Geminis need to be stimulated at all times—whether it's by you, the television, a book, or the telephone; they're always in mental motion.

Take a second and reach out to grab the air around you and then look in the palm of your hand to see what you "caught." Of course air can't be grabbed like a beer; it must *flow*. But if you pull your hand toward you, that creates a breeze that flows right *to* you.

That's how it is with Geminis: they flow to you, then away, then back, continuing in this pattern. They're currents that are constantly moving and changing—even when they're still, their minds are turned on. As Kahlil Gibran so eloquently put it, "And let the winds of the heavens dance between you."

Geminis forget things of an emotional nature rather quickly. They don't remember that you had a great chat the night before and rush home to continue it; they enjoyed it while it was happening. Those of this sign love to be in a relationship and will likely have many friends—and probably flirt with all of them! Like most people, they have feelings that can be hurt easily if you cut the communication lines with them. Geminis' intents will always be clear, and there's a tendency for them to tell you what you need to hear, especially if they feel that they're in "hot water." They're good with words, so use the adage "Actions speak louder than words" when dealing with them.

Gemini Recap

- Must learn to bridge the mental and emotional parts of self
- Feel an extreme sense of elation (immortal side)
- Feel extreme depression (mortal side)
- Often project the dark side onto a situation
- Are easily bored—constantly searching

What Repels a Gemini

- Talking about their feelings
- Commitments
- Intense emotion
- Isolation
- Long stories

What Compels a Gemini

- Gadgets
- Learning something new
- Conversation
- Books
- Language

Cancer

(JUNE 22–JULY 22)

Motive: To nurture (Water)
Mode: Assertion (Cardinal)
Symbol: The Crab

The Myth in 30 Seconds: Achilles' Heel

Achilles was born to the goddess Thetis and a mortal father, Peleus. The couple had seven children, but Thetis didn't want them to be cursed with Peleus's mortal genes, so she proceeded to burn six of them over an open flame to rid them of their flesh. (Myths should have a movie-rating system on them!) When it came to the last son, Achilles, her husband stopped her just in time by grabbing him by his ankles, which was the only part of his body that remained mortal—thus the term *Achilles' heel* came to mean a person's weak spot.

Achilles was called to war and was followed by his mother, who fed him, doted on him, and insisted that he dress in women's clothing. The only time the sulking Achilles showed any enthusiasm was when he saw his friend being killed, which was enough to rouse him from his tent where he spent most of the time with his mom.

Cancer Overview

Thetis wanted nothing but godliness for her children and was willing to kill them in the name of their highest good. This shows how Cancers often believe that they're doing the best thing for the ones they love even if it's painful for everyone involved. Cancers also have high expectations of themselves when it comes to their children: the urban myth of the mother who lifted the car with one hand to save her child is the perfect archetype for the Cancer native, male or female. There's an instinct to build a family, whether it's biological or made up of current friends. You'll hear those of this sign use phrases such as "our people" or "our group," which is their way of acknowledging the family they've created. Their home is vital for their sense of safety and comfort.

This is a Cardinal sign, and you'll find that most Cancers act out the matriarchal energy of the family. Both men and women reflect this quality, as there's an emotional strength running through them that establishes an instant authority.

All Cancers must come to a resolution with respect to their mothers. Some learn to embrace the woman who gave them life, and others learn to leave her, but this is a big issue that won't just walk away without some direct and willing attention.

Those born under this sign are ruled by the moon and therefore appear constantly fluctuating in their moods; this is an issue that's usually resolved by addressing some sort of insecurity.

Cancer LoveScoop

Cancers take their relationships seriously. On the negative side, they may appear controlling and domineering. They think they know what's best for you in everything from deciding that you need to wear a scarf and gloves to forbidding you from buying something you really want. They aren't just trying to be in charge of you—they're trying to control your perception of them as caring and supportive. This behavior occurs because they want to feel needed, perhaps as insurance to cover their deep insecurities. Cancers believe that the people in their lives are particularly special, and they'll do whatever it takes to elevate their status. It's really not about you, though; it's about their need to see you act out *their* own inner gifts. This is very much like a stage mom who wants her child to succeed where she failed.

All in all, you could thoroughly enjoy the warmth that Cancers engender and fuel it with a speck of appreciation. It will tide them over until they find something from their own bounty of creativity that's waiting to be acknowledged.

Cancer Recap

- Must resolve their "mother" issues
- Nurture because they believe they know the greatness within you
- Can control the emotional tone of the environment
- Always have some kind of family
- Are moody

What Repels a Cancer

- Lack of appreciation
- Child abuse
- Camping without amenities

- Being embarrassed
- People who live solely by logic

What Compels a Cancer

- Friends in need
- Children
- Money in the bank
- Humor
- Good dead bolts

Leo

- -

(JULY 23–AUGUST 22)

Motive: To empower (Fire)
Mode: Persistence (Fixed)
Symbol: The Lion

The Myth in 30 Seconds: Perceval and the Holy Grail

Perceval (also known as Parcifal) had a vision at an early age: he saw a cup containing the elixir of life—the Holy Grail—and observed a man giving it to him. This was significant because his father was very ill, so he thought it was his duty to find it. He immediately knew that he had to leave. He walked out on his mother, who begged him not to go, and she died of grief shortly after he left. After many adventures—not all of them good—Perceval found the place where the Grail was hidden, but he wasn't mature enough to ask the question that would

reveal it to him. So he went off and experienced more adventures so that he could go back and ask, "For whom does the Grail serve?" There were many distractions on his journey, including the death of his father, but finally he was given the guidance to find the Grail in a dream, and with it, his grandfather.

Leo Overview

Leos start life with a grand vision of spirituality, a sense that they're divinely chosen. As they mature, they lose much of the memory of that dream. They're usually in a home with a sick or absent father, so they venture away from the nest to reclaim what they feel is missing. It's important to clarify that the actual father may have been an amazing man, but Leos enter the world with a propensity to see him as not enough—lacking in encouragement, support, or strength—and as a result, they set off to find this paternal feeling that they long for, not yet realizing that it's deep within *them*.

Everything outside of Leo natives becomes a potential dad: an audience who loves them, a mate who dotes on them, or a co-worker who looks forward to seeing them. Leos respond to the outside world in an attempt to find acceptance because they have none on the inside. To us it looks like arrogance because Leos can appear self-absorbed, never saying thanks, expecting to be nurtured, and going into full pout mode if they don't get what they want. But what's really going on is the search for admiration, love, and the kind of support they didn't experience; and it may take a lifetime for them to realize that the appreciation they so desperately want must come from within. Sooner or later, they're going to have to face a disapproving world and still have something inside them that reaffirms that they're beautiful just the way they are. In other words, the father within must come forward.

Leos are a most generous sign, with that charismatic fire energy that's very benevolent and caring. They often have the loudest, most contagious laugh that sounds like it's coming from a jolly king.

Leo LoveScoop

Fixed signs (Leo, Aquarius, Scorpio, and Taurus) are inherently loyal. Because they're Fixed, they do nothing fast—including relationships. It takes Leos a while to let you in, but once you're accepted, they're always happy to see you. It's an instant reassurance to them that you approve. Remember: Leos love drama, and most of your time together will be passionate. Whether it's flowers they bring you, a restaurant they suggest, or the stories they tell you . . . the happier they are, the more the excitement will fly. The purpose of drama is to entertain, and they do this very well.

These Lions' Fixed natures make them ferociously committed and possessive, and they'll do anything to protect their pride and all its members. They aren't afraid to take in a spontaneous movie and delight in cooking an outrageous feast for the whole family. They tend to be extremely proud of those close to them, even though they often forget to tell these people so directly. Remember that flattery is gold, so don't falsely compliment them, because that will be perceived as lying and they'll catch you—they're built for it! When your Leo gets hurt, you can expect a cold spell for a while; and when they're angry, it's loud and scary, but over fast.

Leo Recap

- Must resolve their "father" issues
- Have an early spiritual experience
- Take great pride in what they do
- Tend to seek constant approval
- Can have outbursts of great generosity

What Repels a Leo

- Public humiliation
- Disapproval

- Talking about yourself
- Complaining
- Cloudy days

What Compels a Leo

- Adoration
- Optimism
- A good listener
- Gambling
- Being romantic

Virgo

(AUGUST 23–SEPTEMBER 22)

Motive: To serve (Earth)
Mode: Adaptability (Mutable)
Symbol: The Virgin

The Myth in 30 Seconds: Astraea

Astraea, the star-maiden, was a goddess of justice. She lived on Earth in the golden age of humankind. During this period there was great harmony and peace, and the gods and goddesses roamed Earth's accepting plains more freely. However, as humanity grew ugly—with its competition, stealing, wars, and members' disregard for one another—the immortals abandoned Earth, except for Astraea, who tried to help. She was the last to leave, and as each day grew darker with greed, she eventually took up residence among the stars, where she was transformed into the constellation Virgo.

Virgo Overview

Within this little story is the picture of someone who wanted to be of service, to live in the midst of perfection, and who felt the frustration of caring more for others than they cared about themselves. Eventually, she left to be alone, feeling that she somehow failed. The dear heart of Virgo is often plagued with profound self-criticism. The curse of finding the flaw in everything is feeling obliged to fix it.

This "flaw finder" isn't limited to the world outside of Virgos, because it's even worse when aimed at themselves. The inner critic is evidenced in what appears to be a cynicism about life. You can almost feel their caution as they navigate a world that—on a soul level—they left, hurt and disgusted, a long time ago.

To most of us, crime, disease, and cruelty are things that exist in all walks of life. But to Virgos, they're part of the flaw, and people of this sign can't let go of that fact. It's one of their greatest gifts but also one of their most unfortunate curses.

It seems ridiculous to them to eat in a place where you can't see the kitchen, to enter a building where the air-conditioning can transport a germ to every nook and cranny, or to spend hours preparing the self to enter the world only to find that when you get to your destination, your clothes are wrinkled and your hair is a mess. Frugality is born of this very thought.

The self-torture that drives Virgos is the desire for perfection, and this is fueled by a tireless mind seeking a way to stop. The heart of the Virgo dilemma is that they're trying to find the rules for living in a world that's random and chaotic. They're constantly seeking the simplicity of the golden days by trying to fix everything that's wrong with the current moment.

Virgo LoveScoop

Some would say that the phrase "Virgo relationship" is an oxymoron. It's true that Virgos love their time alone and could likely spend the extent of their days on Earth cloistered in their homes because that's not a painful thing for them. There are no messes (save their own) to clean up, and once the place is put in order, it stays that way. Although Virgos pay much lip service to living by themselves, it's important to remember the duality that exists within them: for every stance on an argument they take, there's another side of them saying the opposite.

So yes, there *is* a side to this sign that loves companionship and relating to others. Virgos are generous with their time in a relationship, initially focusing most of their attention on their partners and demonstrating strength as the support people. As time goes on, they start to withdraw into their world of solitude, but begin feeling guilty about this, so they often find something wrong with their partners until they get upset enough to withdraw—only now feeling less to blame for it. This in-and-out cycle is not uncommon for all of the Mutable signs (Gemini, Virgo, Sagittarius, and Pisces), and is usually just accepted as an aspect of their personality.

Virgo Recap

- Love their alone time
- Have a knack with small animals and stray people
- Have a critical eye, but don't like criticism
- Hate germs
- Are frugal

What Repels a Virgo

- Public displays of affection
- Poor hygiene
- Impropriety
- Typos
- Roommates

What Compels a Virgo

- Fresh paper cups
- Pets
- Lint brushes
- Hand sanitizers
- Breath mints

Libra

(SEPTEMBER 23–OCTOBER 23)

Motive: To relate (Air)
Mode: Assertion (Cardinal)
Symbol: The Scales

The Myth in 30 Seconds: Paris and the Golden Apple

Paris was asked to judge the fairest goddess on Mount Olympus and present her with a golden apple; in doing so, he ultimately found love. (This myth and its meaning is covered in detail starting on page x of the Introduction to this book.)

Libra Overview

Libra is the only sign on the Zodiac wheel that's represented by an inanimate object: the Scales. This sign brings in the season of autumn, which is what makes it a member of the Cardinal family. The element it carries is Air, but this doesn't mean flighty or spacey. On the contrary, signs with this motive carry the gift of the mind and have the ability to understand and see life objectively—without emotional influence. Perhaps this is one of Libra's greatest gifts, as represented by the inanimate quality of the Scales: the ability to judge without prejudice and with absolute impartiality.

Libras have a fascination with human beings, and this is common to all Air signs. People are complex—made up of myriad mysteries—and nothing is more captivating to those of this sign than an opportunity to dive into someone's inner world without having to get too involved. With an unbiased eye, Libras can find the good in anyone; and when they focus on what's remarkable about someone, then that part of the person seems to be drawn out.

There are a lot of identifying marks that give away those born under this Venus-ruled sign: they often have dimples, a great smile, and inner and outer beauty—all of which make them safe for most people to approach. Libras seem to love interactions, parties, or gatherings of any kind where they're free to engage in multiple conversations. Being Air, they don't like things to get heavy or ugly, preferring pleasant exchanges ranging in subject matter from the weather to current fashions. The motive is to engage you, explore who you are, and get you to exchange any thoughts or ideas with them. As long as Libras are allowed to feel connected, they're happy.

Libra LoveScoop

Libras need relationships, and if you've chosen to be involved with one, then you've passed the first two tests: you've shown independence (they need the challenge of getting to know you) as well as attractiveness (you must fulfill some external beauty requirements).

These social beings love to stir up conversations and keep a schedule of upcoming activities they'll be attending. And *you'll* most likely be required to attend as well: they love people and showing off their "goods," their partners among them! Although the world will see their charm, they'll save some of the more colorful parts of themselves for your eyes as they become comfortable with you. The good *and* bad news is that you'll be trusted to see the less attractive parts of *them*.

At home, your Libra partner will let their hair down and talk more honestly with you than anyone else. If the phone rings as things start getting a bit heated in one of your discussions, they can turn on their charming Libra voice and offer the caller no indication that anything is wrong . . . without blinking an eye.

If you need your Libra to side with you, there's no greater or more effective tool than reverse psychology. Remember that your Libra is fair and must tilt the scales in the direction of balance, so if you're explaining why you're right, they will, with sheer brilliance, explain why you're *wrong.*

Libra Recap

- Love the pursuit of relationships
- Have an impeccable eye for beauty
- Are horrible at choosing, unless the gain for them is obvious
- Love feeling charming
- Can be utterly diplomatic

What Repels a Libra

- Injustice
- Pictures hung unevenly
- Absence of fashion sense
- Someone's lingering depression
- Vulgarities

What Compels a Libra

- Fashion magazines
- Expensive department stores
- Menus with no more than five items
- Chivalry
- Beauty

Scorpio

Motive: To penetrate (Water)
Mode: Persistence (Fixed)
Symbol: The Scorpion

The Myth in 30 Seconds: Medusa

Medusa's snake-ridden hair was the result of her being horribly raped, and the rage from that experience staying trapped inside of her. So powerful was her anger that all who gazed upon her would turn to stone. Perseus was given the task of killing her to save his own mother, and did so by looking at her in the reflection of his shield. He successfully beheaded her and kept the head in a bag to be used as a weapon against his enemies.

Scorpio Overview

Within this myth we find the constant "reflection" that Scorpio natives practice in an attempt to understand themselves. Imagine being immersed in the depths of the ocean—the real depths, the parts that humans have only fantasized about. The water is black, calm, and completely encompassing; and many things may come to mind while you're floating there. The dark abyss might cause you to envision being surrounded by powerful demons that live there; or you could possibly find these depths tranquil, holy, and serene, imagining a world where you are one of many, even though the others are invisible. Scorpios' sentiments are very similar to these waters: they're still and bottomless, and may conjure fearful thoughts *or* feelings of strength and peace.

Scorpios, by nature, have learned to pay attention to their deep emotions and use them to understand people. By becoming good listeners and investigators, they can begin to uncover hidden information about others, which allows them to feel normal and less guilty. These Scorpions learn to seek the truth and realize the value of secrets, which is why they're magnets for everyone else.

Those born under this sign are trained to look below the surface and discover the lie in any situation—and they always seem to find it—so be as straightforward with them as you can. You don't want your Scorpio finding out a secret years later; time knows no limits when honor is at stake.

Scorpio LoveScoop

Scorpios don't base sexual attraction on the usual standards. On the contrary, they can only be attracted to you if it fits their psyche. To them, there's either chemistry or there isn't—it's black-and-white thinking. The critical piece that they must have in a relationship is honesty; it's vital to them. Even if you don't feel you're getting the full scoop *from* them, always be sure to give it *to* them. They can detect a whopper and are smart enough to catch you with a test question.

When they're hurt, Scorpios recall everything you ever did that wasn't fair or nice, and they let you know about it. Try to remember that when they're angry, they've been wounded, so in their mind it's their turn to hurt you. Once this passes, they usually feel regret and embarrassment. Try to see these situations simply as opportunities for them to vent, because that's probably what's going on. They love deeply and loyally.

Scorpio Recap

- Are on a quest for self-acceptance
- Use others' issues as a way to understand their own
- Make work or relationship choices based on how passionate they feel about them
- Always have a secret
- Never forget any harm done to them

What Repels a Scorpio

- Dishonesty
- Infidelity
- Superficiality
- Too much frivolity
- Bravado

What Compels a Scorpio

- Sexuality
- The colors black and red
- Horror movies or mysteries
- Psychic readings
- Mysticism

Sagittarius

(NOVEMBER 22–DECEMBER 21)

Motive: To wander (Fire)
Mode: Adaptability (Mutable)
Symbol: The Centaur/Archer

The Myth in 30 Seconds: Zeus and Hera

The heart of Sagittarius is found in the myth of Zeus and Hera, the main god and goddess of Greek mythology. The relationship between them was a turbulent one: Zeus looked for adventure, and often immoral play, and Hera lived to foil his plans and hunt down and torture his earthly possessions. Without her, Zeus would have felt bored and empty, as her torments kept the relationship alive and vibrant—and he influenced Hera in the same way.

Alternately, the other most-referenced myth for Sagittarius involves Hercules and Chiron, who was a Centaur (a creature that is half man, half horse) and a healer. These two roamed the countryside, hunting down other, evil Centaurs with poisonous arrows. One day, Chiron fell upon one of these deadly weapons, but survived because he was half immortal, although he remained in extraordinary pain. This mythical being had such compassion that he asked Zeus if he would let his wound replace the eternal punishment that Prometheus had to endure for bringing fire to humankind. Zeus was so moved by this request that he elevated Chiron to a constellation.

Sagittarius Overview

All Sagittarians create a "Hera," or thorn in their sides, in the form of a job, spouse, or cause. The Archers are trying to recognize that there's a downside to being omnipotent: boredom. They love the quest for truth—the kind that thrills you and takes your breath away. Being of the Fire motive, they have an unquenchable thirst for knowledge; and live in a magical realm of myths, kings, queens, and knights.

Those born under this sign are known for carrying a symbolic bow and quiver on their backs that represent the arrows of truth. This can be seen in action when they've decided to offer their opinion about something.

The part of the Centaur that's eternal is the horse, suggesting that Sagittarians have the ability to reach into this immortality and find magic to bring to the physical world.

As a healer, Chiron reflects the innate ability of many born under this sign to cure—whether through traditional means as a doctor or by alternative practices as an herbalist. Sagittarians have a remarkable gift that looks miraculous when used to support others. Bright, witty, and full of fun, these Centaurs of the Zodiac must learn to apply their healing hands to themselves and look within for the revelation that they're sure exists only outside of them.

Sagittarius LoveScoop

Sagittarians aren't eager to settle down, which is why they often unconsciously create circumstances that force relationships on them. Pregnancy, financial support, and even depression are common reasons that press them into long-term commitments. Of course, many find it perfectly okay to engage in a monogamous relationship, but unless there's a reason to stay other than love, it's hard to find one of these Archers who is willing to risk that kind of fear.

If you're beginning a relationship with a Sagittarius, be aware that they will always be active. Perhaps they want to go to night school to learn more secrets of the universe, or maybe they're the "escape to the movies" type. Some of them will even be comfortable enough to stay at home, but they'll most likely have a book in their hands or something that induces learning. Travel is to them what food is to a Taurus; it gives them comfort and a way to sense the expansiveness of the universe.

As for lovemaking, your Sagittarius may be wild in bed, but don't expect a little cuddly-wuddly afterward. Chances are that when they're done, they're off to read, or watch a good movie. Sex serves as an outlet for the immense amount of pent-up energies that they store.

This is a Zodiac sign that always wants *more* as a substitute for feeling the plenty they already have. If you keep your reins a bit tight, you may find that they respond better to pressure than to a long leash. Don't be afraid to be the Hera in this relationship, because your Sagittarius partner is going to need to create resistance somewhere. That's the only way they'll stop and use their magic on themselves and their loved ones.

You can let your Sag escape into their mythological world, and may even be invited to join them. But when it starts to get in the way of their job or other responsibilities, you might have to deliver a firm wake-up call.

Sagittarius Recap

- Enjoy bringing their magic into the mundane
- Love to share their wisdom (sermonize)
- Feel privileged
- Are on a quest for truth
- Always create opposition

What Repels a Sagittarius

- Restraints
- Routine
- Monotony
- Being ignored
- Being wrong

What Compels a Sagittarius

- Spirituality
- Learning
- Sharing an "Aha!"
- Vacations
- Being asked their opinion

Capricorn

(DECEMBER 22–JANUARY 19)

Motive: To build (Earth)
Mode: Assertion (Cardinal)
Symbol: The Mountain Goat/Sea Goat

The Myth in 30 Seconds: Kronos

The mythology behind Capricorn will always involve stories of angry fathers and vengeful mothers. In one of them, Kronos was the husband and brother of Rhea, who armed him with a sickle so that he could kill their wicked father. Kronos castrated him and then spent the rest of his life making sure his own children never lived to do the same thing to him . . . by eating them before adulthood.

Capricorn Overview

You'll most often find that the critical issue for Capricorns lies with their devouring father. "Father" is used here as an archetype; it could easily be a mother, uncle, or relative—someone who made it clear to these Goats at an early age that if they didn't grow up fast, they wouldn't make it.

The important themes for Capricorns to embrace are the need to reclaim the childhood that they never had, to understand that work isn't the definition of who they are, and to remember that they still have their innocence within them, awaiting a time when it's safe enough to come forward.

Most Capricorn natives hide their ages well, and even seem to look younger as they grow older. There are few who will tell you that their lives were easy ones; most had to start working as soon as they could talk, perhaps to care for an ill parent. They always had a list of chores that needed to get done or were forced to watch their siblings. Whatever the task, they started early, knowing that they had to fend for themselves—but being a Cardinal sign of Earth means that they had the skills to do it. They're governed by the teacher planet, Saturn, and follow an internal set of rules. Shortcuts don't exist in Capricorns' minds, and usually the only route for them to get where they're going is the hard way.

Those born under this sign are disciplinarians at heart, and it's difficult for them to understand why any situation calls for suffering or complaining—although they do their share of both. You may often be shocked by their overreaction to a poorly handled business transaction, their overdramatized recounting of a "close call" at work, or their profound disappointment in the face of a deal that fell through. Unconsciously, they're trying to create an obstacle to overcome, and it often means that they're close to success and afraid that it will come too easily.

There's something to Capricorns' symbol—the Mountain Goat or Sea Goat—that represents their multifaceted capacity to handle any situation. This Goat can thrive on the highest mountaintop and in the sea, signifying the ability of those of this sign to survive anywhere.

Capricorn LoveScoop

Capricorns enter every relationship with a purpose; in fact, they do *everything* in this way. If you're involved with one, then you'll be asked to define the intention of your union at some point. At first you'll find that your Capricorn is a traditionalist, liking things done in a slow, respectable way: dating first, talking, and looking to see if this is a good investment of time. They're trying to figure out if they can serve a function in your life or if you will have a future together. Children and family, making money, and working together are all examples of purposes; and when your Capricorn feels that none exist, you risk losing them. Being a Cardinal sign means that they have no fear of activity, but their time must be spent usefully.

Capricorns see everything as theirs and don't like to share the things that are important to them. They're loyal companions, and as the relationship ripens, you'll find them letting you into the more vulnerable components of their makeup. But if there's a moment when they feel too defenseless, they can build a wall around themselves that's virtually impenetrable. When they're scared or hurt, they can look at you as if they'd never met you, which is an eerie feeling.

Capricorn Recap

- Are born mature and get "younger" with age
- Are possessive
- Are entrepreneurial
- Are traditionalists
- Are mature

What Repels a Capricorn

- Small talk
- Shortcuts
- Credit cards

- Gambling
- Breaking the rules

What Compels a Capricorn

- Completing a goal
- Purpose
- Employment
- Taking responsibility
- Making money

Aquarius

(JANUARY 20–FEBRUARY 18)

Jan. 21 23

Motive: To know (Air)
Mode: Persistence (Fixed)
Symbol: The Water Bearer

The Myth in 30 Seconds: Prometheus

One of the ways Zeus maintained power over the mortals was to keep them in the dark—literally. He forbade anyone on Olympus to teach them how to wield fire. Being one of the brighter gods, Prometheus didn't like the suffering this caused humans, so he brought them this forbidden element, forever changing their existence. Because Prometheus broke the rules, Zeus chained him to the top of a mountain and ordered an eagle to eat out his liver—only for it to regrow and be eaten again day after day.

44

Aquarius Overview

The rebelliousness of Aquarians can be found in the myth of Prometheus. This sign follows the more-traditional Capricorn, but these Water Bearers are almost completely opposite in nature: they hate authority, are bursting with new ideas, and are always looking to shatter thoughts and beliefs that they feel no longer serve anyone. Inherent in them is this dance of doing the unheard of and then justifying their actions as being for the good of all.

Noted for their cool detachment and almost unfailing ability to ignore feelings, those of this sign can be notoriously self-absorbed, immersed in a complete identification with the mind. They live in their ideals of how things are—at least how *they* demand that they are. If something doesn't fit their image, it just doesn't exist.

People bore Aquarians, but groups fascinate them; rules are ridiculous to them, but breaking them is divine; emotions are a waste of time, yet they can react wildly if forced to deal with them . . . these are the kinds of paradoxes brought to the most mental sign of the Zodiac. Their gift is in their genius, and their minds have been refined to work wonders. Meanwhile, their sympathy is usually with the underdog, the masses, the hungry, the homeless, and the sick. (Please note that phrases like "the homeless" or "the sick" are labels for groups or categories, not references to individuals.)

Aquarius LoveScoop

Although emotions scare them, Aquarians *do* understand the importance of a promise. If they swear to be faithful, you can usually count on them to keep their word because of what such a declaration means in its conceptual form. Remember, Aquarians are all about *ideals*. If you can always identify with what your Water Bearer is saying below the surface, you'll never lose who you fell in love with. Beyond the mental wall is a person with a true vision of good for the world and a model for the perfect relationship. A partnership is ultimately what Aquarians want, but their powerful minds can easily find another cause they must take care of right now.

45

You can expect a strong companion in your Aquarius partner, meaning that you'll have a good friend who will likely remain in your life till the end. But be on the alert for their more dictatorial shadow; when this emerges, they may become the very thing they're fighting against. Water Bearers like alternatives and are more than happy to settle into your life knowing that *you* like them as well. Let them always tell you their point of view; this will help you navigate the relationship more successfully.

Aquarius Recap

- Have a desire to help the world
- Love humanity, not humans
- Are eccentric
- Are rebellious
- Are brilliant

What Repels an Aquarius

- One-on-one chats
- Traditions
- Rules
- Disagreeing with them
- Narrow-mindedness

What Compels an Aquarius

- Raising funds for those in need
- Alternatives
- The road less traveled
- Fashion faux pas
- Inventions

$\mathcal{Pisces}$

Motive: To feel (Water)
Mode: Adaptability (Mutable)
Symbol: The Fish

The Myth in 30 Seconds: Atargatis

In an old Babylonian myth, two fish found an enormous egg and took it safely to land. Atargatis, a goddess, emerged from it and wanted to reward them. She ordered them to be constellations in the heavens, and their tails were tied together. Over time, one fish became known as Atargatis, and the other her son. This myth also involves mothers and sons who are lovers.

Pisces Overview

The surreal life of a Piscean usually begins at birth. There's a close tie to the mother, who finds her connection with the child to be deep. The young Fish often feels a reciprocal bond with Mom and will genuinely understand all of her inner feelings of isolation, insecurity, and unhappiness; and conversely, her joys, celebrations, and intimacies.

Pisceans must constantly battle to stay connected with the self. The fluidity that exists within them can be overwhelming, and they compensate for this by turning on the mind and identifying with outside thoughts just to avoid the chaos on the inside. Of course, this kind of denial will backfire, and they'll eventually find themselves drawn to individuals or circumstances that pull them into their feelings again—often in an unfriendly way.

On a deep level, Pisceans live with two opposite parts of themselves (all Mutable signs have a duality): one side feels divine and connected to all that's holy; and the other feels conniving, mean, and attached to evil. The symbol of the yin and yang characterizes the opposing yet similar forces at work inside those born under this complex sign. Regardless of their identification with these components, they feel the inner conflict and must make an effort every day to flex the muscle of discipline to create appropriate limits for themselves.

These Fish have no boundaries, so they can easily float into your reality and see life from your perspective without ever realizing it. Lacking confines or a center, they have no way of knowing where home is, so it's important that they take the time to release the absorptions of the day. Whether it's through a shower, a bath, or a long walk, they need to find the part of them within that's the source in their lives.

Pisces LoveScoop

Relationships with Pisceans can be interesting and romantic, but there's a strong probability that they're working out some sort of theme. Its topic could involve a mother/child, master/slave, or protector/defender; the range of possibilities is infinite, but one *will* be present. Those born under this sign are personal yet archetypal, and if you visit them while they're in a relationship, you'll be able to feel that something is going on between them and their partner, but you'll probably have no idea what it is.

These Fish can be extremely romantic, with eyes like watery pools peering deep within your soul. They're looking to merge with you—and, like it or not, they will. It's not uncommon for them to take up your interests with a genuine fascination. You can expect your Pisces partner to be moody, obsessive, and unusually messy . . . unless, of course, *you* prefer neat living quarters.

Pisces Recap

- Have an unusually close connection to their mothers
- Are deeply compassionate
- Have a tendency to self-medicate
- Are creative
- Possess psychic abilities

What Repels a Pisces

- Lack of compassion for those in need
- Criticism of their messiness
- Abuse of any kind toward the helpless
- Prejudice
- Speaking ill of their mothers

What Compels a Pisces

- A hot tub
- Role play
- Consistency
- Random acts of kindness
- Sad movies

PART II

The Compatibility Charts

Introduction to Part II

I often think of each of us as a walking universe—a constellation of planets and Zodiac signs that is formed the moment we take our first breath.

Your unique chart shapes your experiences and shows you the path to wholeness. When your universe comes into contact with somebody else's, a third one is created: the relationship chart. This tells a completely different story, and it isn't just about you as individuals—it deals with your *relationship,* which warns you about potential bumps in the road and maps out paths that can lead to fulfillment. The information found in these charts is at the heart of why you instantly love some people and immediately dislike others.

Since it's impossible to know *all* the relationship determinants, I've simply taken your sun sign—the part of you that you identify with most—and have used it as a guide to suggest how it will mix with others.

The numbers in *LoveScopes* are derived from several factors, but if I were pressed to tell you the most vital component I used to arrive at each score, I'd have to say that it was based on my overall expertise garnered from years of studying the signs and their needs. I was able to determine the common ground that exists for each set of paired energies, making the analysis of each combination highly subjective yet surprisingly accurate!

Clearly, my "prognosis" is limited, but the factors discussed in the following pages are valid elements existing between any two individuals. What you may (or may not) have in your favor is how the rest of your respective charts combine. *LoveScopes* is based on the placement of the sun sign, but at the moment you're born, astrology casts an entire map of all the planets. The rest of the chart refers to all of the *other* planets, minus the sun sign. The extra planetary information tells you more, which isn't always good news. I've given each combination a score, a *LoveScope,* describing the strength of the initial foundation. The rest of your charts will either add to that or weaken it.

By the way, you won't need a book to *tell* you what's happening with you and your love interest—you'll *feel* it soon enough!

So if you're ready (or not), I give you *LoveScopes,* a guide to understanding you and the person you love.

Aries + Aries

LoveScope: 7.8

The Basic Relationship

This pairing conjures the image of Russell Crowe (an Aries) in *Gladiator* and Lucy Lawless (also an Aries) in *Xena: Warrior Princess* living together while in character. Imagine the anger flying each day: "You left the seat up again!" (There's a crashing sound as her sword destroys the entire toilet.)

"Deal with it!" he yells back. "There are worse things you could be wiping up!"

"Yeah? Well, how 'bout I wipe *you* up off the floor, because that's where you're going to be if you keep making me destroy the commode!" (Another loud bang is heard.)

Maybe if you're in an Aries + Aries relationship, you're able to limit the property damage, but you can bet tempers will fly; that's what happens when two assertive Fire signs get together. It's loud and scary, but that's usually when you know it's solid. In fact, I'd venture

to say that the warning sign that this relationship is ending is when it gets quiet.

There's a chance that familiarity could breed contempt, but why focus on the negative? These two signs could give one another *exactly* what each needs.

Aries love their freedom, yet they can be very possessive—something that's hard for people of most other signs to comprehend. This sign mulls it over: *If I let you do your own thing, how will I know you'll come back to me when you're done?* With another Aries, the answer is obvious. Both partners are warriors, and an interesting thing happens when they're with each other: one of them must step down and relinquish control.

Ideally, each Ram can be in charge of a particular area of the relationship. So, if you're the Aries who likes to travel and wants companionship, then your partner, who may not be so adventure oriented, must yield to you in that arena. Likewise, if you aren't so well versed in interior design, then you'd allow your partner to take charge of redecorating the kitchen . . . and so on. It sounds easy, but Aries aren't the best at loosening their grip. When they do, they want acknowledgment for it, and that's where they get into even more trouble.

The Passion Zone

Since Aries is a Cardinal sign, there may be a tendency for both partners to initiate so many things they want to be doing at any given time that they may even look upon *passion* as something to fit in between sporting events, vacations, TV shows, phone calls, or arguments.

The Aries mind never really rests, so sexy endeavors tend to get lost in the to-do lists. There's no lack of heat here, just a lack of time. Both partners may prefer to skip the foreplay, but that's no problem because both will see to it that their own needs are met.

There may be a tendency toward playing psychological games— as in power trips—but overall, this combination works. Aries do everything fast and with a high energy level at first, but their sparks can fizzle out over time, especially if they allow their romantic playtime to become a routine (which would only happen to an Aries as a result of being too busy, thereby relegating it to the to-do list).

Luckily, these two don't require a lot of warming up to get their engines revved, so fitting in passion rarely results in problems. In this arena, Aries are low maintenance.

What Aries Needs to Know about Aries

Aries, your greatest weakness (and sometimes strength) is your inability to lay down your weapons and work for peace. You've come into existence with a predisposition for battle, and that's what you're good at. Surrender, regardless of how noble, is not one of your strong suits; and no matter what you call it, seeking a truce is a form of surrender for you.

Answer this question for yourself: Who's more powerful, the person who walks into a room of enemies with full armor and weapons fully loaded, or the one who strolls in wearing jeans and a T-shirt? Your initial instinct might cause you to say the first person, but you have to admit that the second is braver and more self-assured, as people respect that kind of self-confidence. Be the first to put your weapons down and encourage dialogue . . . it shows more strength and will consequently bring you more honor.

LoveScope

This union can lead to a great relationship that has a good chance of lasting. It will be a solid foundation to build on because each partner innately understands the motivation of the other. Whether they're acting like primitive Neanderthals or tame intellectuals, the bond between them is based on one thing: ruthless honesty. These individuals assume that both of them are doing exactly what they want without apology, and that kind of basic groundwork makes for a long-lasting structure!

HOW TO KEEP THE ARIES YOU LOVE

- Tell them to go on without you a couple of times a week.

- Make reference to how much you love a "natural" look.

- Create dual savings accounts and challenge them to earn as much as you do in a month.

- Casually remark on how ridiculous hair salons are.

- Ask their permission about something that you know they'll say no to so that they'll feel like they're in charge.

- Occasionally disagree with them so they can feel the rush.

- Start to cry, then quickly toughen up.

- Don't "play" after sex.

- Hire someone to clean the house, and lie about the cost.

- Make fun of someone who wears makeup.

Aries + Taurus

LoveScope: 6.7

The Basic Relationship

Just like a fertile oasis in the middle of the hot, dry desert, this love is usually met with huge appreciation and relief. The partnership of Aries and Taurus is akin to a haven in the sand. Aries is obviously the heat in this combination—since the sign has the motive of Fire—and that can either represent passion or scorching pain. Taurus is the refuge of comfort symbolized by the trees in the oasis, but this sign is only seen as such because of the extreme conditions of the surroundings—suggesting that the contrast is what's important here.

Aries and Taurus are Zodiac neighbors, which is an asset to their relationship. Taureans somehow innately understand Aries' innocent and impulsive behavior, and seem to have great patience for it. Aries aren't so tolerant of Taureans, but they aren't patient with anyone; that's just the way they are.

We've established that Aries need a battle and that Taureans need stability and security, so it's hard to imagine that they have anything

in common—but they do. Each holds something the other wants: The Bulls deeply desire more energy and assertion, and the Rams want to feel the security that Taureans carry with them. These desires are strong enough to create a deep attraction.

It's rare for Rams to feel that their anger *won't* be hot enough to melt its object, but Taureans can certainly handle the heat of their tantrums. Aries will expect to be tested and pushed against, and this is an area where Taureans will be full of surprises. The Bulls have no interest in testing them, and know how to get what they want. This factor alone makes them almost irresistible to the Rams.

So, if it's all so wonderful, why such an average LoveScope score? Over time, Aries will begin to see the Taurus stability they originally revered now as stubbornness; and when Rams see a wall, there's only one thing they can do about it—bring it down!

The important thing for Taureans to remember is that Aries abhor stagnation. Bulls are notoriously immovable to the point of inertia, and Aries treat immovability as if it's a direct challenge.

The biggest bone of contention between them will be agreement about the pace at which they take on life. If they can strike a happy medium, then there's a good chance of long-term survival—but neither one of these individuals is big on bending.

The Passion Zone

Aries lovers can bring Taureans new things to adore (including their love). They can open up the horizon for these Bulls to see the vast and wonderful qualities of the world that they often overlook because of their desire to cocoon or anchor themselves in one location. Likewise, Taureans can help Aries enjoy the luxuries of the body and the joys of sensual play. They revel in slow, erotic, well-timed lovemaking, while Aries would rather get it done without the restraints of timelines and the buildup of anticipation. When Taureans are finally ready, Aries can be far off on the horizon pursuing something else.

Nothing will make Bulls change their pace; it's up to Aries to slow down long enough and let Taureans unveil their seductive magic.

There's no denying, however, that the incredibly satisfying and considerate attention of Taurean lovemaking makes Aries feel cherished and secure. This factor can be used to help the relationship become empowered and long lasting. The Rams just need to curb their quick, fun, flash-in-the-pan passion and concentrate on a slow sizzle. Taureans will delight in the foreplay and stimulation of making love, even if their Aries partners sometimes find it tedious after the novelty wears off.

What Aries Needs to Know about Taurus

The harder you push, the thicker the wall! You love challenges, but when it's to push your Taurus more quickly than they're ready to be moved, you've met your match. Don't see the resistance as defiance or you'll just keep running into the same roadblock again and again. Make your request, state your desire, and then remove your attention and let it all process through their slow but sure way of making decisions.

What Taurus Needs to Know about Aries

Aries aren't trying to control you—well, actually . . . yes, they are. But you need to understand that it's not so they can be in charge. They want you to move as fast as they do, but you can't—nor should you even try. The problem here is that if you *feel* that they're trying to exert dominance over you, then you'll never budge. Eventually, you'll only react if you feel they no longer have a vested interest in your action. Lighten up and understand that Aries have a buzz inside of them that makes it hard for them to relax.

Lovescope

Since Taurus is the sign after Aries, the Bulls have a head start in understanding some of their quirks . . . but it doesn't make them 100

percent accepting of them. Because these signs are so vastly different, each is required to put away the old ideas of what makes things work and be open to different ways of relating.

A LoveScope of 6.7 is a great foundation, and suggests that the strength of this relationship is more than two-thirds of the way to a perfect 10. Now you just have to use the last one-third wisely.

Aries + Gemini

LoveScope: 8.2

The Basic Relationship

The elements of Fire and Air have an obvious compatibility: Air feeds Fire, and Fire motivates Air. When one of those elements is an inspired go-getter and the other is a flexible communicator, it's hard not to imagine a high-speed combination that loves to connect.

There's a comfortable degree of ease between Aries and Geminis: Aries are quick, easily bored, aggressive, and sometimes pushy; whereas Geminis are quick, easily bored, diplomatic, and flexible. You'll notice that where Aries are aggressive, Geminis are diplomatic; and where Aries are pushy, Geminis are flexible.

These two energies enjoy a certain flow between them. Aries like the fact that their partners are smart enough to understand them and easy enough to move with them, and the Twins like the chance to adapt to an always-on-the-go Ram. Geminis are smart; and Aries are no dummies, although they put little time into the trivia that Geminis

so love to pursue. Every now and then, the Rams will get in a bind that the Twins can pull them out of—just by virtue of the vast amount of information sitting in the their brains. Conversely, no one can push a Gemini out of harm's way like Aries, whose protective nature *loves* fending for their airy partner.

The Passion Zone

The elemental combination of Fire and Air seems like it would be obvious: Geminis can fuel and intrigue Aries' passion, and the Rams' unmistakable spirit should please the Twins. This partnership is full of hot, juicy passion—at least at first. The problem is that they can have a fleeting sex drive. It's like, "Let's have fun and move on." The key to these two lasting in the bedroom is to keep it interesting without glomming on to each other. Don't expect couples of these signs to spend the entire day in bed, because both have other things to do.

What Aries Needs to Know about Gemini

As an Aries, you must remember that the rules of the warrior don't apply to everyone. To you, Geminis will seem to avoid dealing with things head-on . . . but that's not the case. The Twins are communicators and need to understand and feel understood. So put away your sword and talk to them—but be gentle at first. Gemini is an Air sign that will take leave until the pressure isn't so intense. You should also remember that your Mutable friend is quite easy to hang around with—until the *other* Twin emerges. Then you have to keep in mind that it's not a response to something you did wrong—which you hate—but rather a natural cycle that can be expected from Geminis.

What Gemini Needs to Know about Aries

Gemini, you must understand that Aries is an "act first, think later" kind of sign. Sometimes when the Rams get momentum going, the only way to stop them is to be firm and clear. You probably hate being put in the position of having to call forth intense emotion, but it's the language Aries understand—and you're all about language. Every once in a while, express your anger and stick around to see the positive result.

LoveScope

This union is as comfortable as a pair of worn Nikes, yet it's always in motion, and there's a constant need for entertainment and newness. Both signs have a love of activity and share that "Go, go, go" mentality. But this partnership hits the skids when it comes to money management or planning for the future. Also, the responsibility of having children could cause this relationship to crumble—but then again, it could actually inspire one or both to buckle down and commit to stability.

Aries have no problem being alone, and Geminis usually prefer to be with someone. It's a great duo. Together, these two can remind each other how much fun and full of mystery life can be. Each has special tools to solve the big problems *and* create plenty of minor ones, which will keep enough stimulation going to last a lifetime. There's a high rate of relationship survival among these Rams and Twins, and an exciting road ahead should they decide to remain together.

Aries + Cancer

LoveScope: 5.9

The Basic Relationship

The union of Aries and Cancer is an attempt at bringing together two assertive signs with completely different motives . . . at least it may appear that way on the outside. There's the warrior, Aries, with the maternal figure, Cancer—at first an unlikely combination. Mothers are great fighters, and warriors can be super nurturers, making them strange, but not all that different, bedfellows. On the surface, it seems that these two should just stop now and take their chances with someone else, but there *is* chemistry here.

Aries are Fire, full of inspiration and warmth, and unable to sit still. They're always in need of something to occupy their ADHD-like personalities and will never be caught bored with a situation, because they will have moved on before it gets to that point.

Cancers are Water: full of nurturance and passionate stirrings, but always scanning for the next possible breach in security. When the tide isn't moving in their direction, they can create those nasty under-currents that will catch their partners off guard, making them wish that they were anywhere but in this sea of emotions.

Aries get the rap for being competitive, but this is true of all asser-tive signs. The difference is that they're more blatant about it—they want to beat you at your game, whatever that is. Cancers are a little more subtle in their ambition to come out on top. They want the title of "the one who knows what's best" for you, but they know they won't win it by announcing their intentions. They'll take the crown by looking innocent, letting their watery nature track their target unno-ticed. Then they'll use their superior *feeling* skills to stealthily anticipate what their companion needs. Their behavior hardly *looks* competitive, but it definitely has its origins in the need to take command. Both of these Cardinal signs want control, and they'll typically use anything in their power to get it.

Cancers nurture by tickling emotions; Aries support by tackling fears—different motivations, same goal. Crabs aren't afraid of their partners' dependence; Rams aren't scared of their *in*dependence. Alas, the potential clash is obvious.

The Passion Zone

As I've already said, assertive signs require a certain amount of con-trol to get intimate. Cancers must feel that they're going to be taken care of if they surrender, and Aries need to know that their partners will still be their conquest the next time they make love. So, Crabs could use some toughening up and Rams have to soften in order to experience the kind of passion together that they both want. This relationship can be physically *hot,* as long as these conditions are met.

The problem is that this combination can start out strong but quickly lose steam if Cancers realize that not only is their assistance unnecessary to Aries, but it's also not appreciated (at least not in the desired way). Crabs need to be adored and like to give pleasure, but Rams don't linger after a passionate encounter and enjoy satisfying their mates a bit less. Despite these variances, there's a high attraction

level because of the completely different approach to life each sign has: Cancers find Aries' strength to be sexy, and Aries find Cancers' unique perspectives to be intriguing.

What Aries Needs to Know about Cancer

Cancers approach life in a totally different way than you do. They feel every nuance of emotion coming from everyone they encounter and base their self-esteem on the ability to nurture and support. You're trained to see this quality as a weakness and control it. A simple shift in thinking could allow you to see your Cancer as a powerful warrior of the heart, offering them the same respect you would a comrade in your battalion.

Aries, you must appreciate (and find a way to show that you do) the sensitive nature of your Water partner. Imagine that there's really someone in the world who cares that your feet are cold or that you might get sick if you don't wear your coat. You may never understand *why* anybody cares about these things, but your Cancer partner undoubtedly does.

What Cancer Needs to Know about Aries

Aries will tend to see you as weak, Cancer, if you continue to let your feelings be hurt by their actions that appear insensitive. (I say *appear* because they aren't *trying* to be brash; they're just used to having a thought and then acting on it.) Rams are warriors and love knowing that you're going to fight for their right to be emotional—that's the kind of strength they can trust.

It's also important to remember the gifts of your Aries mate. Who else would go to battle for you over the smallest thing or map out a trip that they want to take with you? It doesn't matter if they don't do dishes or make the bed; they're showing *love* the best way they know how . . . and you can bet that's what it is if they look you in the eyes and tell you how much they appreciate you in their life—even if they never actually say the words.

LoveScope

These are two very assertive signs that could learn a lot from each other, but they both need to establish trust and awareness within themselves first before finding a common space. There's a lot of sacrifice that each needs to make in order for this connection to work, but neither is short on courage, strength, or conviction—and that definitely benefits the relationship.

Aries + Leo

LoveScope: 8.1

The Basic Relationship

The Ram and the Lion ignite because they share the element of Fire and the desire to deliver inspiration. Here we have signs that are insightful, brash, unpredictable, and hot in the areas that count . . . but there are some differences in this seeming land of nirvana. Their modes aren't the same: Aries is Cardinal, and Leo is Fixed. This means that Aries will likely *look* like the pushy ones and Leos will *seem* more tolerant. It's enough to make Aries run, but they can't. If confronted with a challenge, it's common knowledge that they're slaves to the temptation of a difficult test, although absolutely nothing else—and no one—could ever confine them.

Both signs have father issues to work out. Rams have to remember that they're almost always in a state of proving themselves. In this case, it will be to the always-in-need-of-attention Lions—who like the role of giving approval. Contests are to Aries what dramatic roles are to Leos: neither can resist a chance to perform.

Aries easily project their image of the unaccepting father onto Leos—regardless of gender—who, in turn, assume that the Rams don't care (just like the Lions experienced with their own fathers). This chemistry leaves each extremely grateful to hear a voice of genuine gratitude from the other, making for a great equation: low expectations plus thankfulness for any recognition received equals a happy relationship!

As a positive for this union, Aries bring enthusiastic appreciation to Leos, who then express their generosity. To outsiders, this probably won't look like your typical lovefest, but make no mistake—it is.

The Passion Zone

When two Fire signs get together, it spells one word . . . *hot!* Yes, they're in the red zone, and this can be sexual—or even angry—passion. These two have intense emotions in droves, so when they're not mad at each other (which they often are), they're capable of wild fun—and we're talking loud and often volatile behavior in the bedroom or in battle. Whether the heat is caused by jealousy, rage, or sheer sex appeal, this pair is a great match between the sheets. Leos need to feel appreciated, and nothing sends this message better than satisfied Aries who have stopped long enough to focus their attention on their partners. These two signs likely coined the phrase "makeup sex."

What Aries Needs to Know about Leo

Aries, there's little point in giving you advice, except to say that showing gratitude or recognition gives remarkable rewards.

Remember that there's another person sharing this partnership, and even though your Leo is pretty accepting of what you do and seems in need of little, they do thrive on appreciation. You aren't good at giving it directly; you just assume that if you're hanging out with someone, it's obvious that you like them or you wouldn't be there. Just remember that this isn't always clear to a Leo, who needs overt demonstrations that you care.

You have a hard time resisting the urge to charge through any boundaries that are placed before you, but there's one that you should try to refrain from pushing against: when your Leo tells you that they've had enough. If it's gotten to that point, what they say is probably true, and you don't want this Lion to start roaring, because it will take a long time to get them to cool down again and purr.

What Leo Needs to Know about Aries

There *is* only one king of the jungle, but you must tone it down in this relationship, Leo. You may even need to let your Aries believe that you're lending them the throne for a while—just because you can. Whatever it takes to keep the peace must come from you—Aries won't yield just because they feel it's expected of them. Since you are, after all, the one with the crown, you have the ability to demonstrate considerable tolerance for your subjects by knowing when to criticize and when to keep quiet.

Aries are good companions, especially if they recognize that they're being given lots of space to do whatever they want. It's not like they'll run off and start another relationship; for them, one is plenty. They want to feel that they can focus their attention on other interests (which may hurt you). Actually, you're giving them a chance to fully embrace who they are without restraint. The truth is that not many lovers have the courage to do that, so bravo to you.

LoveScope

This is an incredibly passionate coupling because it's so *fiery* by nature. There's a strong potential for long-term connection because both signs understand the difference between goading for fun and pushing the limits—at least, in *theory* they do.

Both Leos and Aries are resolving father issues, so with a little compassion, there's a chance for feelings of inadequacy to diminish as each experiences this kind of deep acceptance from a fellow Fire sign.

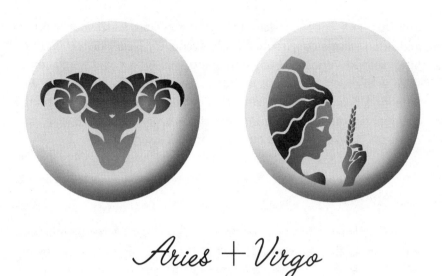

Aries + Virgo

LoveScope: 5.2

The Basic Relationship

A Ram and a nun . . . quite the image. It's not the complete picture, but certainly part of it. Aries are by nature hunters, and seek thrills through conquest. They also appear to be outsiders because they move to the beat of their own drum and dislike stopping for anyone. Virgos *are* loners, and definitely prefer privacy over cohabitation. Aries don't follow orders, are *Ram*bunctious, and love chaos; Virgos live by the rules, are docile, and love order. So why would these signs hook up? It's actually not so hard to understand when you consider that Rams love a challenge and Virgins come to the relationship presenting all sorts of them.

All warriors seek a battle to test their abilities, and trying to fit into such a different lifestyle would certainly be one of the bigger accomplishments . . . should they be successful. For Virgos, there are unbreakable rules that aren't written down anywhere, not to mention myriad codes of conduct that must be honored. Respecting these guidelines

isn't that hard once or twice—take your shoes off, wash your hands, and so on—but a daily routine could eventually wear down even the fittest soldier. Virgos love to fix anything, and Aries come to relationships with much that needs mending. The Aries nature is somewhat unrefined, especially when compared to Virgo, the sign of perfection. Many accidents take place in Rams' homes, and lots of repairs are required. This keeps Virgos busy, but not necessarily happy.

The Passion Zone

Virgos' innate duality allows them to show up as either the nun or the whore in the bedroom. It's always a surprise for Aries to discover which persona will be sharing intimacy with them tonight. This union can be wild and untamed, based on this element of surprise. For Aries, conquering the Virgin means a chance to meet the "un-Virgin," and that battle is one worth winning; while Virgos are tantalized by the idea of being ravished by that Ram passion. When it's over, though, it's easy to guess which one will politely slip away, clean the sheets, and make the room look like it was never touched! Lots of heat gets generated, but nuns aren't as spontaneous (and that's really an understatement), so there can be lots of disappointment as well. Virgos are precise about what they like and don't like, and Aries just love pushing against all those rules to see how far they can get.

What Aries Needs to Know about Virgo

Aries, there's no doubt that you're particularly klutzy, although you may not have been before you met your Virgo. When sharing a space with them, something may happen to the way you see yourself. All of a sudden you'll feel messy, notice your faults, and sense that somehow there *is* something wrong with the way you're doing things. Virgins often give off the self-righteous message "You're wrong!" But that's not what they're really saying. If anything, they blame themselves for not being able to fix the problem, including the flaws they perceive in you—which they're sure they unconsciously brought forth.

Remember, if you have a service-oriented Virgo, they'll come to life when appreciated; otherwise, they'll summon the evil, nagging part of them . . . and trust me, nothing feels worse than when Virgos are being real pills.

What Virgo Needs to Know about Aries

Not all Aries are messy, but they tend not to worry about details the way you do, Virgo. They may try to get you to lighten up about your personal standards, but that can just cause you to become stricter. The problem with this strategy is that Aries *must,* almost automatically, try to break all rules. So if you add more, you'll end up creating a Ram on a mission—and not necessarily the kind you're hoping for.

Remember that Aries don't respond well to criticism. In fact, being castigated will likely trigger feelings of not being appreciated, which they'll bury deep within them. Encouraging words will work wonders and also help keep you from sinking too far into your critical mind. Just remember, Aries couldn't care less about half the minutiae you're thinking about every hour—or minute—of the day!

LoveScope

Basically, these two could overcome great adversity as a couple and respect their individual characteristics—or they could just annoy each other. The biggest hang-up here is lifestyle—one cares about details; the other doesn't. And both are good at leaving, which is what will happen if they each don't try to acknowledge the gifts that the other has to offer. Virgos get irritated at Aries' self-absorption; meanwhile, Aries are only aware of what *they're* doing, basically proving Virgos' point. Virgins can feel quite overlooked, while Rams don't want a nag.

Understanding is the most powerful tool that these two have to work with, or soon they'll figure out that they can do fine on their own.

Aries + Libra

LoveScope: 7.8

The Basic Relationship

Even in astrology you can count on the idea of opposites attracting
. . . and you can't get more opposite than Aries and Libra. They live
on totally different sides of the Zodiac wheel, but get along because
of this. Aries is a Fire element, and Libra is Air. Both signs long to be
inspired, enjoy an engaging chat, and take pleasure in the pursuit of
life and love. Libras are after relationships, and Aries are on a quest
for the unattainable, but both need a challenge. Aries is a self-focused
sign, which doesn't necessarily mean selfish—Rams are just attentive
to what's in front of them and how things will affect them. Libra is an
"other-focused" sign, which means those born under it are constantly
measuring and evaluating people. Whereas Aries are instinct based,
Libras are mental, and what one does may create fuel for the other's
reaction—for better or worse.

Both of these signs are Cardinal, which means they're leaders.
On the one hand, they respect independence and know that they'll

both take care of themselves; on the other, problems arise when either believes that they're right and the other is wrong. Assertive signs vanish at the first indication of negative accusations because it's just too hard for them to sit there and sort out—they'll each back away until things have cooled down. We have two hunters in this relationship: one that uses brawn and the other beauty. When they're in sync, it's a perfectly matched party.

The Passion Zone

There's a lot of sexual tension between these two signs, and that means things can get hot. Aries see beauty as strength, and Libras see strength as beauty, making it a perfect setup. Neither is afraid to steam up the room with passion, which is easy to do when Air and Fire get together. When the lovemaking is over, there's little cuddle time, because both will be off to the next adventures.

What Libra Needs to Know about Aries

First, it's important to realize that you're both warriors. Yes, you may be more diplomatic, Libra, but Aries have fought for justice and fairness since the beginning. Although *you* may prefer more refined battles, you'll enjoy theirs just as much. In fact, not only are they aware of your love of conflict, they can see right through that sweet voice of yours that's usually reserved for strangers—but be sure to understand that they're not judging.

Aries love shortcuts: "Why fold clothes when you're just going to wear them anyway?" "Why do the dishes when there are still clean ones available in the cupboard?" Consider creating a system that gratifies your Ram's desire for immediate satisfaction if you want them to participate in good housekeeping practices. (For example, hampers underneath basketball hoops throughout the house could actually work—just a friendly tip!)

It's important to remember that Aries value allegiance, so if you start to take someone else's side—and do your *fairness* thing—that needs to be explained to help keep the peace. Try to always delight in, rather than feel disdain for, your Ram; this might take a bit of work, but it will surely pay off.

What Aries Needs to Know about Libra

Libras aren't being condescending when they talk in that "nice" voice. Rather, they truly are trying to maintain balance. That tone often implies that they're tired and need some time alone, but the world's demands won't let them have it—even though sounding pleasant may be all they have left. Conversely, they're appalled by temper tantrums and petty emotions like jealousy and rage—but these things fuel *you*. If you can't keep your more abrasive side under control, then take a walk with your cell phone and call a friend. That way, you'll get a chance to rant, and your Libra will know exactly what you did (believe it or not), and why. This will please them very much because you didn't make *them* see that side of you, and they'll probably reward you somehow.

LoveScope

Libras truly appreciate Aries' frankness, desire to prove themselves, and raw honesty. Aries love Libras' charm and understand their need to be liked. This starts a strong foundation of understanding. Both signs are aggressive, and although there isn't a lot of glue holding them together, this union can last if they remember they're both warriors—they just "fight" differently. This relationship will allow Libras to see that there are usually no repercussions for being honest, and Aries might finally learn that you can catch more with honey than a clumsy bear trap.

Both of these signs make great friends and supportive partners once the need to control is replaced with compassion. Since each can survive in the world alone, they must know that the other is in this by choice. These two could redefine "relationship" because they both love trekking across new topography. The terrain for Libra and Aries is a rough one to navigate, but few signs are brave enough to attempt to scale such a mountain. Kudos for the willingness to give this potentially powerful combination a chance.

HOW TO LOSE THE ARIES YOU LOVE

- Ask them, "Can we just stay indoors and reflect on life this weekend?"
- Make more money than they do.
- Hide their "sword."
- Give them a list of chores.
- Smile and act patronizing when they brag.
- Win (at anything).
- Have your own to-do list that doesn't include the things you need to do for *them*.
- Let them overhear you telling a friend that you like "gentle" sex.
- Look bored when they start a fight.

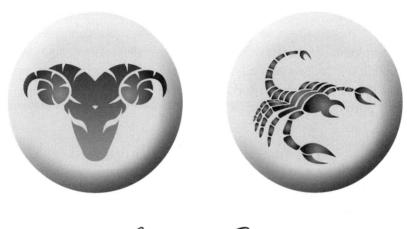

Aries + Scorpio

LoveScope: 7.8

The Basic Relationship

Before Pluto was discovered, Scorpio and Aries were both ruled by the warrior planet, Mars. Appropriately, it follows that these signs pursue what they desire with a zest that leaves many others in the dust. However, because of their elemental differences, their motivations don't match.

Aries will go after any challenge, regardless of their attachment to the cause. If there's a battle, they'll pick a side, grab a weapon, and jump in. Scorpios aren't afraid to fight either, but they have to be passionate about the cause—or at least have an emotional tie to the people involved. Therein lies the difference between these two scorching signs: Scorpios sense danger and plan an attack; Aries perceive a threat and jump right into action. Rams not only love the battle, they love the *battler*. They abhor weakness, and Scorpions will repeatedly show that they're far from weak.

Scorpios are constantly seeking the truth, and Aries have no choice but to tell it. There isn't much that Scorpios wouldn't do for others once trust is established, but all the honesty in the world won't stop them from testing people from time to time to see if their faith is still merited.

Scorpios also love the "what you see is what you get" style of Aries. This innocence is crucial for them because they tend to believe that everyone is hiding an ulterior motive. Certainly, they'll go through a distrusting phase with their Aries, but these suspicions will quickly dissipate once they figure out that their partners can't possibly be that calculating.

Both signs are comfortable with anger, but they each arrive at this emotion in different ways. Aries have flash-in-the-pan rage: if something makes them mad, they see red. To Scorpios, it's always the result of being hurt. When they're upset, they've been wounded and are still feeling the pain.

The Passion Zone

These two signs are astrological "kissing cousins" and share the same passion levels. (By the way, Aries are completely fascinated by Scorpios' deep, mysterious nature, which results in some steamy romance when these two get interested.)

Scorpios thrive on sexual energy . . . not just sex, but the energy created by desire. Aries are always ready for a romp in the hay, but may not understand their mates' complexity in this relationship. When Rams are done, they're done; but with Scorpions, there may be some deeper meaning in what took place, and they'll be watching every nuance to ensure that what they just experienced was safe. When this combination is in harmony, it's incredible; when it isn't, there could be a dangerous test of wills.

What Aries Needs to Know about Scorpio

Scorpios are more complex than you, Aries. To them, life is filled with mysteries and secrets that they must uncover for their own survival—it's just not something you'll ever understand. They're always searching with a low-level radar that tracks your every move and motivation. Treat this probing with as much respect as you want from *them* when you go on *your* quest for a challenge or a battle. You may not give the people in your Scorpio's life a second thought, but *they* will, and allowing their exploration without judgment will prolong your lives together. Last, remember that Scorpions are extremely private and don't ever want anything personal of theirs exposed—regardless of how harmless you may deem the information. Restrain yourself from telling friends any relationship secrets or engaging in locker-room talk.

What Scorpio Needs to Know about Aries

You *must* understand that not everyone self-analyzes their every motivation, especially Aries, who don't have much of an attention span—it actually depresses them if they have to evaluate things too much. You must have an inner sense of security when in a relationship with Aries because they're not going to give you an ounce of reassurance outside of "I'm with you, aren't I?" And it's true, they *are* with you—and that means a lot in the *Aries Manual of Love.* Some creatures just don't go that deep.

LoveScope

These two signs are very similar. There's enough mutual respect for each other's needs here for this relationship to really work in the long term—although there will be some bumps in the road. Scorpios are Fixed Water (deep and emotional), and Aries are Cardinal Fire (fast and inspired). Keeping this difference in mind may help them work out any early misunderstandings. When a good foundation is in place, these two can have a very special friendship—one where loyalty is respected and given. It will also be one where Aries can nudge Scorpios past those inner doubts, and then be taught how to respect others' feelings.

These two could be dynamic as a team, but a certain amount of maturity is required if the relationship is to prosper. If Scorpios let someone in, that person has a friend for life. If an Aries does, the individual in question will be ruthlessly supported in being all that he or she can be. This can be an amazing union if both parties take charge of their own baggage and remove any expectations of each other.

Aries + Sagittarius

LoveScope: 6.3

The Basic Relationship

We have two Fire signs, so let's start with what they share in common: both can be warm and inspirational, but also abrasive, unpredictable, easily bored, and intolerant . . . and both can exhibit gigantic egos!

Aries is an assertive (Cardinal) sign, and people born under it like to keep things moving because they're easily depressed when feeling trapped. They get a primordial urgency about them that silently screams: "Hurry, let's keep moving before they come for us!" But Aries don't even really know who *they* are.

Mutable Sagittarians don't feel that same urgency. Rather, their own inner beliefs are that they're somehow *chosen,* or special. As a result, they tend to hang around waiting for the gifts that they expect to be laid at their feet. Both signs bring inspiration and amusement to the partnership, but their styles of delivery are a far cry from each other. Sagittarians must know that they made a difference in your spiritual life and that they somehow moved you. Aries just want to know that they're liked better than anyone else.

Self-absorption in both is so strong that it can feel like there's a vacuum of space around them. The competitive energy flourishes between the two, so there's little room for anything else. And in their world together, nothing else *exists.*

The Passion Zone

These two can have a lot of fun together, if they can get over themselves. Luckily, each loves sex as well as feeling like the object of the other's affection. The foreplay alone will keep the passion interesting. Sags truly believe they're gifted in the bedroom, while Aries *know* that they are. Egos run amok, sheets get torn, and backs get scratched—and it all makes for wild fun that's fast, hot, furious, and done when it's done (if you catch the drift).

What Aries Needs to Know about Sagittarius

Sagittarians love to hear themselves talk, so, Aries, you must tell them up front to keep their stories to ten sentences or less, or you'll have to explain your impatiently tapping foot. The Archers respond to direct communication, but seriously hope that their beliefs make life better—this means you must be tolerant when they want to explain their spirituality. Oh, and Sagittarians are flirts, so you're just going to have to deal with it.

What Sagittarius Needs to Know about Aries

Sag, you must realize that Aries are warriors by nature and will seek a battle that can be fought and won. Stepping out of the way is a good strategy for you, but your Ram may get off balance if they

can't duke it out. Remember that spirituality is an internal process that can't be measured on the surface, so if your Aries intuits that you're trying to bully them into accepting your belief system, you'll never get them to open up to new ideas. They can sense when you expect something from them, and you won't get what you want if they feel your pull. Learn to stay connected to your Aries by focusing on the things you love about them. The space for a more spiritual connection will emerge on its own.

LoveScope

This relatively low score may surprise many of you since we're taught that compatibility means similarity. In fact, it can have more to do with our differences. Aries and Sagittarius can see themselves in one another too easily, and that doesn't make for the most passionate kind of connection.

Both appreciate life and love, and have more than enough energy to share these things together. They're independent motivators who seek stimulation and understand that in each other. Neither will feel like they wear a ball and chain when they're together. Certainly, an Aries + Sagittarius relationship can work, although it *will* take effort, which isn't news that any Fire sign welcomes. This can be turned around, but both will have to desire real growth.

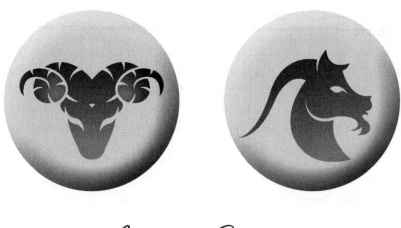

Aries + Capricorn

LoveScope: 5.5

The Basic Relationship

Rams usher in spring, and Mountain/Sea Goats bring forth winter. Both require a formidable amount of energy to do their jobs. They're aggressive, quick, and inspired; and neither likes being told what to do. Therefore, when they decide to engage in a relationship, all sorts of things are started, but no one knows what will get finished. Both signs are initiators; that's their cardinality, as demonstrated by their seemingly endless energy. But one is Fire (the Ram), and the other is Earth (the Goat). Unless there's a conscious effort to work together, Capricorns could get burned, and Aries stand the chance of being smothered.

Aries love independence and spontaneity; Capricorns need purpose and practicality. Aries have hot tempers that, in this relationship, will be met with a cold, calculating wall. The Rams hate routines and love a good shopping spree; whereas the Goats thrive on procedures

and habits, and believe that a day of "impulsive spending" at the mall is an oxymoron.

The essential ingredient in this combination can be found in the word *father.* Aries' issues are with the dad who competed for power, and Capricorns' stem from the paternal figure who drove them to be productive, but had little compassion. This results in an interesting entanglement where each party is likely to project these issues onto the other.

The Passion Zone

Whatever issues exist between these signs in the outside world tend to dissolve inside the bedroom. Capricorns hold a secret surprise in this realm: beneath their matter-of-fact exterior is a passionate and powerfully sexual lover—and one who isn't afraid of that power . . . and this is an instant turn-on for Aries!

The desire between these two horned beasts hits hard and stays with each of them long afterward. Aries see stoic strength and sensuality almost instantly in Capricorns' eyes . . . and the irresistible challenge has begun. At first, the Rams will probably be the aggressors, but it won't be long before the Goats are making the decisions in bed—and Aries can leave at any time if they have a problem with that. Capricorns are used to doing without, but Aries really don't mind relinquishing control to someone who will take charge.

What Aries Needs to Know about Capricorn

Aries, remember that your Capricorn will provide for you, but won't let you control them. They don't like shortcuts and phone calls to friends in high places just to get out of a parking ticket. If you must pull strings, it's better to convince your Goat that your motives are practical and get their endorsement, rather than lose their respect.

You must also remember that every sign has its limits. Your tendency is to push boundaries (it's what warriors do), but you may want to bring consciousness into your relationship here so that you can offer the much-needed component of gratitude.

What Capricorn Needs to Know about Aries

Capricorn, this warrior has as much need to control as you do, so the more you butt heads, the more they'll lock horns with you and fight back. Use logic in your approach to capturing their attention by making it clear that your way is the path of least resistance. But if they insist on working harder rather than smarter, learn to let them expend their energy without resenting it.

You might also try to understand that Rams are fiercely independent . . . but don't assume that they're running from your support. They simply have the intense heat of a furnace burning inside them, which combines with their innate desire to be liberated. Sometimes just doing the smallest thing on their own is enough to satisfy their self-reliant nature—so let them be.

LoveScope

The foundation that this relationship can stand on is respect. Both signs are ferociously autonomous but share a love of raw determination. This is a great place to start, but it's not enough.

Cooperation is possible *if* respect for the other's differences is maintained. Aries get an incredible sense of support from Caps, which helps them create wealth and stability in life. Rams' spontaneous natures help Goats break the rules (an amazing feat in itself) every once in a while, and this allows them to feel the freedom of a walk on the wild side.

These signs have conflicting motives: one seeks to inspire, and the other attempts to build. Unless they're willing to turn their own willfulness down a notch, the foundation will get shaky.

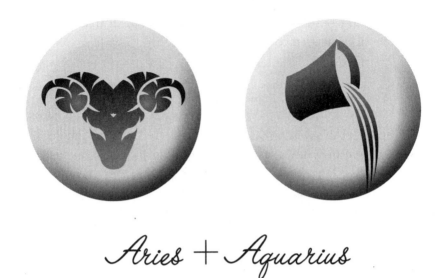

Aries + Aquarius

LoveScope: 5.7

The Basic Relationship

There's a sexy thrill when a rebel and a pioneer come together in a relationship. Both Aries and Aquarius are bold signs that seem to inadvertently call attention to themselves. Neither will shy away from a good fight, although their reasons for the battle and the ways they enter into it will differ greatly. Aquarians will think through the entire strategy *prior* to marching to war, whereas if Aries give any thought to it at all, it will come *after* the battle has been fought. This difference creates a tension between these two that keeps their connection alive.

The campaign of Water Bearers is usually one that embraces humanitarian issues like ending world hunger or raising money for The Humane Society. They tend to think and act globally, and their ideals can seem so removed from the individual that it becomes hard for the very personally motivated Aries to feel connected to them or their causes. An Aquarian relationship remains with the cause and the group—not with a person.

Aries want to be inspired rather than sitting around all day thinking of solutions—which is just too painful for them to imagine—so they'll simply react to a problem. They might go to a rally for a movement they believe in, but will probably end up arguing with the person who blocked their view because they *need* a fight. For Aries, this compulsion is actually felt physically in their bodies and must be expressed. (Do you remember Rosie O'Donnell, an Aries, loudly expressing her liberal views on TV or her fights with Donald Trump about his toupee? That's what I'm talking about.)

Both of these signs fear commitments that are too binding, giving them a mutual desire to create alternative ways of relating. Consequently, they rarely end up with a union that looks *normal.*

Aries are conquerors and love (but also hate) the brick wall Aquarians so easily sit behind. Rams will work extra hard to please in this relationship because the Water Bearers are so difficult to read. Those of this Fire sign would rather overcompensate for the sake of their own pride than be accused of not stacking up! Aquarians are so amused by the seemingly juvenile tactics that Aries are willing to employ in order to be seen as "the best" that they end up hardly noticing the sex but thoroughly enjoying the show!

The Passion Zone

Aries is Fire and Aquarius is Air, so there will likely be fast and furious passion that could flare up but die down quickly. Although the heat might not linger long, these two can ignite their desires in the moment. One note: Both of these elements often view physical intimacy as something to fit into their schedules. They love the sex they share, but once they're done, it's back to the activity that was set aside to make time for their sensual play.

What Aries Needs to Know about Aquarius

Aquarians worship the mind and will probably see your spontaneity as reckless, which to them is a weakness. You may detect

condescension in your partner's voice as they try to hide their disdain for your impulsivity. Let them know that you're fully aware of what you're doing, because they need to know that you're acting with consciousness—but if there's any doubt in their mind, it would be good for them to ask. Also, be aware that Water Bearers love their causes and will expect you to be on board with them. If you don't believe in what they're doing, politely decline to participate . . . otherwise, you'll just resent it later.

What Aquarius Needs to Know about Aries

Aries are smart—mentally quicker than you might imagine—so remember this when you talk to them. To you, Aquarius, they seem impulsive and mindless of details. That doesn't mean they haven't taken notice; it just means they don't make the small things a priority. They'll tolerate your control to a point, but if you aren't aware that they loathe it, you'll be caught off guard when they reach their tipping point and suddenly leave you. Make a habit of acknowledging what your Aries partner does well.

LoveScope

Both Aries and Aquarians love feeling supported, but neither really needs it. Sometimes it's easier to go it alone rather than fight to stay connected. Water Bearers love control and Rams abhor it, which could be a match made in hell. Their LoveScope score edges just past the halfway point on the 1–10 scale, suggesting that the partnership has a slightly better-than-average chance of success. If the relationship makes it through the initial obstacles that this Zodiac combination may present, there's a good probability of longevity because both signs share something vital to the survival of commitment: individuality.

Aries + Pisces

LoveScope: 2.8

The Basic Relationship

Pisces is the quintessential Water sign: accommodating completely and containing volumes of mysteries. Those born under it are the perfect opposite of Aries, who see conformity as weak. On the surface, this is an unlikely duo—Aries is the first sign of the Zodiac, and Pisces is the last.

However, beneath this surface lies an uncanny understanding, which makes sense if you follow the astrological calendar in order and imagine that the sign just before yours contains wisdom that will inform your own. In this case, Pisces contains the insight of all 12 signs; and since Aries follows Pisces, it's bestowed with a deep understanding of that same intelligence. Unfortunately for the Fish, the Rams shake off all that knowledge and use their powerful aggression to remain singularly focused on their own current reality.

Pisceans understand that the world is filled with people in pain. Usually characterized as caring and considerate, they cope with their

experimental knowledge of everyone else's struggles in one of two unusual ways: (1) they consume mind-numbing substances; or (2) keep their bodies completely pure so as not to absorb others' energies. Their compassion has a price. Meanwhile, Aries have an innate capacity to completely block these empathetic feelings by identifying with their warriorlike intensity. This makes Pisceans feel safe enough to create and connect with their own desires. Their ability to "swim" into this protected world allows them to feel an independence that isn't part of their natural realm of existence.

The Passion Zone

This is an inspired mix in the bedroom. Aries know that they'll be provided with whatever they want, while Pisceans are assured that they'll be able to read their lovers. Luckily for Rams, Water Bearers are fluid and often take on the traits of their mates. In intimacy, the forceful nature of Aries will often be met with equally aggressive Pisceans, who have emotionally merged with their partners. Aries love the adoration from Pisceans, who, in turn, are enamored with their Rams' strength and bravado; this is irresistible to these warriors. Meanwhile, the Fish live in a lush, watery world and may not need that much sexual satisfaction—whatever needs are *not* being met will be satisfied within their own inner fantasy worlds. Aries love to conquer, and Pisceans love to surrender. The biggest challenge here is finding ways to keep the Rams interested.

What Aries Needs to Know about Pisces

Aries, it would serve you well to understand the gentle nature of Pisceans. They have a deep-seated belief that the more suffering people experience, the more capable they are of taking away the pain of others. This concept might as well be taught to you in a foreign language because you aren't likely to understand it.

Pisceans tolerate your anger effortlessly, but this does have an impact that may show up after a stiff drink or in a few days when they can't work because their stomach hurts. They absorb what you put out, and the more conscious you are of this, the more kindness you'll be able to bestow upon your partner. Know, too, that your Pisces is faithful, but won't always perceive the flirtatious advances from others for what they truly mean.

What Pisces Needs to Know about Aries

Aries can be selfish. They know what they want and go after it . . . and assume that you'll do the same thing. When you silently allow them to push forward without first thinking of you or others, you're suffering for them and they'll never know it. Sacrifice isn't your conscious motivation (you really just want recognition), and you are *not* required to make any. It *is* a sacrifice when you bite your tongue when someone jumps in front of you, interrupts you, or inadvertently hurts your feelings. Assert yourself to your Aries, or at the very least, let them know that you altered your behavior to accommodate them. It will help them see how conscious and considerate you are in areas where it would have never occurred to them.

LoveScope

I wish I could rank these two higher, but there are problems here—not the least of which is the idea that Pisceans' compassion is totally foreign to Aries. It's up to the Fish to adapt and conform. Rams usually aren't invested enough in others to bring a full level of commitment to this relationship. There's much to be gained if both have a willingness to work for it, and if the moon and rising signs are considered. Alas, without the support of other planets in their charts, these two could have fun in the short term, but for the long haul, it's an unlikely pairing.

WHAT MAKES ARIES AWESOME?

- How they are a true friend who will go to bat for you when everyone else is against you
- Their boldness in saying "I'll go first" to prove to you that it's safe
- Their way of having just the right size foot when they need to give you a motivational kick
- Their knowledge of the fastest way to get somewhere during rush hour
- Their bravery in going where angels fear to tread
- Their courage when you have none of your own
- Their way of never outstaying their welcome
- Their insistence on being independent
- How they constantly find new and better things to do
- Their appreciation of the sun

Taurus + Taurus

LoveScope: 4.9

The Basic Relationship

At first, it might sound a little bit heavy to have two immovable, Earthlike objects plunked together trying to have a relationship—both unwilling to give up their positions or ideas and stimulated by their personal comforts. It's really not that bad, though. Taureans are motivated by their own desires, it's true, but their partners are included in that—or they wouldn't be with them (trust me on this). This union can hit points where someone has to bend for compatibility purposes, but that's true for all relationships. It's just harder for Bulls to yield, which is where it gets interesting. Here we have two natives of the most Fixed (stubborn) sign of the Zodiac trying to figure out how to cooperate in a mutually satisfying way, and surprisingly, they can usually pull it off.

Taureans are practical and gentle, and full of desire for wealth and the luxuries of life. This love of the material world—especially goods

of the finest quality—equips them with the skills they need to get what they want. These abilities don't necessarily include savvy business minds, but they are quite adept at the art of seduction. No one understands how to go about it better than Taureans, which ups the ante in this relationship! With most other signs, Taureans have the gift of making their mates feel honored to do things for them. However, with another Bull, the skill gets highly developed, and both partners have built-in support to improve it even more. When they need or desire something, it's up to each of them to tell the truth and not just anticipate assistance, but expect to *give* some as well.

The Passion Zone

Sensual Venus always heats things up, and when two signs ruled by this planet are involved, it can mean "Pleasureville" in bed. Unlike those of the Fire and Air motives, who are noteworthy for their quick and easy romps between the sheets, these two may turn lovemaking an event that lasts the whole evening (or day!). It may start with food of some kind—perhaps a great dinner or just some strawberries to feed each other, but it will be a feast of the physical in some capacity. Candles, baths, massages, or anything that feeds the body will be part of the ritual. There are no "quickies" for these two—just long, mutually sensual delights—and don't forget that they'll spend an hour cuddling afterward.

The worst part of this connection in the bedroom happens if one of them gets angry or closes down. Taureans have remarkable memories and can hold a grudge for a long time. When two are in the house, one could decide to give up their resentment, but then the other may just decide to give them a taste of their own medicine . . . thus, the cycle continues.

What Taurus Needs to Know about Taurus

If you two decide that you have different ideals or paths, it will be almost impossible for a relationship to work, because there will be a stalemate. An unhappy Taurus can stay that way for a long time (*you should know*), but you can melt your disgruntled Bull with appreciation and understanding. You both soften at the sign of a gentle touch or kind word, but *only* if it feels genuine.

If you two don't learn the art of putting desires aside in favor of more immediate acknowledgment of what you have now, a standoff will prevail. When you understand that being still and feeling the moment could give you a perspective that you've never known, then bliss is possible. This can be a relationship filled with hope and stability as long as each of you takes personal responsibility for giving yourself what you so desire from the other.

LoveScope

It's great when partners are similar to each other, but it's also hard when there's too much likeness—it can actually stunt the growth of the relationship. Certainly, with the entire birth chart involved, each may have a different personality, but when all is said and done, they're both motivated by the desire for security. There's no doubt this can be a successful union, but the mediocre LoveScope score reflects the difficulty they face in bringing ease and joy into the partnership. If anyone can do it, determined Taureans can—but getting them to *want* to do it is another story.

HOW TO KEEP THE TAURUS YOU LOVE

- Cook them a great meal from scratch.

- Give them neck massages.

- Buy them the most expensive version of the gift they want when it isn't on sale.

- Don't make them answer right away (unless you want them to say no).

- Don't lend them money—give it to them.

- When they say their mind is made up, believe them.

- Think of something you appreciate about them every day, and then tell them what it is.

- Let them sleep in when possible.

- If you have to wake them up, do it with the smell of hot coffee or tea (no yelling).

- Don't use *their* things.

Taurus + Gemini

LoveScope: 4.0

The Basic Relationship

At first glance, the idea of immovable Earth and blowing Air may seem ridiculously incompatible. One is grounded (pardon the pun) and steady, and the other is flitting around from one person to the next, but this is the kind of difference that can actually work. In a way, it's like those sci-fi movies that are so bad that they become endearing cult favorites—all right, this union is not *that* bad, but Taurus and Gemini are an odd couple at the very core.

Geminis love to be in nonstop motion, as they require constant stimulation. Taureans are almost the complete opposite: they're slow, giving thought to each word's meaning, and they love bilateral appreciation—the kind they can both give and receive. The Twins easily use words that sound appreciative, but Bulls are purveyors of quality, and they know the difference between ordinary utterances and those coming from the heart. Taureans, being Fixed, have a harder time trusting

that Geminis, who just can't take root as deeply as their mates, have the best of intentions. If they do stop long enough to really comprehend something, they get nervous. It's not that they can't *feel*—they just need to *move*. If forced to stay in one place for too long (either mentally or physically), they'll become claustrophobic.

The airy winds must blow, but when left alone, the Twins will always set their autopilot to home. Taureans, whose element is Earth, evaluate trust on consistency, and the only thing that never fails about Geminis is that they must change. In the worst-case scenario, if a Taurean is forced to maintain low-level distrust for very long (because the Gemini is acting uncommunicative or sneaky), that sentiment gets planted in the Bull's Earth and will take root and grow. That's something no mate wants to have happen—once an idea sprouts in a Taurean's mind, it takes nothing short of divine intervention to change it.

So on the one hand, you have an airy Gemini who loathes being cornered; and on the other, an angry Bull who won't budge until it feel safe. Taureans need their partners to remain still, which Geminis abhor; and Geminis insist their mates be more flexible (equally detestable to Taureans). If these requirements aren't met, this union often results in an impasse.

The Passion Zone

This relationship usually has a strong initial zing, but sadly, it tends to fade quickly once Geminis' minds move on to something new and different. Taureans will eventually need more affection and connection, and the Twins will need more change. But instead of dwelling on that, it's better to look at what makes the pot boil . . . in that steamy sort of way.

Because they're a sign that inherently seeks security, Taureans often become creatures of habit, to the point of even boring themselves. Before they realize it, they've mindlessly completed a task to perfection without really paying attention because they've repeated that same one a million times. Then they meet this flickering firefly of light chatting wittily with friends, showing such apparent interest and knowledge about *everything* . . . and it's a Gemini with twinkling eyes and a dashing smile. It's Air all right—*fresh* air—and Taureans love how this feels!

Geminis find that most people are easy to talk to (for them it's like breathing), but when they meet Taureans, their natural tactics make them shine. Bulls don't smile just because they were told a great joke that perfectly relates to their beliefs (how do Geminis *do* that?); they do so because someone stopped and noticed them. The Twins met them at the Taurus door, and they didn't even have to speak first.

Yes, these two feel it right away; it's keeping it *going* that they find hard.

What Gemini Needs to Know about Taurus

Gemini, you need to know that your Taurus partner truly values security, more than you might realize. Eventually, the Taureans who become attached to you will begin looking at how you manage your finances. Even if they don't need it, money matters to them, and trying to brush these issues aside won't help. Even though Taureans will hold on much longer than most other signs, many won't tolerate what they consider to be a discourteous Gemini. It's important that they can see evidence of your ability to stay in one place (with certain freedoms, of course).

What Taurus Needs to Know about Gemini

Taurus, there are two important things to know about Geminis: (1) they need some space, and (2) they'll perceive you as a control freak. Those are two indelible facts, which means you must accept them or be willing to leave.

You have to let it sink in that Geminis need freedom, but they also want to know that there's a place waiting for them that's safe. It's not enough for you to be the stable one while they play their fields of

flirtation; you have to know that you can't put them on a leash and then expect them to be happy. They need stimuli that you may not totally understand. Underneath all the playful dalliance, they're terrified of any kind of commitment. So why are they with you? Because you're a little more self-absorbed. It's the perfect extra person in the Twins' relationship, and Geminis love threesomes!

LoveScope

It's true that these two have strong initial chemistry, but the everyday routine might not add up to a good mix. Taureans may need a daily massage or cuddling for hours to know that their partners care. Geminis are looser with their schedules, but they also need to know that their Bulls will be there with no strings attached. Although the Twins love their freedom, they always come back to what's familiar. And no one makes things routine better than Taureans.

Taurus + Cancer

LoveScope: 9.2

The Basic Relationship

There's ease when someone is involved with another person who's two signs away from their own—and it doesn't have to look like a picture-perfect couple holding hands and whispering sweet nothings throughout the day. This calmness is about two people being completely comfortable with who they are when in each other's presence.

In the Taurus-Cancer relationship, their elements—Earth and Water—are compatible, and the recognition that each has of the other is greater than most. They both understand the softer side of life: the world of feelings, senses, emotions, and caring. Both are sensitive to the needs of the ones they love. Cancers love to have a role in their mates' development and want to be provided for, and Taureans adore being nurtured and supportive. Crabs tend to their partners with encouraging affection, and Bulls do so with understanding. When

these two are in the flow, it can be delightful, but when they're out of sync, Water and Earth can seem like mud, causing the relationship to feel stuck and stagnant. These two have to be careful to maintain the proper amount of distance between them to ensure a refreshing connection.

The Passion Zone

This is the beauty of the every-other-sign relationship. There's an instant understanding between the Bull and the Crab. Cancers' insecurities are laid to rest by the solid assurance of Taureans, whose *love* of being loved is met with consistency. Under the wrong circumstances, the elemental motives can make "mud," but they're more likely to create a garden that will produce an abundant harvest of love. Their passion is tender, mutual, and erotic. Each person can bring bliss to the other and enjoys the prospect of doing so. Cancers are imaginative in the bedroom and secure with partners who don't turn their attention to the TV after sex, and Taureans love surprises that stimulate their bodies and the richness that their mates bring to intimacy—it's definitely a good match.

What Taurus Needs to Know about Cancer

Cancers are of the Cardinal mode, which means they're leaders who like to nudge and push, but in a way that's always for the highest good, Taurus. Being Fixed, you won't be pushed under any circumstances, even if you agree that it's in your best interest. It's an inner reflex for you to dig in your heels when you feel pressured. Unfortunately, Cancers feel safest when the person they're in love with has total faith in them. Know that standing your ground is certainly not a statement of trust when seen from their perspective. For you, it's surrender, and if you really believe in them, you'll do as they wish—even if it doesn't feel right because that's just not how you work. You have to feel things for yourself and in your own time, but for a Cardinal Crab, that could just feel like downright rejection.

What Cancer Needs to Know about Taurus

If you pull the rejection card, Cancer, your Taurus may have to deal with your range of emotional reactions, from tears to a major withdrawal into your extremely hard shell. Possibly feeling unappreciated and perhaps even attacked, they may now explode. That's right—sometimes Taureans erupt in loud, out-of-character bursts of rage! And if you've ever seen an angry Bull, you know how scary that is.

If you two let things mount up, hurt upon hurt, it could be a long time before they lighten up and are ready to resume in the usually comfortable state. Too much pain will send you home to Mom and your Taurus out to eat!

LoveScope

In their normal states, these two can bring much happiness to each other. Taureans' stability is a refreshing security to Cancers, who like to know that they're safe from the dangers of the world—something that Bulls are more than happy to offer. Taureans want the peace of mind that they'll be cared for and even spoiled just a bit by their "Cancer momma" (male or female), who will do whatever is necessary to protect and support as well. Two nurturers offering the necessary tools to live successfully in a harsh world is the major gift that they can bring to each other. Bulls will need a push every now and then, but Crabs know just when to do it, in spite of the complaints of their often-complacent partners. Cancers will need a reminder every now and then that love and encouragement are different from control. With this in mind, the relationship can work like a charm.

HOW TO LOSE THE TAURUS YOU LOVE

- Ask them to return that item they borrowed from you.

- Buy them a pleather briefcase.

- *Lovingly* pat their belly.

- Order fast food for your night on the town.

- Sell their favorite chair in a yard sale.

- Tell them that they're not unintelligent, just "slow."

- Borrow money and don't pay it back.

- Give gift cards from the dollar store.

- Leap out of bed after sex.

- Buy them flowers from the sale rack at the grocery store.

- Make fun of how they dance.

Taurus + Leo

LoveScope: 7.9

The Basic Relationship

Leos are the kings (or queens) of the jungle, and feel an inherent right to benevolently allow the other beasts to feast on their goods. It's part of that Leonine generosity, which is bestowed willingly as long as the recipient acknowledges that it's the Lion's territory. Taureans are Bulls, and if they hear what the king or queen is saying about the jungle, they might just respond in words true to form and say, "This is *bull!*" They aren't ones to take kindly to feeling controlled, especially regarding their most valued prizes: food and material comforts. It's easy to see why it may take these two a while to trust each other's position. It's not impossible, though. In fact, when it happens, it lasts forever—Fixed signs do everything forever—but getting there takes a lot of understanding.

Since both Bulls and Lions are Fixed, there's a tendency for them to dig in their heels about everything. Also, they tend to keep a close

eye on their own needs. Taureans have definite wants, and their goal here will be to tame those bullish desires. Leos have needs as well, but theirs are for their partners to like them and see them in a positive light. Since both are focused on their own issues, it's common that each will overlook the attention that the other needs. At its worst, these two will resent each other's apparent self-centered approach to the relationship. Because signs of this mode tend not to trust other people right away, their self-centered attitudes add more fuel to the fire of mistrust. Taureans need to be showered with appreciation, but Leos will only give it when they feel that they're "received"; however, Bulls won't welcome Lions unless *they* feel gratitude. As with all Fixed signs (especially when the elements are very different), someone has to bend first.

The Passion Zone

It's been said that the degree to which there's frustration in a relationship is the degree to which there's passion, and these two are destined for extreme passion. Leos are highly receptive to Taureans' sensuality, and return the favor by showering them with a generous dose of their warm lovemaking. Both are very "giving" in bed, as long as there's an equal exchange. The Lions are fascinated by the receptivity of the Bulls, who love the kingly manner of their partners—so expect "off the charts" chemistry. Just remember that between the sheets, Taureans love appreciation and Leos cherish adoration, so someone has to take the first plunge. There's definitely incredible sexual tension here that can last a long time.

What Leo Needs to Know about Taurus

Leo, your Taurus doesn't want to steal your stage, throne, or thunder—that would be counterproductive. They simply want to know that what's yours is also theirs. It's just a psychological thing, and if you really *are* in a relationship, why not make it a fact? Taureans love to feel spoiled, and yes, they will sound dictatorial and demanding as they tell you what they want. When you put your foot down, though, they'll stop and reconsider their behavior. Just make sure you speak in those nice "*I* feel that . . ." phrases. It ensures that they won't feel attacked, which only delays the possibility of a gentler turnaround. Once you state your complaint, let it go so they can "digest" it in their bodies for a while—they'll come back with a resolution.

What Taurus Needs to Know about Leo

Leos love your approval! You can't let them know how patently true this is or you'll embarrass them. . . . Oh, never mind—really they want what they want and don't care if the entire world knows it. No one gives appreciation like you do. You can make your Leo feel royal one minute and like a peasant the next. Try to stop this blatant control because it will eventually lose its power.

The worst part of Leos is their never-ending need for acceptance, and the most unfavorable part of you is your ceaseless manipulation of that point. When you're with your Lion, think generous thoughts. It will pay off in the long run.

LoveScope

This is a very common combination, and one destined for a successful future. Once these Fixed signs can enter each other's realm of trust, they'll be the reigning royalty for a long time to come. It takes a lot to break up this dynamic pair because neither likes change. Leos' loyalty to their Taureans—and vice versa—make for one of the sweetest unions in the Zodiac; and with a small amount of consciousness, this lovely combination will withstand the test of time.

Taurus + Virgo

LoveScope: 9.0

The Basic Relationship

It would be easy to assume that this combination has a high Love-Scope score because Taurus and Virgo are both Earth signs. Although there is some truth to the fact that signs of the same element have a certain ease with each other, that doesn't always translate to a good relationship. In this case, though, it does.

Taureans need a certain amount of reassurance. They get it from their belongings: a nice car, a cozy chair, or even their old trusty leather bag. Whatever *it* is, it's important to their nature. Virgos tend to comple-ment this earthly Taurean desire by being people who also care about material possessions. They seem to think that everything has a place, and can devote their lives to the idea that one person's trash is another's treasure. By their very natures, these two suit each other. Bulls believe that their things are priceless, and Virgins also treat their stuff in that way. You'll never see Virgos secretly giving anyone's possessions away, and that makes the rather materialistic Taureans feel good.

Taureans are truly self-absorbed, and Virgos are the loners of the Zodiac. That makes for a match made in heaven. Neither sign likes to be bothered . . . at least until something comes up that just can't be overlooked. The Bulls will be the ones to take the last morsel of food from the leftovers in the fridge, and have no problem leaving the empty plate right where they found it! This initiates nagging from Virgos that could irritate a saint, but that's how these two hear each other. Virgins know that there's a thick wall around their Bulls, and sometimes it takes loud explosives to get through!

The Passion Zone

It's the detail-oriented, fastidious Virgos meeting the sensual and materialistic Taureans. Together this can make for incredibly fun adventures when it comes to sex, because both get to unleash their hidden wild passions. Bulls are accepting, and Virgins love that. They share an extreme attention to detail: Virgos will keep the sheets clean, and Taureans will make sure that they're 1,000-thread-count Frette.

For Virgos, it's a chance to act out their own inner duality (the nun and the harlot). Depending on how "good" they've been, they'll be equally and diametrically "bad" in the bedroom. In every Virgo lurks the desire for untamed abandon, and simultaneously, for purity and order. Taureans love sensuality and touch, and when Virgos are ready, those things will be provided. When all is said and done, though, a shower is in order, and those expensive sheets need to be cleaned. Taureans appreciate the cleanliness as long as they don't have to do the laundry (which Virgos don't really mind), but they must shower . . . before *and* after!

What Taurus Needs to Know about Virgo

The Virgo world is one built on order. The Virgin also has an active mind that doesn't miss a trick. Taurus, when your Virgo starts nagging, it's a sign that they've overextended themselves. That means it's

time for you to pull out the appreciation card and take them to dinner. No sign shows gratitude like you do, so make sure to give them all they deserve. Just don't do it too blatantly, and make sure there's plenty of sincerity!

What Virgo Needs to Know about Taurus

Taureans are capable of letting you do everything if you let them. Since you love being acknowledged for your efforts, you could find yourself doing all the household chores, from dinner to laundry, with only a meager "Thank you" or just a nod of appreciation in return . . . or nothing at all.

Your Taurus loves to feel safe, and the way to make them fully secure in all areas of life is to push them out into the world. This won't be easy, but once you get them to their first job interview and back, you've hit a jackpot of progress.

LoveScope

This is a really solid couple, and these two appreciate being on the same page in life. Virgos are the service-oriented ones who won't leave until the job is done. Taureans will avoid change at all costs, so they'll also hang around for a long time. Together, this pair can create a lot of wealth, and if nothing else, own a lot of "stuff." Collecting and cleaning it could be fodder for hours of quality time for this relationship.

Taurus + Libra

LoveScope: 5.8

The Basic Relationship

It's hard to repress the image of *Beauty and the Beast* when thinking of the union of Taureans and Libras. Certainly, neither is beastly, but their styles of living show that Bulls never lose touch with their fundamental urges, while those represented by the Scales are way too refined to even think about anything primal.

Both signs are ruled by the planet Venus and have strong desires. Those yearnings take shape in very contrasting ways. The difference here is the elemental focus: Taureans are Earth and concentrate on physical issues, whereas Libras are Air and therefore fixate on relationships. They each possess an inherent curiosity about the other, but often have difficulty finding a balance of understanding. Taureans like the finer things in life, such as good food and high-quality products that will last a long time. Libras relish what's beautiful in life: people, art, and parties where they can don their most elegant clothes and

network. The Bulls can enjoy sitting in their top-of-the-line La-Z-Boy all evening, but their partners need the social connections with others. Libras are Cardinal (assertive) and like to set a pace; Taureans are Fixed (persistent) and like to plant their roots where they are. Both hate conflict and love appreciation (a plus when arguing), but Libras have less patience for those things that Taureans will easily wait for.

Libra is the only sign of the Zodiac represented by an inanimate object: the Scales. It's a testament to Libras' clear, unbiased minds and the ability they have to remain objective—regardless of the intimacy involved. Because they're an Air sign, they form pictures in their heads of the perfect relationship: romantic, conflict free, and most of all, light and easy. Taureans are very different in this regard. The Bulls like a close relationship with one person and treat their beloved possessively (like everything else they "own"). Libras like that their mates are there for them and are always where they say they're going to be.

The Passion Zone

Venus, the planet of love, rules both of these signs, so they have each other figured out right away when it comes to what happens in the bedroom. Their mutual appreciation of beauty and quality ignites their passions; however, there might not be enough sexual tension here after their strong initial attraction fades.

Libras are Air and like intimate encounters to be light and pleasant. They seek beauty in the body and personality, and are seduced by charm and grace. When Taureans' attractiveness captures their fancy, the sexual chemistry can be great. But Air does not like to be clung to—nor does it like to be caged—and that can be an issue, because Bulls like to "own" their partners. Up front, though, they have all the allure and grace a Libra could want. A Taurean could revel for hours in a sudsy bath for two, and that's just the foreplay. The purely sensory delights enhance the physical pleasures, and they become erotic delights for both. At first, it can be a tantalizing experience for Libras; but as the familiarity increases, they'll want the encounters to be lighter, with just a few sprinklings of tenderness.

What Taurus Needs to Know about Libra

Taurus, you need to stay conscious and understand that your Libra partner must fly off to experience what the planet has to offer, but be assured that they'll always return home after their brief excursions. You can rest in the comforts of home until your butterfly returns to you.

Libras like to charm, flirt, and find magic in every person; and they seek connections with different people on a regular basis. It's not because they're dissatisfied with you, but rather because their Air nature sends them whirling around—thinking, connecting, and making decisions about what's fair in the world. Meditating on all of this is exhausting to them, and they need lots of rest in the meantime. Give them room to fly, and remember—you'll never win a debate with them.

What Libra Needs to Know about Taurus

Taureans like to revel in what they have and dream of what they can obtain. It's a solid, practical way of looking at the world. They have incredible staying power, and if allowed, would lie in bed most of the morning and start their day at 2 P.M. Libra, your Bull likes to be moved from an inner drive—a deep sense that what they're doing won't hurt or surprise them or throw them off their game.

Taureans have a remarkable ability to take criticism, and you're remarkably good at finding faults (especially if you've spent the day being nice—those Scales need to balance). Be careful, because you may not notice the accumulated effect your criticism is having on your Bull. They have an amazing capacity to endure almost anything without showing any signs of breaking. But if you administer that last straw of complaint, the one that sends your Taurus into a rage, it's not over when the shouting stops . . . their anger can last for months. Know that you've been warned.

LoveScope

These two see much of the world the same way, so they'll have a great friendship that's based on an understanding of what constitutes a good quality of life when it comes to food, places, and people. Unless their charts are extremely compatible, they might perceive each other as selfish and unsupportive, but this pair can also form a bond of mutual admiration grounded in compassion that can last a lifetime.

Taurus + Scorpio

LoveScope: 8.8

The Basic Relationship

At first glance, these two signs look vastly different. Taureans seem simple and grounded, with a focus on material comforts. Scorpios appear complex and brooding, concentrating on sexuality and watching for things that could hurt them. In reality, there's little difference between these two Fixed signs that just happen to be exactly opposite each other on the Zodiac wheel.

Taureans are Earth and Scorpios are Water, so there's a basic level of understanding that allows this union to be without the typical strife that either would face with the other two signs of the Fixed mode. If Scorpions aren't passionate about something, they simply can't be interested in it. Similarly, if Bulls can't *feel* something, they won't act on it (sense equals sensual). So one is sexual and one is sensual, and that's a pretty good start for these two oft-maligned signs (Taureans get the rap for being stubborn, Scorpios because of their obsessions),

as it means that both of them rely on a deeper-felt response before they act. This process engenders trust for each of them.

Taureans need to have the assurance that their partners will be there for them and know how to reward them for their "good behavior." It's a gift from Venus, their ruler. Scorpios are curiously turned on by the Taurus desire—it's a language they share. Both *feel* intensely and need to believe that they're the source of their partners' deep sentiments. Once they pass each other's tests (and there *will* be tests), these two are in for a long and comfortable ride.

The Passion Zone

Scorpios and Taureans are both fascinated by the process of intimacy. That means they'll have some really fun, passionate encounters where the sexual meets the sensual. Bulls won't flinch at Scorpions' "dark side," and Scorpios are wild about Taureans' almost psychic knowing of what feels good. *Passion* is Scorpios' middle name, and not many on the Zodiac wheel can allow this watery sign the depths that it needs. They want to envelop their partners completely. Taureans aren't afraid of that kind of desire, yearning for a completely sensuous experience—touching, feeling, embracing, laughing—and the complete range of physical pleasures . . . and Scorpios can meet those requirements without blinking. These two can make sheer magic between the sheets. The hard part is learning to leave bedroom antics behind closed doors and assigning different rules to daily living.

What Taurus Needs to Know about Scorpio

Taurus, Scorpios want to feel a sexual connection with you at all times. That's not to say they want sex, but typical Scorpions rate their commitment to you on an inner feeling of intimacy. That feeling, however, can translate into a constant monitoring of the connection that may have you feeling stalked and intruded upon. It's important that you remember to explain your need for some distance (if you can) so that your suspicious partner's fears are allayed.

Another thing to remember is that sometimes your Scorpio partner will say something very cruel in the heat of the moment; this is often followed by intense remorse, and is usually the result of their harboring a hurt inside them. Try to find out what that issue is before you lose your cool, too. Speaking of being mad, Scorpios tend to trust you when you're communicating from a place of anger. They don't realize how dangerous that is since you don't defuse very easy.

What Scorpio Needs to Know about Taurus

Scorpio, your Taurus doesn't like to act immediately on problems or fears. You do react right away in order to release the obsessive thinking that would result if you didn't. Bulls must let the truth that they base their decisions on come from a different place, and this doesn't usually happen instantaneously. So don't think there's disinterest or apathy when their reaction is merely to stare at the computer screen or television. They feel everything that's going on, but need time to process it.

The other thing to know is that once Taureans get to the point of expressing anger, they don't show it the same way you do. It's not likely that they'll go into a place of remorse for getting something off their chest, but instead will probably stew in those incensed feelings for a while. If they tell you they're starting to get angry, believe them.

LoveScope

If there are concessions made by both, these two can find a lifelong bond that's virtually impossible to break. The passion here is almost off the charts, but the tendency to get stuck in particular feelings can be the hardest thing to overcome. Taureans must remember that communication is as important as trust to their Scorpions. Scorpios must remember that their Bulls have a tendency to feel more secure with material things, and that it's not a reflection of their commitment

to the relationship. Fixed signs must, more than ever, learn to bend when they're involved with someone born with the same mode. The old cliché "A tree that bends will not break" is advice that will work wonders for this couple! Once they open up to each other, they have a hard time letting go. This is a relationship of sensuality, sexuality, consistency, and commitment that can prosper.

Taurus + Sagittarius

LoveScope: 4.4

The Basic Relationship

At first this pairing, between a Bull and a Centaur, seems an unlikely one. Sags bounce around and are optimistic and hopeful, spreading messages of inspiration and (often exaggerated) joy. Taureans root more patiently into the earth, nurturing those who happen to cross their paths. When they catch each other's eye, there's a moment of remembering an energy not their own. The Bulls are actually uplifted by the antics displayed by Sags, who are often drawn to the safety they sense in their partners.

Sagittarians are roamers, while Taureans are planters. Centaurs inherently trust that life will work out for them, and Bulls don't give their trust anywhere near as easily. In fact, they're more likely to remain in a state of mind that prepares them for the worst. Sags take risks and sometimes hit a jackpot, but other times may hit rock bottom. Bulls don't like risks and abhor the thought of falling on their faces. But

there is a twinge of attraction in this relationship, a hint of wanting to have what the other seems to embrace so confidently. That's what draws these two to begin their journey together.

The Passion Zone

Sagittarians may grow tired of the same old routine of lovemaking and require something different—not necessarily a change of partner, but maybe a new scene. "The bed is too boring," complains the Sagittarius. "How about we make love on a gondola in Venice?" After all, the city of canals has its root word, *Venus,* right there. Being ruled by that planet, Taureans would feel an immediate draw. That's what Sags do: they inspire . . . unless they feel held back. Then that uplifting nature can burn their mates to a crisp. The Bulls have lovemaking down to an art form, and for all the worldly traveling Sags have done (sometimes just in their minds), even they will be surprised by sensations in their bodies that they never knew could be so wonderful. No matter how far they wish to journey, there's something addicting about re-creating those breathtaking feelings.

What Taurus Needs to Know about Sagittarius

Taurus, Sags are dreamers! They never tire of coming up with hopeful ideas and alternative ways of doing things so that outcomes might be different. More often than not, the results disappoint them, but it's important for them to have the hope. Centaurs abhor the idea of being stuck in the physical world and don't easily understand people who like it. They're known for their stinging criticisms and whining complaints about the things they imagine are holding them back from their true calling. You are a fine target for that disappointment, but their blame never lasts longer than the momentary annoyance of a child who might as well be cursing the sun for being hot.

What Sagittarius Needs to Know about Taurus

Taureans understand the importance of the world around them more than any other sign. They aren't so willing to change or move—and that could frustrate you, Sagittarius, because you may feel that there isn't time to waste. Bulls do tend to focus on what *could* go wrong, always fearing that their securities may be taken from them. It's this lack of faith that you understand the least. After all, you're all about believing in yourself, and Taureans are about trusting that their lives work.

LoveScope

It's tough to believe that things are one way and then see some-one doing the opposite. That is often the foundation for this pairing. Taureans love stability; Sagittarians hate it. Centaurs need spontane-ity; Bulls despise it. But knowing these things in advance should make for a wonderful connection, because the hidden expectations will be wiped away. These two can make a go of it if they're able to give freedom of expression to each other, but it does take flexibility and willingness from both.

Taurus + Capricorn

LoveScope: 8.9

The Basic Relationship

Earth signs such as Taurus and Capricorn have an automatic understanding of each other. These two are comfortable with the material world, even though their approach to it is remarkably different. Taureans love comfort: an easy chair, a new car, a cozy pair of slippers, and let's not forget great food! Capricorns love building whatever it takes to have those luxuries, but they aren't usually as interested in the actual *things* as much as in the power to get them.

Capricorns grow up early; they have to for myriad reasons, ranging from a dysfunctional family (or one that's too large) to having to cope with a tyrannical parent, and all the other possibilities in between that cause someone to mature earlier in life than normal. They learn the ropes, and as soon as they can earn money, they'll usually start their own lives. Taureans seem to have had things a bit cushier. Most Fixed signs stay right where they are and have things brought *to* them, and

Taureans are no exception. That's not to say that Bulls didn't have a difficult life; they just maintain a certain level of expectation or entitlement when compared to Caps' more stoic approach.

If you give something to Taureans, they'll happily take it if it's money or "stuff." Capricorns have a difficult time appreciating anything they didn't work for, so it's harder for them to accept charity. Bulls love being brought gifts, and Goats enjoy providing them (within reason), and that's a good enough place to start for compatibility!

The Passion Zone

Earth signs understand each other's need for physical contact. Taureans are renowned for their sensual desires, but what most people don't know is that Capricorns are sexual tornados! Yep, underneath that mature, handle-anything demeanor is a vault of desires they're just waiting to unleash on their partners. They like their sex sturdy and aggressive, and if they know what you want (and they probably do), you'll be shocked by their to-the-point, compelling sexuality. Whew!

Bulls will provide endless reasons for Capricorns to return to the bedroom—there's just not much Goats can dish out that Taureans can't take, and vice versa! So expect pure, sensual pleasure, because these two signs give it to each other in spades.

What Taurus Needs to Know about Capricorn

Taurus, the worst part of Capricorns is their ability to close you out. They'll build an impenetrable wall and keep you at bay—especially if you've violated their boundaries in some way. Capricorns are also possessive (Cardinal Earth) of the people in their lives. They were trained to either control them or lose them. They need to have a particular purpose—one that doesn't make them feel like they've succumbed to a life of leisure. It's not that they're judging your Taurean ways; they're just afraid of that inability to move forward again once they've stopped.

What Capricorn Needs to Know about Taurus

Taurus is a Fixed sign, which means that those born under it don't take orders or obey authority very easily. Capricorn, Bulls have an inner mechanism that dictates when to take action, although they seem to have an unconscious desire to be pushed. It's always a good idea to figure that out before you start nudging them. They also harbor deep feelings and are trained to experience them. You aren't, so try not to judge them for the very things that guide their lives.

Taureans love to be provided for, and you have an automatic response to that part of their personality—but don't make things too easy for them. They have a problem with inertia, so once they put on the brakes, it's hard to get them going again.

LoveScope

These two are masterful at setting goals and watching them come to fruition. Each understands the needs of the other, and they can easily manage a working relationship. Capricorns love to create and build, and Taureans love to turn those creations into functional tools for living more comfortably. Goats long for things to be traditional and stable, and no one understands or appreciates steadiness like Bulls! If this couple can avoid the pitfalls of greed and selfishness, they can share a remarkably compatible life. Caps will rarely tire when the foundations of the relationship have been laid and adhered to, and their partners thrive on the same commitment.

Problems can be overturned quickly if these two remember that it's likely that neither is trying to provoke the other. It's important that both remember the ambitions they have in common and let the day-to-day quirks simply dissolve. Also, when they share material wealth, these signs have even more reason to stay together. Their kids, nice homes, and good cars remind them of what their union gives them. Setting goals will ensure that their future is successful.

Taurus + Aquarius

LoveScope: 3.9

The Basic Relationship

These two very different signs are the "poster couple" for how to make things interesting . . . or difficult, depending on your perspective. Taureans focus on their possessions, and Aquarians are intent on maintaining their freedom *from* them. Bulls love to feel their bodies and be grounded, moving slowly and methodically; whereas Water Bearers hate the heaviness of the physical and love to float around in the ethers—and are fast and anything *but* methodical when doing so. Taureans don't think; they sense. Aquarians don't sense; they think. Taureans live for touch, but lay a finger on Aquarians, and it's at your own risk!

Okay, maybe it's not *that* bad. There's that theory that the attraction between opposites actually creates chemistry . . . these two have that for sure. They're so very different, but are certainly curious about each other.

The Passion Zone

There can be an amazing amount of passion between these two rather "hard to get to know" signs. Taureans are closely connected to the goddess of love, Venus, and understand the value of appreciation, touch, sensuality, and desire. There are certain requirements that need to be met for them to offer these gifts in an erotic way; and ironically, they are appreciation, touch, sensuality, and desire. Yes, they want to get what they give. It's not that Aquarians can't supply those things; rather, it's just that they have to make the jump from the mind to the body in order to do so, and that could be a giant leap of faith.

This relationship can turn into a battle of wills in the bedroom. Bulls want intimacy to be a sensual embrace; Aquarians want it to be idealistic and quick. But in that moment when the lighting is right and the mood is perfect, these two could partake in what can only be described as *fabuliciousness*.

What Taurus Needs to Know about Aquarius

Aquarians really do live by the pictures in their heads, Taurus. It's as if they have an inner tutor who explains how things are supposed to be. Once these absolutes are learned, they won't acknowledge anything that doesn't conform to them: tantric sex is better than Western sex, the lunar landing was a conspiracy, sex during a full moon can lead to Alzheimer's, and on and on they go with their "ideas." You aren't meant to try to change their minds (that would be next to impossible); it would be more productive to distract them with more relevant issues. Once you realize that your Water Bearer is doing what they do, you can stop seeing it as control (which it is). Just view it as unconscious action, and that will make it better—sort of.

What Aquarius Needs to Know about Taurus

Taureans who aren't getting what they want will remove the Venusian quality from the relationship (appreciation, warmth, and understanding) and can hold out for an eternity. It's true, Aquarius, your Bull has every bit as much of the tenacity you have for *your* ideals and the things you desire. You must realize that even though material objects may mean nothing to you, for an earthy Taurus, they're the essence of security. Indulge your partner whether you understand it or not . . . and they'll reciprocate the favor.

LoveScope

With compassion stirred into this soup, these two can be lifelong partners. Each would have to understand that a fulfilling life starts with the individual, and then a whole person meets the other whole person. Taureans who've established a sense of personal safety and security, along with a good dose of self-gratitude, can see more clearly that their Aquarian friend shows appreciation in massive doses, too, but uses a different "language." It's sometimes hard to see, but it's there—in, say, the single organic bloom that a Water Bearer may have brought home the other night that's still in its pot of soil so it can be planted. Never mind that Taureans would like to display it in the center of the room because it matches the sofa; it's the thought (literally, the mind of Aquarius) that, once understood, can be fully appreciated.

When Water Bearers, who abhor buying into cultural standards, come home to find that their Bull just incurred a huge debt in order to buy the leather chair that's sitting in the living room, they should remember that every once in a while the individual matters, too.

If they support each other, these two can find a rich love life. If Aquarians aren't emotionally cold and Taureans don't remain emotionally immovable, these different worlds can come together, and with some consciousness, truly pull it off.

Taurus + Pisces

LoveScope: 8.5

The Basic Relationship

Pisces and Taurus sit apart from each other on the natural Zodiac wheel, separated by one intervening sign. Typically, that's a good omen for compatibility . . . at least at first glance. Pisces is a Water sign, and Taurus is Earth. Both are "feminine," or receptive, regarding the issues of others. Pisceans are very susceptible to the energies of the people they're in contact with, and Taureans are as solid as a rock, aware of those around them but not easily influenced. Fish like having a solid structure in their lives—someone who knows what they like and don't like and who cares enough to create a protective boundary around them. Bulls fit that requirement like a glove without really meaning to. Their innate ability to remain steady until they "feel it" is easily perceived by any outsider as stable, if not protective.

Neither of these signs are strangers to escapist tendencies, and they can lean toward overindulgences if they're not careful. Taureans and Pisceans understand comforts and can support each other in achieving them. There's a strong chance of developing codependency here, where each sign needs the other in order to feel "right" inside. If allowed to get too intertwined with this feeling, a depressing, heavy tone can develop in the relationship. So it's important for one of these sensitive beings to know how to open the psychic window and let some fresh air in when things get too emotionally burdensome.

The Passion Zone

Taureans don't mind being seen as romantic warriors. A magic spark can exist between these two signs as a result. When Water and Earth combine, the results can be rich, fertile soil, or just mud. These two may never leave the bedroom once Bulls discover the flair for fantasy that exists in their Fish. It's no different for Pisceans, who find great passion in the solid Venusian sensuality that exudes from Taureans. This is a great match for romance, and the sizzle factor is one that can't be ignored.

What Taurus Needs to Know about Pisces

Pisceans are extremely fluid. Some days they seem gentle and sweet, and others they're cold and removed. The fluctuations are a function of Water in its Mutable, or flexible, form. However, its effect on you, Taurus, who are in need of attention or appreciation, can be disturbing. It's something that your Piscean will insist they have no control over, and it's true. Fish have a hard time recognizing what's responsible for their seemingly fickle state. Sometimes it's a disappointment they experience, or it might simply be a snarling colleague's mood they've absorbed. For an outsider looking in, it appears somewhat self-indulgent.

Don't take your partner's mood in any particular moment as a reflection of their feelings for you; rather, encourage them to go relax in a hot bath or take a nap. They need to release daily accumulations, and it's best when they don't take them out on you.

What Pisces Needs to Know about Taurus

Pisces, your Bull needs appreciation, but this is something that you don't give out very easily. While you can offer it to the homeless guy on the street corner or your best friend who needs encouragement, there's something about expressing it when it's expected that tends to stop the generous flow. Taureans aren't *expecting* your appreciation; they just respond to it . . . remarkably. Next time your Bull does something to make your day better, please let them know. They'll just do more of it, which is a win for you.

LoveScope

Together, there's a chance for this couple to build an empire based on compassion and understanding. There's also an automatic strength to this union, which makes it easy for Taureans and Pisceans to commit to each other; and once attached, they rarely decide to leave. If either feels life together is stagnant, with no growth, they'll want to pull away for a while—both need fresh air and must infuse it into the relationship. Ideas and imagination flourish between them, making for an extremely creative pairing built on the magic that they both believe in.

WHAT MAKES TAUREANS AWESOME?

- The way they teach us how to trust our senses
- Their sexy voices
- How they make their partners feel like they're the most important people in the world
- Their eye for quality and comfort
- The way they nurture, and provide safety
- The way they give gifts
- Their unending tenacity
- How they find simple ways to solve the most complex problems
- Their movements
- Their cooking
- The way they can make any experience a sensual pleasure
- Their natural elegance

Gemini + Gemini

LoveScope: 6.3

The Basic Relationship

You'd think you could double your pleasure when two sets of Twins come together in a relationship, but is a foursome really such a great idea? Remember that Geminis have two distinct personalities (just ask anybody who's dated one). One can be bright, light, and chatty, and supply anyone willing to listen with a wealth of random information. The other is a deep, brooding loner who wants nothing to do with people. Boy, with two characters like that inside of them, who needs a partner? Well . . . Gemini does.

Those born under this sign crave communication. The Twins love information, and they acknowledge their ability to flit from one idea to the next. What's more, they appreciate having someone there who can track all this mental activity.

The planet Mercury rules Gemini. It's known as a messenger as well as a trickster, and both nicknames describe the Twins perfectly.

Put two Gemini natives together and it's like a TV sitcom, with all the comedic one-liners they'll toss at each other. This is an important trait for them to use as an antidote for their poison, which is boredom.

The Passion Zone

Some astrologers would go so far as to say that passion in this connection is an oxymoron, and they'd be far from the truth. Just because Geminis tend to translate their feelings into thoughts, it doesn't mean they don't feel; it's as if eroticism for them is a mental connection. Now, it's true that this cerebral exchange can lead to so much rapport that there's no mystery left to fuel any desire. In other words, this couple can get to know each other so well that the romance starts to fade. And although this can be true for any sign, it's particularly so for Gemini.

That being said, two Geminis in a relationship together can be inherently youthful and playful, giving them years of frolic in the bedroom. They need to play and keep things light, which will hold those dark Twins at bay.

What Gemini Needs to Know about Gemini

As with any pairing, a lot depends on the other planets that are activated in your respective charts, Gemini, but looking just at the sun signs indicates that there's a need for constant change or stimulation. That's not bad unless one of you subconsciously agrees to play the "dark" Twin and the other takes on the "light" persona. In that case, you each have denied one of your own inner Twins and projected it onto your partner. If both of you aren't willing to work on reclaiming those projected parts of yourselves, then little growth will occur.

In other words, if you're the happy Gemini, you must accept that your dark side is being acted out through your partner, and then you'll eventually have to claim it for yourself. The same issue applies if you're the depressed Gemini who's cast your joyful Twin onto your partner.

The insight that you'll gain about each other is easily translated to an understanding of yourself. So before you cast that stone at your partner, recognize whom you're really throwing rocks at and who's yelling "Ouch!"

LoveScope

Gemini times two represents an enormous amount of mental energy for one household, but it can work. Now they'll both have someone to gossip with and help them enjoy all those gadgets they love—and then they'll gossip some more! It's nearly a perfect match when it comes to friendship. They're two peas in a pod, with twice the connection.

Geminis will need to be prepared, though, to assume a role they're not used to in this relationship (needy and dependent—yikes!). It's a necessary part of the growth process, and one that they'll appreciate if they use it to understand that how they perceive one another is actually how they judge themselves. That may sound like pop psychology, but the truth is, it's a powerful way to take charge of this complicated connection. Also, Geminis shouldn't fret if they notice that passion is being replaced by friendship. That's a natural outcome for people of this Mercury-ruled sign, because they'll have so many intriguing things to bring to each other that passion may well be the lowest on the list. Having a compatible partner who understands the need to fly and multitask while still maintaining their own interests counts for something.

HOW TO KEEP THE GEMINI YOU LOVE

- Don't ask them what time they'll be back.

- Act interested when they complain about work.

- Ask *them* before you Google something because they're natural fact finders.

- Don't hover over them when they get depressed . . . they'll lose their patience faster.

- When you say "I love you," don't linger around waiting for a response.

- Ask them if they want to talk about it.

- Praise their minds.

- Don't ask them how they feel about you.

- Don't tell them what you don't want their friends to know.

- Give them the TV remote.

Gemini + Cancer

LoveScope: 5.2

The Basic Relationship

When we're comparing the compatibility of signs that are adjacent on the Zodiac wheel (which is the case with Gemini and Cancer), it's important to note the metaphoric direction that we're taking. Gemini prepares us for the coming of summer. Its Mutable mode allows it to handle the ranges of temperature from wet and cool to dry and hot. Cancer is the start of summer, and therefore needs a tremendous force of energy to bring it in.

Geminis are airy and often light, while Cancers are determined and emotional. The Twins are magnetically pulled toward the energy of their partners in this union, but too much Water may make them run for cover. This is a learning relationship: the Crabs figure out that there are certain situations in life that can't be controlled, and Geminis come to understand that there are things worth attaching themselves to for a long time.

At first, Cancers are attracted to the Twins' apparent disinterest. The Crabs notice and feel *everything,* so they're drawn to those who appear to be unaffected by their emotions. Geminis' gifted minds can relate to almost anyone, and Cancers find that quality reassuring. After all, they're used to playing the protective "bouncer" who only has their mates' interests at heart (that's what they tell themselves, anyway). In Gemini, they feel that there's a person who understands them and can help lighten them up.

The Twins find the lush inner world of Crabs reassuring as well. After hanging out in a realm of facts and figures, they can bathe in the soothing waters of this nurturing sign. There are pitfalls, however, and they mostly have to do with Cancers' desire to pin their Geminis down—which is a Cardinal no-no.

The Passion Zone

Gemini natives love the *idea* of sex. It's just recreation designed to keep them stimulated by new experiences. Afterward, it's time for a movie, a bike ride, or a quick read through a book or two! Conversely (and yes, it couldn't be more opposite), Cancers see lovemaking as a merging of two beings, which allows them to feel completely loved and supported . . . if only for 20 minutes. They like the cuddly sense of security that comes from having their partners hold them until they fall asleep. (And if Cancers are able to keep their Geminis in the room after reading this, they're doing great!)

There's great attraction here, but Crabs will have to learn that protection isn't going to be found in the arms of the Twins. There's just too much mental energy moving in their heads for them to stay still that long. It's also helpful to remember that a sexual relationship involving two signs that reside next to each other on the Zodiac wheel is often a little flat—like being kissing cousins. It's not bad, but it's not hot either.

What Cancer Needs to Know about Gemini

Gemini natives are anything but consistent. They're close to you one moment, Cancer, and will need to be far away the next—but it's nothing personal. They sense your tentacles (and let's face it, you use them to track your partner like a submarine uses radar to track whales) and, quite frankly, they're freaked out by being followed—even if it's just psychically. They're aware of your vibe! Also, the last thing Geminis want is to be cornered, backs against the wall, and asked to examine how they feel. This will give them the impression that they're being suffocated, and they'll likely do what any self-respecting Air sign does when feeling caged . . . leave. This doesn't mean that Geminis don't *have* feelings, but it does mean they don't have to look at them just because you want them to take a peek. It's important to remember that their security only appears to come from another person. In reality, their true safety originates deep within themselves.

What Gemini Needs to Know about Cancer

Gemini, your Cancer partner is a bit of a worrywart. They're apprehensive about harming you, and even more afraid that they might get hurt. It's not that they're fragile (Cancer is actually one of the most resilient signs of the Zodiac); it's just that they perceive *everything.* They're not trying to control you . . . well, actually, they *are,* but that's how they feel safe. It may take some time for you to realize that all you need to do is make them laugh or give them enough attention so that they understand that you do see them. Your Cancer is worried about a lot of things, but mostly they're just troubled about the possibility of not having someone who loves them or whom they love. It's less scary if you go after the fear first.

LoveScope

Once Geminis comprehend that feeling trapped is just a defense against feeling *anything,* they can easily see the benefits of being in a relationship with an emotionally based sign. There's no quicker way to understand others' sentiments than being immersed in them. Geminis can teach Cancers how to loosen their grip and let heavier concerns mix with airier viewpoints. The Twins don't really understand how to nurture the same way Crabs do, but that's the point. Support, like love, comes in many guises, and that's a healthy lesson to learn. Just remember that if these two take each other too seriously, that in itself might become the greatest obstacle to overcome. But Cancers' gift of laughter and Geminis' propensity for lightness are a bridge to help these two walk over any troubled waters.

Gemini + Leo

LoveScope: 7.9

The Basic Relationship

In the Gemini-Leo household, there's probably no shortage of children. Geminis, at their most lovable, have a childlike innocence that's probably one of their most attractive assets. Leos are more notorious for being child*ish,* mostly when they make demands that require others to pay attention to them.

When these two come together, there's a tolerance granted that bypasses the need for either of them to change. Geminis accept that their Leo partners need a certain amount of reassurance, so if they can offer a nice compliment on their way out to "play," they'll be glad to oblige. It's worth it when the reward is a shining smile and an exceptionally good mood.

Gemini and Leo are one sign apart on the Zodiac wheel, which implies a good foundation right from the start. Gemini is Air and Leo is Fire, and each fuels a degree of inspiration in the other. The Twins understand something about the Lions, who appreciate that fact. Geminis can laugh at Leos' boastful self-absorption, largely because they're also busy being egocentric. Leos want to be taken seriously and need attention, and their mates can accommodate both of these needs. Geminis don't have many requirements outside of the desire for connection, and Leos can give them that, as long as the focus eventually lands back on them!

This can be a delightful union provided the Lions understand that the Twins may enjoy playing with others as much as they enjoy playing with them (well, maybe not *quite* as much). The relationship is easy, playful, and has a lot of growth potential, with one caveat: neither must feel that they have to change to make the other one happy.

The Passion Zone

This couple can have a lot of fun together, especially when they're both in good spirits. That's true for all signs, but there's something really awful about either of these two being depressed: it feels most unnatural when Geminis are dispirited, and an unhappy Leo is like having the sun disappear. These smart signs know that about each other, and more often than not, won't get passionate until the time is right. Between them, sex is intuitive, easy, dramatic, and over when it's over (20 minutes is *plenty* of time). The only thing they need to guard against is boredom. Geminis hate anything that becomes a routine, whereas that doesn't bother Leos at all.

What Gemini Needs to Know about Leo

Leos are trained to look for approval from the world around them, which is something they learned during childhood—and should *un*learn as adults. So, Gemini, in the beginning there will be a lot of questioning of your trustworthiness. "Why are you going out again?" or "Do you ever consider *my* feelings here?" You have to remember that they aren't trying to cage you. They're testing you to see if you'll

still like them once you've seen this insecure part of them emerge. If you can use your gift of words to convincingly say what's needed, you'll be surprised by how quickly this phase will pass.

What Leo Needs to Know about Gemini

Geminis need a certain amount of communication. Leo, if you're too absorbed to give them the connection they need, they'll take off. And for the record, you can always *threaten* to leave, but we all know that Fixed signs (of which you are one) *never* do. To Geminis, the world often seems cruel and makes too many demands on them. Don't let their negativity erode your Leo optimism; counter their complaints with your brilliant and positive perspective. In time, they'll start believing you.

LoveScope

When there's a proper balance in this relationship, a lasting connection is likely. For the most part, these two are comfortable with each other, providing enough differences to keep things fresh, and adequate harmony to keep it all together. The Lions must remember to indulge their mercurial Gemini companions with a long leash, which means allowing the Twins to make the diverse connections with their friends that they need—and with all the various gadgets that will be floating around the house. Geminis must remember that Leos want to be seen and acknowledged for the generous things they bring to the relationship—including those times that they keep quiet when they'd really like to share more about their day, or not pouting when their Gemini partners have too many appointments. Overall, this is an easy pick for compatibility.

Gemini + Virgo

LoveScope: 4.5

The Basic Relationship

The interesting thing about two Mutable signs getting together is that there are really four: each party brings in two distinct pieces of themselves. Virgos' offering to the relationship involves the archetypes of the nun and the "nympho." One is righteous and pure; the other devouring and sexual. Geminis bring both the optimist and the pessimist, making for a total of four complex characters.

What makes these two different from the other Mutable signs is that they share the same ruling planet, Mercury, which is all about communication. In Greek mythology, Hermes (called Mercury by the Romans) was the messenger god, but he was also the trickster—the playful boy who loved messing with unsuspecting lives. This attribute is easily seen in Geminis, but is less obvious in Virgos, where it shows up in the guise of a very dry sense of humor. Virgo natives can come across as completely serious, but then surprise you with their hilarious wit.

When two Mercury-ruled signs come together, the one common area that emerges is communication. Both of these signs love discussion. Geminis like to talk about almost anything, but Virgos keep the focus on things that matter to them: "Why does the dirt on top of the refrigerator seem more concentrated than the dirt, say, in the bathroom?" There are other disconnects, too. For example, the Twins are curious and social, and they love gadgets; Virgins are skeptical loners and enjoy *destroying* gadgets.

The Passion Zone

Anytime the androgynous planet of Mercury is strongly involved, it's easy to assume that passion will require a certain amount of conversation. Geminis and Virgos can swing from nonsexual to completely insatiable, but it will depend on their moods. The Twins can usually strike a chord in their partners so that the Virgins see the cute, often light reflections of someone who truly makes them laugh. Conversely, Virgos' humor is unmistakably dry and piercing, and easily overlooked if people aren't paying attention. Geminis not only hear their quips—they understand them. Because both have such a strong mental orientation, it's likely that these two will become good friends, veering way beyond passion to acting more like siblings.

What Gemini Needs to Know about Virgo

Virgo is a sadly misunderstood sign. Within your Virgin is an uncontrollable urge to be of service and assist you with anything you need, Gemini. Simultaneously, they have an equally irrepressible desire to be alone. Being of the Earth element, they care about what's taking place in their surroundings and may feel attacked if that environment is misused. Even a messy Virgo has a system of functioning that belongs to them and isn't easily shared. They're the most self-critical of all the signs, and consequently, the most prone to retaliate if criticized by others.

What Virgo Needs to Know about Gemini

Virgo, your Gemini can be critical, but the complaints won't be specific. Most people born under this sign hate their jobs, but can't give a good reason why (the lack of clarity may drive you crazy). When the Twins aren't happy, anything can be the target of blame. Try to remember that they'll respond to a different perspective if you first make a connection with them. Yes, it does sound like you're dealing with a child, and that's because in many ways you are. Keep in mind that Geminis understand the world in much the same way you do, but they just aren't as adept as you at working it. They're also pack rats, so you'll just have to deal with that. Rather than complain, find a way to help keep their useless bits of information organized.

LoveScope

As with any relationship, when both people take full responsibility for their needs and wants, there can be harmony. Virgos simply must own that their criticism is a way of saying "I'm not happy" or "I'm picking on you to stop judging myself." Geminis must acknowledge that they have a hard time staying present and dealing with the more mundane routines that Virgos love.

As they each recognize their habitual responses and realize that they're unproductive, they can start communicating, which is what they do best. Once these two start, they can talk all day and night, and this solidifies their bond and their trust in each other. Every conversation brings them closer together and nearer to the realization that they aren't that different, which can actually help them see the quirks within themselves that cause unhappiness. This means that each can help point the way to the other's happiness, and *that's* a relationship worth considering. Just don't forget that familiarity breeds . . . creativity. Virgins are so self-critical that having a supportive perspective from the Twins is a great gift.

Geminis can go anywhere that their partners' minds can go and present the opposing argument, making it safe for Virgos to take risks.

Virgos can chase the Gemini depression away with brilliant quotes and surefire wisdom that just can't be denied. These two are best friends and could stay that way forever. Many people would say that this is all a good relationship needs; and if that's true, then this combination is perfect. On the other hand, if someone is looking for more passion, sex, and sensuality, they may want to keep moving.

Gemini + Libra

LoveScope: 8.9

The Basic Relationship

When Geminis and Libras meet, there's a big swirl of energy that explodes between them. Each almost instantly likes the other's lightness and ability to chat about anything. Past-life connections start surfacing, and all of a sudden, there's love. Libras love the childlike look of Geminis, who adore the beauty and charm that is Libra. To Geminis, Libras know what they're doing and where they're going, and that's a big plus for a sign that tends to get distracted easily from its own path. Libras believe that their partners know how to handle any situation, and love the innocence that's portrayed in the Twins' sparkling eyes. From breakfast to a midnight snack, these two keep the energy refreshing and usually unencumbered. The key word here is *usually.*

The Passion Zone

With Air signs, the passion is deep, fast, and furious . . . and often used as a way to turn off their active minds. Geminis and Libras love sex, especially when there are no strings, which allows them to play even harder and with more drama—as long as they both understand that neither is getting too attached. They share an extreme commonality in their desire to connect, and commitment is thrown to the wayside by Geminis' interest only in the moment. (One note: both are horrible cuddlers.) This could easily turn into one-night-stand-like sex between these signs—totally light, airy, and fleeting—if they allow it.

What Gemini Needs to Know about Libra

Libras love connection, but unlike you, Gemini, the association they seek is more specific. You've been known to talk to solicitors just to fulfill their quota, but you'll never see Libras move outside of their motive: establishing fondness for a potential partner. It doesn't matter if they're in a committed relationship, because this type of connection isn't about finding a mate. Libras want to form an attachment with others so they can bring out the beauty that people hold deep within themselves. They love thinking that they had something to do with facilitating these wonderful expressions because it promotes their image of themselves as fair, balanced, and knowledgeable about all things beautiful.

What Libra Needs to Know about Gemini

Geminis hate the feeling of having to conform to anything, and that's exactly how they feel when you, Libra, start your idealistic mission to make everyone and everything beautiful. The sad part is that you don't see just how *ugly* it becomes when you put your mission ahead of the people involved.

Unlike you, Geminis will never have a difficult time making decisions, but this doesn't mean that they don't care. Your own reaction to their quick judgment usually means it's worth taking a look to see if, by making them feel bad about their mercurial nature, *you* don't have to feel so bad about having such a hard time making choices yourself.

LoveScope

These two recognize the joy that exists quite easily in each other. Reflecting on the lightness of life, both in this union can be relied upon to bring a sense of balance and friendship. This is valued deeply by people who have to remember to *breathe* and *feel* just to make their experience on this planet real. Air signs hate commitment, which is a four-letter word to them. They're actually terrified of it, but because there are *two* who are frightened in this relationship, they can usually hang out together for a long time since long-term devotion usually isn't required. They find safety in this no-demand zone they've created together. But if either gets bored enough to seek another type of connection—and they both love newness—this relationship will hit the skids.

Gemini + Scorpio

LoveScope: 9.0

The Basic Relationship

At first this might seem like an improbable pairing: the light, play-ful, childlike Gemini embraced in the arms of the deep, brooding, entrancing Scorpio. After all, the Twins abhor going too deep into uncharted feelings, and Scorpions live for the chance to explore the darker side of emotions.

Many couples of this combination do quite well. It could be that opposites *do* attract, since these energies seem so vastly different . . . or it might be that they actually feel better just being together.

One of the Gemini Twins loves connecting with all that's super-fluous and light, but the other insists on visiting the more sinister side of Air. This is the part that *does* perceive more deeply and needs a strong emotional embrace. Hanging out in a feeling place is hard for either Twin, and they'd avoid going there at all costs if they could. They also know that navigating any scary place is safer and easier when you have a guide, and no one knows the caverns of the inner world like a Scorpio.

Scorpios are afraid, but they have a compulsion to move *toward* fear . . . it's how they feel safe. They aren't very good at letting something be that seems to pose a threat (I believe we call this *obsession*). In other words, Scorpions compulsively keep their attention on potential dangers, making it very difficult for them to be at ease even when they aren't dealing with a crisis.

So, this actually does seems like a good pairing: Geminis can show the way to lighten up, and Scorpios demonstrate how it won't kill someone to hang on to their feelings.

The Passion Zone

This is one of the most common combinations. It brings together light Air and deep Water, resulting in an unforgettable attachment that's both passionate and intriguing.

Scorpios are looking for a reflection of themselves that affirms that they aren't as bad as they feel. Geminis, who naturally don't dwell anywhere for very long, are perfect candidates for that reflection. Scorpions discover solace in the Twins' eyes; there's a youthful playfulness that even the most brooding Scorpio finds ease in. The fact that Geminis like to stay close to the surface when it comes to emotions actually provides great incentive to keep things lighter, which creates just the right amount of tension for some serious passion.

What Gemini Needs to Know about Scorpio

Scorpios must learn to trust themselves, which will allow them to have faith in others. Gemini, you must understand that when Scorpions get angry, they're really just hurt. If you can get them to remember this, you can help them stop the growing ball of rage that carries them down their emotional hill.

Scorpios feel things deeply and trust their own perceptions. You'll never be able to shake them from their emotions by being flip or

dismissive—that kind of response will only make them think you're hiding something. Just assume that they're going to look for the worst-case scenario, and then speak with them about it. You're good at talking, and they're good at listening.

What Scorpio Needs to Know about Gemini

Scorpio, you must remember that Geminis abhor direct confrontation and will do whatever it takes to avoid it. This behavior isn't necessarily an attack as much as it is about survival. Moreover, to hover obsessively over any emotion is torturous to the airy Geminis. They really can't fathom the answer to questions like "How do you feel about me?" or even the more basic "How do you feel?" This forces you to deal with your mistrust. If you can remember that Geminis love to discuss their perception of a situation, you should relate with them on that level. It would be good to let them feel connected to you from this mental understanding before you react emotionally to your own assessment of the event.

LoveScope

As the trust grows between these two, the possibility of a long-term union becomes realistic. Geminis are Mutable, so they're able to adjust to Scorpios' frequent outbursts. More important, the Twins eventually realize that they have a certain permission to get angry that won't even shock or hurt their Scorpio partners. Also, Geminis can tolerate the seemingly obsessive rituals of Scorpions, who have many quirks. Scorpios provide a consistent introduction to a new way of thinking, which is perfect for the always-curious Gemini mind.

The Gemini-Scorpio combination tends to facilitate deep understanding—the kind that's difficult to see without the reflection of a partner. This is a spirited relationship that can last a lifetime.

Gemini + Sagittarius

LoveScope: 5.5

The Basic Relationship

Sagittarians and Geminis share many characteristics: both are on a quest, like to talk, and have dark sides that tend to overtake them for short periods of time.

The essential difference between them is their motives. Sagittarians need their partners to be inspired in order to reflect back to them their rightful inheritance as children of Zeus. Geminis just want to borrow your phone and discuss the different features that your service gives you. The Archers long to travel in order to experience and understand new cultures and religions. The Twins are satisfied with watching a good documentary on their new high-definition television.

Sagittarians love sharing their adventures with anyone who will listen, and Geminis love to share their knowledge on topics that might be of help to anyone within earshot.

Neither of these two is likely to fit what the other needs right off the bat, but with some adjustments and gifts from planetary birth alignments, anything is possible!

The Passion Zone

This couple has great bedroom chemistry. Sagittarians create a mythology, and Geminis embellish it. There's nowhere one of them can go that the other can't follow. A sense of perfect rhythm and harmony exists in this relationship—all the way down to the fact that when they're done, it's over. Lingering is not an option.

What Sagittarius Needs to Know about Gemini

Sag, your Gemini friend won't always follow you to your grand inner sanctuary where you enjoy being revered and adored. It's hard enough for them to maintain any daily routine, let alone face having to be reminded of how insignificant they are next to your brilliant light. The Twins want to feel connected to someone, and you'd get a lot further in your relationship with them by being interested in their day—regardless of how trivial its events may seem to you. Geminis have a need to feel that someone sees their world, but the clincher is that they'll never admit it (and likely don't even know it).

What Gemini Needs to Know about Sagittarius

Sagittarians are capable of initiating antagonistic, yet *seemingly* innocent, verbal attacks that appear to come from nowhere. Things may be going great, and then suddenly you'll get an earful about how devastating it's been for them to hear you blow your nose every night once the lights are out. According to them, Gemini, you make that horrible honking noise that sounds like a wounded bird. Remember that Sags are known for exaggeration. It's their way of letting you know that you aren't seeing their magic.

The Archers thrive on feeling that they inspire you—or anyone around them, for that matter. It's a lot like your need for a connection, only they want to *know* that you believe in them. You can go into their inner world with them, but leave your cynic at the door. The reward for inspiring your Sagittarius is worth the minimal effort it takes.

LoveScope

Both Geminis and Sagittarians are skilled learners. Geminis catch the minute details, and Sags see the big picture—together they don't miss much. The Archers live in the world of gods and goddesses, and the Twins can take that vision and write epic poetry about it. Between them is a fellowship that will survive the most difficult passages of time. Sags must learn to listen and stop proving what they know, and Geminis need to understand that they often let their negative viewpoints bring too much realism to someone who lives for fantasy.

Together, these two can confront and solve any problem because there's trust here. That belief in each other goes beyond the present and into past and future lifetimes of familiarity, and this is where they find that they're inherently not all that different. The Gemini-Sagittarius relationship has a fighting chance if both partners are willing, and open up enough, to consider that what they see in one another is possibly an important issue they need to reclaim in themselves.

Gemini + Capricorn

LoveScope: 4.2

The Basic Relationship

This relationship involves the eternal child and the eternal grown-up. It's amazing how different these two are, yet remarkable how important it is that they know each other. Every Capricorn understands the value of responsibility, and every Gemini knows that of play.

An interesting polarity is created when a Gemini (who values youth) is in love with a Capricorn (who appreciates the importance of maturity). There's also a certain irony in the fact that Geminis are exactly what Capricorns must become—and vice versa. The Twins are learning that commitment and duty aren't as draining to their lives as they appear to be, that there's value in the here-and-now, and that any good foundation takes time to build. Capricorns are beginning to realize that living in the moment and enjoying reality isn't irresponsible —it's actually acceptable as a contrast to the routines they rely so heavily upon.

There's a natural attraction in this relationship: the Goats know that inside the Gemini world is a secret they must learn, and the Twins can see that Capricorns have a plan that holds the key to happiness.

The Passion Zone

Although the attraction is initially strong, Capricorns usually won't continue to engage in passionate lovemaking unless there's a purpose. It's as if sex triggers an inner voice that says, *Okay, what are we doing? What are we building? What's this going to lead to that's productive?* Of course, this line of questioning doesn't diminish the fact that there's a hidden cache of intense sexuality within Caps. Geminis love that, as long as the intensity begins and ends in the bedroom . . . but it usually doesn't.

What Gemini Needs to Know about Capricorn

Gemini, although you have no problem handling intense passion, you should keep in mind that Capricorn is a very possessive sign. The focus is on attaining ownership of everything. Goats prefer to do things the hard way and expect the same from you, too. You'll find, though, that there are instances when they're receptive to a legitimate shortcut (like using the Internet to find a phone number rather than dragging out the two-ton yellow pages). They're sensitive to people trying to take the easy way out, so if you're attempting to be inventive with a project to save time, it might be best to keep that to yourself until it's done. Capricorns love to feel useful, so be sure to accept their help if you need it . . . and even if you don't.

Building is one of the many things that Capricorns have learned how to do. Specifically, they know how to create walls around their hearts if they're hurt or offended. Goats have an amazing ability to reject all they've known and loved about you as a defense against feeling violated. Violations are considered to be things that aren't done within their definition of propriety. For example, if you become

involved in a get-rich-quick scheme that could perhaps be considered shady, or flirt just a bit too much with someone you just met, they may consider that a breach of trust and erect their infamous wall.

On the other hand, if Capricorns get too bogged down by life's more negative perspectives and try to lay a guilt trip on you, you'll probably take some course of evasion for a while, which will look like you're leaving. If there's little or no communication between you two before things start to escalate, then there will likely be a separation. Both of you have trouble admitting fault, but neither has any problem blaming the other.

What Capricorn Needs to Know about Gemini

Geminis thrive on the idea of freedom. They like to use their innovative minds to make tried-and-true traditions more efficient. That's a challenge to your basic nature, Capricorn, as you tend to dismiss shortcuts as the result of laziness. But there's a difference between innovation and cutting corners, and you'd do well to try to understand that difference when you evaluate the behavior of your Gemini. Another thing is that when you do assess their actions, you may notice something else about the Twins: they abhor scrutiny.

LoveScope

When these two are in harmony, much can be accomplished. Capricorns can provide stability without making their partners feel claustrophobic; and Geminis are able to bring a smile to Goats' faces, which not many others can do. Appealing to Capricorns' business sense, Geminis are a good investment—with the Twins, they're getting two for the price of one!

Unfortunately, the commitment level between these signs is usually horrible. Capricorns perceive a lack of responsibility in Geminis, which will make the Twins want to run; and the Goats have an aggressive side to them that their partners don't appreciate. It's an extremely challenging relationship when these two signs come together. Magic can be found, but it will be a difficult search.

HOW TO LOSE THE GEMINI YOU LOVE

- Hide their phone.
- After one of their long monologues, ask, "What were you just saying?"
- Tilt your head and ask them how they're feeling.
- Question them about what time they'll be home.
- Sign them up for a ten-day vow-of-silence retreat.
- In the middle of an argument, say, "I'm not going to talk about this."
- Ask them if they love you.
- Shred all of their stored magazines.
- Downgrade to a dial-up Internet connection.
- Tell them you have a tendency to fall asleep mid-sentence.

Gemini + Aquarius

LoveScope: 7.8

The Basic Relationship

There's not a lot to complicate the energies between these two signs . . . given that all is well within the rest of the chart. Geminis breeze in like a light rainstorm, and Aquarians throw in the thunder and lightning. Aquarius is Fixed Air, and Gemini is Mutable Air, which makes for a good detour from intense arguments. Water Bearers search for a bigger truth that's larger than life, and the Twins look for many small ones—or, shall we say, "non-lies." It's not that Geminis can't be honest; they just see so many relative truths. It all depends on perspective. Geminis have any number of different outlooks, depending on their mood, and Aquarians usually have two: *truth* or *un*truth.

The chemistry here is easy and light. There are no dark closets to open (except the literal ones in Geminis' houses, which may not be dark but are generally a mess!), and there isn't too much excess baggage. The Twins usually make friends with their exes, whereas Water Bearers typically never see theirs again. Communication is the gift between these two Air signs, although Geminis will always win any arguments because of their ability to take both sides: Aquarians are really up against two very different personalities within their partners.

The Passion Zone

What Aquarians need most in the bedroom is someone who can stimulate their brains and follow them into the realms of the Water Bearer universe. No one can do this better than Geminis, who are great at connecting their minds and bodies in a relationship, creating experiences where fantasies are welcome.

Sex for people of these signs is light, fun, and breezy. They don't let things get too heavy, and both see it as a release of pressure from the daily accumulation of facts. Aquarians can become jealous after committing to their mates, and there may be a few problems with Geminis' flirtatious nature. It's nothing that the Twins' quick wit can't explain away in just the terms their Aquarius needs to hear.

What Aquarius Needs to Know about Gemini

Aquarius, your Gemini is likely to be unhappy with certain aspects of their life, and you're not going to be able to change that. It may be frustrating for you to realize that none of the brilliant solutions you offer will work because there's a part of them that *needs* to push against these negative thoughts. It's one way in which they create momentum. Don't take it personally or you'll end up dismissing them as not being serious about their life, which could actually create more problems because you're disconnecting from them.

What Gemini Needs to Know about Aquarius

Aquarians rely heavily on their thoughts. As a result, they can get stuck on an idea and may find it difficult to stop obsessing over it.

This notion is usually about how things *should* be, and your Aquarian friend is good at dismissing any view that opposes it . . . so be careful in this arena. You, Gemini, are a master at looking at things from every angle, so you can try to be the devil's advocate or the main line of support, but your Aquarius has a hard time seeing all those points of view. Be patient. The less you push, the more willing they become.

LoveScope

When Air signs get connected, there's a certain lightness around them. They seem to know when to be close to each other and when to stay away. Geminis can be most charming and childlike when they're in the presence of someone they respect, and they do tend to highly esteem their Aquarian partners—who, in turn, appreciate being seen from such a positive perspective. This relationship is a keeper and will last, as long as both partners can keep their lips moving and their eyes toward the future. There's love, compassion, and support here, but also a need to take the time to establish these things.

Gemini + Pisces

LoveScope: 3.5

The Basic Relationship

Pisces is a Water sign, and therefore ready to fill whatever container it's poured into. Most Fish don't realize it when they've begun to morph into the energy of the people around them, but that's what they do. Geminis change, too, but don't usually move toward those they're involved with; on the contrary, they tend to pull away from them. Geminis like to keep things light and need their space; Pisceans enjoy heavier affairs and adore closeness. Pisceans see the pain in everyone, while Geminis think everyone *is* a pain.

Both signs are Mutable, so each has two sides: Geminis comprise the happy Twin and the depressed Twin, whereas Pisceans are made up of the nice Fish and the mean Fish. In essence, there are four people trying to live together, and that's not an easy feat in any relationship.

The Passion Zone

There's a strong initial attraction here, thanks to the changeable nature of Geminis and Pisceans; and they even exhibit multiple personalities in the bedroom. The passion is new and stimulating—and will remain so for a long time—with enough flexibility to create real excitement. Both signs have different needs and desires, but are willing to accommodate . . . within reason. Pisceans are more likely to develop an attachment to this union, which could scare away the fickle-but-fun Geminis. The Twins, on the other hand, also have their share of dependencies and love the look of acceptance that radiates from their Pisces' eyes. There's a natural connection that's only likely to be awkward when the relationship is over.

What Gemini Needs to Know about Pisces

Pisceans live in a world of emotions and are very attracted to those who *don't* live there. Gemini, you're the perfect hook for them because you don't attach to very much and tend to leave your feelings by the last bed you slept in. Your Piscean will be very interested in what you're doing—and you love that—but be careful not to make them think that accommodating you is their only function. They'll rebel against such expectations.

Please know that your Fish has a magical, watery reality that supports them; and they'll want to share it with you. However, if you overanalyze and rationally criticize it, the enchantment dissolves and they'll feel alone and insulted. Pisceans have addictive natures, so be respectful of fad diets and their latest interests that are so important in the moment, but will fade once they're obsessed with something new.

What Pisces Needs to Know about Gemini

You can easily pinpoint the Gemini motive, Pisces. They're easy for you to read, but don't always see themselves as clearly as you do. Try not to assume that they know what they're doing—they often don't. Gemini is a sign that loves change and unpredictability, so it's important to let them spread their wings and go out with their friends once in a while. They respond to your attention to them when it's positive, but they don't like it when you're disappointed. You can add sparkle to their analytical thinking with your natural enthusiasm and encouragement—something they need but won't *admit* to needing.

LoveScope

In this household, things will be strewn all over the place, with hardly a nook or cranny that's not filled—but each person will know where every single item is. This is love in the Mutable world—a place where care is in knowing where the hammer is, and lovemaking can happen in the middle of cooking dinner. To most of us, these two might look weird, but to each other, there's no one better when things are good. Each partner accepts the quirks of the other—and there *are* quirks—and brings special twists or idiosyncrasies to the union that, like any chemical reaction, create something completely different when mixed together. Although transformations happen in all relationships, they're particularly significant with these two. After all, there are four aspects to contend with here.

Geminis and Pisceans need to avoid falling into a commiserating frenzy of self-pity, something that can be easy to do if they aren't careful. It's just as effortless for them to fill each other up with positive thoughts and affirmations, but this certainly isn't natural for either. These two can make a strong go of it, but it will be harder than other combinations. It calls to mind the phrase "Something worth having is worth working for in life."

WHAT MAKES GEMINIS AWESOME?

- Their true acceptance of others

- Their readiness to lend an ear and give good advice

- Their childlike innocence, regardless of age

- Their willingness to be flexible when you aren't

- Their talent for finding the perfect solution to the most obscure problem

- Their knack for telling a joke just when it's needed

- Their ability to see the positive when you can only see the negative

- Their gift for translating the most complex issue into something quite simple

- The twinkle in their eyes

Cancer + Cancer

LoveScope: 8.6

The Basic Relationship

Whenever two people born under the same sign come together, it's important to consider their full charts. Cancers are ruled by the moon, which makes them funny, moody, and altogether unpredictable. Whatever guise they take, the caregiver characteristic will be the common denominator. When two Crabs first form a partnership, each genuinely appreciates the heart-centered warmth the other exudes. Whether they're pouring coffee or making sure food doesn't get cold, they're constantly reacting to one another's emotional responses and needs. Most of this tender nurturing is because they're control freaks . . . although they'll never admit that. They like to have things their way because it makes them feel safe, which is a big reason why these two are fond of each other.

Mother issues will abound, and likely create a palpable love-hate situation for this couple. Whichever one of them broke free from

Mom—or at least moved out of her house—will determine who's the stronger partner, at least with regard to emotional control and rational thinking.

These funny little crustaceans are adorable when they're enamored with someone. They bat their eyelashes, look sad or shy, and make it safe to approach them. Because of their instant familiarity, there's also an instant attraction.

The Passion Zone

Cancers are like big pools of imagination. If they're in a passionate mood, their partners will be the most beautiful in the world. Together, their sense of humor will be off the charts; and their ability to respond to each other's needs will make their space feel like there's no better place on Earth . . . and no other person they'd rather be with. For Cancers, this is what true lovemaking is about.

The only problem they encounter is timing—when both of them are "feeling it" at the same moment. It starts out easy in the early stages of their relationship, but as things progress, it becomes increasingly difficult for them to be in sync. The issue is in the nature of their moods; no one—not even Cancers themselves—knows why they happen to be "in the mood" for love or "not in the mood" to talk about something . . . or why they feel sad, depressed, lonely, happy, safe, or insecure. Mating becomes a roulette wheel of chance. Naturally, when their sentiments don't coincide, there's little chance that sex will happen, and both Cancers know this to be true.

What Cancer Needs to Know about Cancer

This is a sign that's loyal, caring, and supportive. You like to get what you give, so if you're expressing these feelings, you probably expect them in return. This is also a very committed sign. Each of you has a set of "hang on until you die" pinchers, making your bond four times as strong as superglue. You should realize, however, that

172

emotional honesty is the toughest thing in the world for you. Sure, your partner will let you know they're in a bad mood, but as for the reason . . . well, that's anyone's guess. Crabs can get through the rough patches by realizing that no one makes a home more "homey" than their Cancer partner.

Imagine two Cancers under one roof. The house is now more than just a house; it's a shrine—a place to eat, sleep, shop, learn, and entertain—and the residents will never leave it . . . ever! Crabs always get what they want, and when two are together, it's just a matter of who can throw out the guilt generator first:

> **Cancer 1:** "Honey, I'm going out with the guys tonight."
>
> **Cancer 2:** "But I thought we could stay in and watch Disney movies. I had such a hard day and already planned the whole evening."
>
> **Cancer 1:** "I'm sorry, but I've waited a month for this card game. I need a night out."
>
> **Cancer 2:** "Okay, go. You're right. I just miss having someone to talk to. You've been working late, and I've been working *and* cooking. But you're right . . . you go."

Of course, Cancer 1 stays, but will get his way the next time—there's no doubt about that!

Remember, Cancers, you need to be needed. If you don't *need* your partner, they may find a flaw or a problem that they'll just have to take care of . . . including how to make you a better person. On the flip side, it's easy for you two to get along because you understand each other's strengths and weaknesses.

LoveScope

This is an awesome relationship, even with a few missteps. Cancers provide great support for their fellow Crabs. The greatest gifts they can offer each other are understanding and compassion, combined with valid and tangible reasons why they're not in danger. Knowing that they're safe when they don't feel that way and having someone there to keep an eye on them when they retreat are gifts beyond what words can express. Cancers are loyal and will show their appreciation by being their mates' biggest fans. Home is everything to Crabs, and perfection for them is to have one filled with love and support.

HOW TO KEEP THE CANCER YOU LOVE

- Don't pinch their cute cheeks.

- Pay them back if they loaned you money.

- Don't make fun of their friends.

- Let them determine how to dole out discipline.

- Know the foods that nurture them.

- If they say, "I don't know what you'd do without me," reply with, "I hope I never have to find out."

- Don't talk negatively about their mother, even when they do.

- Give them monetary gifts.

- Be nice when they tell you a long story. It means that they're afraid to ask you something.

- Act like you don't notice their mood changes.

Cancer + Leo

LoveScope: 7.3

The Basic Relationship

The sun (Leo) and the moon (Cancer) are the two luminaries of our solar system, and they share old wisdom. Cancers reflect the optimism they find in their Leo partners, making them great mirrors for the royal Lions. The happier Leo is, the more the Crab shines!

Cancers almost always have kids; and many times their friends, felines, or canines will fall into this category. Leos are often called the children of the Zodiac because of their ability to be childlike—and sometimes even child*ish*—but that's not the only reason these two come together. Cancers are watery creatures, meaning that they live in the world of emotions. They have a hard shell that protects their mushy interiors, and they tend to worry a lot. When they meet a bright Leo, there's an attraction that's almost instant. If the Lions are strong enough to show their vulnerabilities while radiating their sunny optimism, then they'll be partners that Crabs can't easily resist.

The Passion Zone

Cancers are wildly imaginative and coy, and Leos pretend to be unaffected by any positive attention that comes their way. When Crabs start doing their sideways shuffle toward Leos—who, by the way, pretend not to see Cancers' obvious interest—the Lions stand firm, but psychically invite the cute lunar crustaceans in. Cancers, feeling safe and encouraged, will get the permission they need to lavish their hungry Lions with passion. This relationship is magic, at least until Leos become demanding and grumpy, which causes Crabs to withdraw. Then it becomes just a test of time to see who will reemerge first, followed by crazy makeup sex so they can do it all over again.

What Leo Needs to Know about Cancer

One of the big setups for Cancers is their need to mother. It can be among the most nurturing experiences you can have, Leo, but there's a catch: you'll become one of their children if you let them take care of you; and eventually, they'll want some support in return. Cancers need to know that you have their backs—that if something happens to the mortgage, you have a backup plan . . . and one that you believe in. They absolutely must know that they don't have to shoulder all the concerns of the relationship (after all, they're already carrying a shell for protection, and that gets heavy!). Their moods aren't personal, so try to take yourself out of the picture every now and then. Cancers don't know why they get like that, but if you flash your security plan in their face, it's a sure aphrodisiac.

What Cancer Needs to Know about Leo

It's not that Lions aren't caring or generous, Cancer; they just don't like to be told *when* to be those things. In fact, they don't take kindly to orders of any kind. If Leos get mad enough, you may not *see* their temper, but they'll withhold their sun for a while—and you can say good-bye to that safe feeling. They love to know that you think highly of them, and in return for your approval, they'll romp around in child-like happiness. Just what you need . . . another kid! But it *is* what you want, because you can now wield acceptance as your weapon. Use it wisely, though; if you abuse your power, they'll just withdraw without warning.

LoveScope

It's a beautiful sight to see these two getting along. Crabs are good moms (regardless of their gender), and Lions make for good kings and queens. As long as Leos remember to recognize their Cancers for all the doting, and Crabs remember to encourage their partners to be children, these two will feel the magic. Both signs need their mates to stop every now and again to take note of the remarkable things they've accomplished. Cancers' warm words of encouragement can help build the often-insecure Lions' manes of pride into coiffed master-pieces, and Leos' praises can coax their Crabs out of their shells. When these two are doing well, the room is filled with laughter; when either is hurt, everyone loses out on the sun and the moon . . . and that can be tragic.

On a happier note, Cancers and Leos each appreciate the loyalty that the other provides, and both are ferociously protective. Laughter and a deep sense of familiarity give these two years of staying power. This astrological combination is the best of the planetary light givers. It's traditionally a sweet blend of tolerance and encouragement that makes for a union that likely withstands the tests of time—and each other.

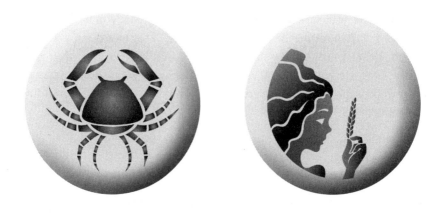

Cancer + Virgo

LoveScope: 7.8

The Basic Relationship

We have a case here of "likes" attracting. Both signs are care-givers who are funny and love safety and comfort—but Virgos are ruled by Earth, and Cancers by Water. What makes Crabs feel safe is a bit different from Virgins, who are secure as long as there's some kind of order (Earth). Whether it's a neat house or another sharp mind, they find comfort knowing that there's a system of organization. For Cancers, on the other hand, it's a *feeling* that makes them safe. Their environment could be in complete chaos, but if it seems like home, they're happy.

For the most part, these two have fun together. Virgos can get a little dry, and Cancers have fun dousing the Virgin with a little imagi-native humor, or even a funny tale of how they torture themselves taking care of the world. Both signs take pride in supporting others, but Cancers have a deep respect for the propriety that Virgos bring to the task. Crabs may see what's needed and provide it, but Virgos are more likely to follow the rules that were agreed upon.

The Passion Zone

There's a lot of initial sizzle here as these two caregivers of the Zodiac provide for each other in the best way they know how. Both accommodate their mates' likes and dislikes, but the big problem here is the onset of familiarity over time. Eventually—and often quickly—these two will form an attentive bond that transcends sexuality, which may transform the relationship into one of friendship rather than love. Ironically, neither of these two are likely to care because both understand the impracticality of sex!

What Virgo Needs to Know about Cancer

Virgo, remember that Cancers hold your opinion in high esteem. For some reason, Cancers consider you to be an authority on a lot of subjects. But if you become too critical of something they're doing or unsympathetic to the work they've put into a project, then you risk losing them to their shell for a while.

You don't have to sell your opinion to a Cancer. Just give it and let go; the rest will happen naturally. Also, Cancers won't easily resolve their mother issues, so you're just going to have to accept that as an inevitable fact. Let it be something that should only be broached if you're prepared for the consequences.

What Cancer Needs to Know about Virgo

The Virgins have no trouble retreating to their ivory tower. In fact, they have an absolute *need* to do this occasionally, and it's in your own interest to let them, Cancer. As Virgos tend to overextend themselves, retreat is their only defense against the influx of demands being placed on them—and not all are coming from you (at least not consciously). They tend to feel what's needed from everyone, and then provide it with what seems like an effortless ability.

Unfortunately, you may not notice that they've reached their breaking point until the complaining begins. Once your Virgo goes

on a rampage of criticism, it will be clear that they've neglected time for themselves, and this energy must wear itself down before anyone can relax! When it comes to arguing, don't try to be right, because you'll never win. Virgos have already thought about their positions for a long time and will counter anything you have to add. It's best to graciously accept defeat.

LoveScope

Virgos eventually learn that perfection means accepting that this is a world of chaos. There is, after all, an order to disorder. Cancers eventually learn that when Virgins want to be alone, it's not a personal rejection. And they shouldn't be discouraged if they have to sleep in a different room or learn how to line up their shoes in the closet. It's a small price to pay for the steel-trap commitment that's developed between these two signs.

Virgins can easily understand and be warmed by Crabs' sincere appreciation, and Cancers love the protection provided by someone who—although usually skeptical—believes in *them*. Each partner can fill a room with laughter and show the other gratitude for years to come if there's flexibility within the relationship.

Both have large capacities for compassion and can offer the securities needed for them to thrive for many years. These two will share an endearing and enduring friendship, and can support each other through thick and thin (Cancers tend to be "thick," and Virgos are "thin"). This is a long-term powerhouse of love—that nonpassionate kind that finds camaraderie in mutual complaining. Just watch out for too much grumbling because it could lead to martyrdom and negativity, which even the most optimistic signs find hard to cope with. Both parties are guilty, not only of being negative, but of actually *feeling* guilty. Otherwise, they have a great foundation to build a strong connection.

Cancer + Libra

LoveScope: 4.8

The Basic Relationship

This is a story of two people of the Cardinal, or aggressive, mode who came together because each has a great deal to learn from the other. Cancer brings in the season of summer, and those born under this sign have the innate ability to affect emotions—either their own or someone else's. Crabs are natural caregivers with a talent for gaining love through giving. Libra brings in the season of autumn, and the people the sign rules have the inherent talent to connect with just about anyone. They have an instinctive capacity for seeing the good in all people, which is one way they feel accepted.

These strong signs have a lot of respect for each other, but it's usually kept at an arm's length. Cancers love the charm of Libras, who in turn fancy the Crabs' emotional, protective strength. But a battle ensues when it comes to their individual approaches to life: Libras forgive and forget, and are able to see both sides of every story and

maintain a (seemingly superficial) level of courtesy. Cancers approach others cautiously to sense their motivations and are quite willing to make quick judgments. Libras may notice this behavior, but won't encourage discussion on anything that "isn't nice." Cancers look for alignment and love the personal, while Libras seek objectivity and aren't so friendly.

The Passion Zone

There's definite intrigue that exists when the emotional meets the intellectual. It will be a strong attraction that quickly fizzles when Libras don't quite want to go where their partners want to take them, and vice versa. Libras have high standards of beauty—so those they've taken an interest in have passed a crucial test! They also find the emotional lushness of Cancers intriguing, and when these two first meet, there's instant respect for the strength each feels in the other. Good sex is defined differently by this couple, and they won't be satisfied if both aren't willing to adjust in some way.

What Cancer Needs to Know about Libra

Your feelings will get hurt if you don't understand that your Libra must flirt, Cancer. It's how they've learned to value themselves. It's not personal on any level, so just try to step out of the way of their mission, which is to get love reflected back to them. Libras abhor being scrutinized and will feel controlled if you aren't careful. They also have a way of fighting unfairly (ironic, I know, for a sign represented by the Scales) when they sense they're being judged.

Try to remember that they're the diplomats of the Zodiac. If you're wrong in their eyes, you're wrong whether you two are a couple or not, and they'll be compelled to tell you what they think.

What Libra Needs to Know about Cancer

Cancers *feel* differently than you do, Libra. They actually "morph" so they can experience the emotions of another person, whereas you just objectively translate others' sentiments (which is what makes you fair).

You may lose patience with how your Crab partner tends to take on problems that aren't their own, but your disapproval will only send them into their shell . . . and they *will* hide from you. It's best to be supportive, with the understanding that your Crab will eventually shape-shift to sympathize with your point of view as well, creating the change you want without the nagging. Also, Cancers tend to never speak directly about anything, which is how they manipulate outcomes. If they tell you a long story that ends with "So, can I use your car now?" consider yourself "worked."

LoveScope

Water seeks to fill containers, and Air tries to be freed from them. If these two can trust each other enough to do something different from their natures, there can be a great bond of respect and support. Libras want to be seen as loving and gracious, and Cancers prefer being portrayed as kind and supportive. They both give what they really want for themselves.

The inherent clash between Cancers and Libras is that they have individual missions to accomplish. Both signs are born with a desire to push their partners in the direction they believe is best, but neither will easily admit that self-interest usually turns out to be what's behind this.

Libras are ruthless in the pursuit of their goals for a relationship; and being Air, they hate it when things even start to look routine. It's hard for them to admit this in a lighthearted way, but it's absolutely true. Cancers are unyielding in their need for safety by seeing to it that their mates are dependent upon them. Sure, this is unconscious, but it makes it hard on people who are trying to be self-sufficient.

Making this relationship last could be worth the effort, but it will take work and a desire for growth. It can be done—and *has* succeeded—but the initial foundation isn't a strong one.

HOW TO LOSE THE CANCER YOU LOVE

- Tell them they resemble their mother.
- Comment on their weight gain, and then act like you meant it as a compliment.
- Use up all their bubble-bath soap.
- Tell them that you're not going to engage in baby talk with them.
- Complain about their kids.
- When they're sulking, ask them if they have someone they can call for support.
- When they show you their photo album, laugh at their baby pictures.
- Take them camping without a trailer.
- Remove the TV from their bedroom.
- Take them to a buffet on Thanksgiving.

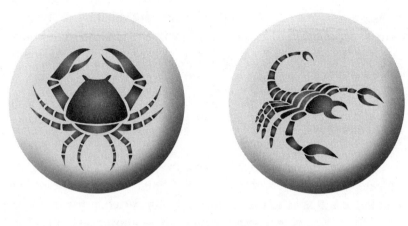

Cancer + Scorpio

LoveScope: 9.4

The Basic Relationship

The magic of this union lies in the element of Water, because signs of this motive feel a certain safety with each other. There's a natural understanding of the changing moods that are inevitable with them (Pisces, Cancer, and Scorpio), and an innate awareness of the sometimes murky depths to which emotions can run.

The *modes* are what separate these two: Cancer is Cardinal, and Scorpio is Fixed. The Crabs are the movers here. They're able to feel inside the cauldrons of the intense Scorpion mind and offer safety and security. Scorpios seem to insist on living beneath the surface of everything and don't change their position easily; they'll hold firm to a particular emotional viewpoint.

Scorpions often think in terms of worst-case scenarios and will set up tests and provoke anger just to see if their partners can really be trusted. Cancers love the depth of Scorpios, who tend to find comfort

in the warmth of Crabs. Since Cancers are motivated by safety, they relate to Scorpios' need for security as well—and have no trouble providing it. The Scorpion's naturally ferocious protection is like music inside a Crab's shell!

The Passion Zone

If these passionate Water signs are in sync, there's no end to the intimate depths they'll reach. Each encounter will be more intense than the last, thanks to their ability to be immersed in the moment. When these two signs come together, there's an uncanny familiarity between them. They allow their partners to follow their emotions to any depths, without fear of judgment. Crabs' capacity to create fantasies is enlivened by Scorpios' inclination not to be shocked by anything. This is a great combination that will need to set an alarm for when it's time to go back to the real world.

What Cancer Needs to Know about Scorpio

Scorpios have an inherent distrust of people, Cancer. The closer they feel to someone, the more intense their suspicions become. The doubt is merely a reflection of that old Scorpio wound in which they believe that they're born with some inherent flaw; and they fear that if you get too close, you'll see it. That's why they have to control how close others get to them. Rather than seeing what's good about a situation, Scorpios try to anticipate what could go wrong. It's not personal, but it can be offensive if they're out with you and see someone they don't like. Suddenly, all of their obsessive thoughts are now back on the past and how they were hurt by this person. If you realize that this isn't happening because of anything you did, you'll be able to pull them back to the here-and-now . . . but it won't be easy.

What Scorpio Needs to Know about Cancer

Crabs are known to walk in a sideways shuffling motion, and they talk in that indirect manner, too. It's their defense against not being able to control how you feel, Scorpio. They're not *lying* to you; they're trying to *protect* you. It's important that you understand this round-about way of relating, or you'll never come to trust your Cancer. They also worry a lot about their own safety. If you can, try not to discuss your conspiratorial views during their more vulnerable times. It will help you keep the peace in a big way!

LoveScope

When they're healthy, this combination can create a unique bond of acceptance and give each other the strength to face the fears that Water signs deal with every day. When the apprehensions are at bay, these two will embrace each other with a comfort that's indescribable. Their psychic bond is evident when one says "Bless you" seconds before the other sneezes.

Cancers are forced to be direct and honest in this pairing, and Scorpios can share their secrets confidentially. This relationship will be worth all of the arguing it took to form it. Both partners have rich imaginations. Crabs love that Scorpions easily understand their dodgy way of communicating, and Scorpios know that Cancers will cancel out any negative voices that ring in their ears like bells of doom.

The commitment factor is high here, and the mutual loyalty these two share is priceless. It's hard to leave a connection with such telepathic exchanges because it feels extremely comfortable for both. Looking into each other's eyes and knowing that secrets are safe is a wonderful thing to share.

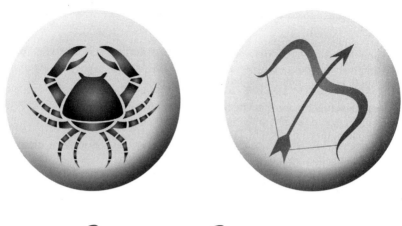

Cancer + Sagittarius

LoveScope: 5.5

The Basic Relationship

There's an odd kind of attraction between Cancers and Sagittarians, because they both see something that they're simultaneously drawn to and repulsed by. Archers are usually happy people when you first meet them. Their element is Fire, so they have an inspired air about them. Chatty and self-focused, Sags are rarely without a good story or a few words of encouragement. Crabs, even though they're Cardinal, are usually shy when first meeting people. They want to feel someone out before exposing any parts of themselves. Usually, Cancers' initial impressions are that Sagittarians are a bit unpolished—and somewhat self-absorbed—but there's a bit of magic that can be felt as these two approach each other with a hard-to-extinguish curiosity.

The Passion Zone

There's a natural intrigue that these two have for each other, which is common to all combinations that are five signs apart. If the other planets in their respective charts support it, this enchantment could grow and linger; but if there are too many other clashes, the initial burst could fizzle quicker than baking soda and vinegar.

The key here is that when Fire signs are passionate, it's usually fast and furious heat (pun intended), but those of the Water motive express their emotions as deep desires that envelop both partners. The pace is usually slow and intense, because Sagittarians rarely let their inner wounds emerge—the ones that remind them that life is tough since they're children of Zeus. But in this intimate setting, with Cancers' watery eyes looking at them, the Archers feel that they might be understood at last. Crabs see Sags' wounds, and their propensity for nurturing gets activated. It's one of the rare places where these two see something special that can't be found anywhere else in their relationship.

What Cancer Needs to Know about Sagittarius

When Sagittarians are hurt, they can sling openly embarrassing barbs at you—not really understanding your sensitivities. Unfortunately, Cancer, being embarrassed isn't something you're comfortable with, but it's important to understand that it's happening because your Archer doesn't know how to express their own hurt. One of the things that Sags are sensitive to is your dismissal of their dreams as nonsense—that's opening their wounds a little too much. Remember, Sagittarius is the sign of excess, so encourage healthy alternatives if you're with a partner who tends to go overboard with refreshments of the not-so-healthy kind.

What Sagittarius Needs to Know about Cancer

Your Cancer is extremely sensitive, Sag. They're especially affected by (and appreciate) approval and displays of gratitude and support. You tend to pay a lot of attention to how the world is receiving you, so it will take extra effort for you to recognize the caring work of your Cancer friend. It will also mean slowing down to embrace their impeccable nurturing, even if you see it as control. Crabs don't always know what they're up to, so start with appreciation, and then move your discussion to a gentle exploration of what happens when you feel controlled. This style of relating to your partner can engender years of loyalty and respect.

LoveScope

Understanding is always the recipe for making any relationship work. Cancers must understand that Mutable Fire wants to be wild sometimes and needs a lot of freedom. Archers are flirtatious as a means to fuel their inner engine, but will develop a deep loyalty if they stop long enough to trust their mates. Cancers don't have as much physical alacrity and will require a certain amount of reassurance to feel safe. Sagittarians are happy to provide this when they're sure that they're not responsible for their Crabs' feelings, which do change frequently. Sags need to listen more, and Cancers need to let go a bit—this is an important key between the two of them.

Each has an amazing sense of humor and can fill a room with laughter. Crabs love family, and to Archers, the whole world is one big happy family. These two can bring hope to the hopeless. It's about faith and love, and this combination has plenty of it!

Sadly, there's nothing to keep these two together on their own merit. Commitment must come from a deep recognition of the gifts each has in the other. If this pair chooses to make a go of it, the resulting relationship will likely be an amazing one.

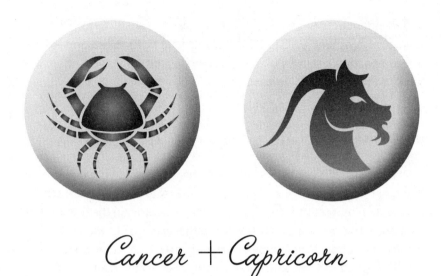

Cancer + Capricorn

LoveScope: 8.1

The Basic Relationship

Here's a situation where both signs are aggressive, yet the elements are compatible (Cancer is Water, and Capricorn is Earth). It's easy to put this relationship into more archetypal images: Cancers are mothers who provide emotional security, and Capricorns are fathers who supply the material security. Both are caregivers with different fields of expertise. Crabs were often responsible for the emotional stability of their families when they were children—more specifically, they took on the role of the mother. Goats had to fend for themselves and grow up quickly to help provide for the family so they weren't a burden.

Capricorns are traditionalists and trust in order, the way things used to be, and the proprieties of life. Cancers are sentimentalists, aggrandizing a past full of warm memories and home-cooked meals (even if they didn't get either of those things). When these two meet, there's safety and respect because they feel for each other. Both are

independent in their own way, yet they have the ability to form lasting bonds with others. Unlike the other Cardinal signs (Libra and Aries), these two don't mind pulling together to combine their efforts to make a family or build an empire.

The Passion Zone

There's an almost instant attraction here because what one needs, the other naturally provides. These two can create passion and sustain it longer than most of the other signs, and the chemistry in the relationship is about a 10 (on a scale of 1–10). Being the "parents" of the Zodiac is a powerful mix, too. When these two signs get together, there's a desire to be productive, and reproduction is certainly part of the plan.

The sexual excitement can be about something larger for this couple from the start. Both parties approach lovemaking from a caring place and focus on the feelings of their partners. Crabs are safe in the boundaries presented by Capricorns. Meanwhile, Goats believe that they can express what they feel inside. Both provide extreme passion, and it's not surprising that they find their sexual appetites put to good use. This is an important ingredient for future success.

What Cancer Needs to Know about Capricorn

Capricorns are stern and can easily build a wall of protection around themselves if they get their feelings hurt—or if they think that they're being controlled. They're also very possessive of what they own, and in relationships, *you're* considered their possession, Cancer. They expect a certain amount of self-control and willpower, and are quick to tell you that you're spending too much money or being too sloppy with your emotions. Although that might be true, Goats can be unyielding in their opinions and cold when they don't get what they want. At worst, they'll be extreme in their dominance, and this may feel cruel when they're out of control. You must have the courage to confront them when and if it's needed. Sometimes it's the only language they can hear.

What Capricorn Needs to Know about Cancer

Cancers are very possessive and tend to rely too much on manipulating their partners to "feel" a certain way. They can be stubborn in their pursuit of control and often won't give up until they're emotionally hurt. Capricorn, you must treat your Cancer as someone who has your best interest at heart, even if you don't agree with their methods. This isn't about condoning absurd plans; it's about realizing that if they don't believe you, they won't lift a finger for you. So if your Cancer is attempting to assist you in some way—even if it's not *your* way—it's a good sign of affection. Occasionally, they need you to be vulnerable so they can kiss your wound and put a Band-Aid on it. Sure, you can do this yourself, but this is your chance to *share.*

LoveScope

When they're aware of the potential pitfalls, these two can build an empire of support for themselves and their chosen ones. Capricorns, in understanding the needs of the emotional Cancers, can demonstrate how safe it is to occasionally break the rules and color outside the lines. Crabs will understand the necessity of self-discipline and patience. After all, what's the fun in spending money that you haven't really earned (a Capricorn question)? Cancers can teach Goats about the joys of sharing, or about tearing down what they've built if it comes to represent a wall between them. They'll also show Capricorns how to donate unused goods to the less fortunate . . . and then will get an immediate explanation on how to add that generous donation to the tax return.

What's most important is that there's trust here. These two inherently understand each other and naturally offer what the other person needs. A few heated arguments are nothing compared to the opportunities that each will provide when it comes to living a full and captivating life.

Cancer + Aquarius

LoveScope: 3.7

The Basic Relationship

A relationship involving Aquarians and Cancers can certainly be one of the sweet mysteries of life. There's Cancer, the Cardinal Water sign, and Aquarius, which is Fixed Air. It's a curious attraction between these two: Aquarians seem assured, confident, strong, and silent; and are off in their own world, with just the right amount of woundedness to bring Crabs out with a purpose. Cancers are enigmas to Aquarians (who like enigmas), with their watery eyes and sensitivities. They're also off in their own world and are just wounded enough to call on Aquarians' sense of humanitarianism. Did that sound repetitive?

It's true: as different as these two can be in nature, they're drawn to similar things for separate reasons. Aquarians think in pictures; Cancers think in images. It doesn't sound that different, but an image is part of the imagination, and it's fluid. A picture is a static, real, detailed object. Cancers change with the moon's cycle, while Aquarians do so when they feel like it. Crabs have faith in their feelings, and Water Bearers trust thoughts. Yes, this couple is different enough to be intriguing.

The Passion Zone

Cancer is an insecure sign by nature. A gamut of feelings drives their lives, and passions come from a deep reservoir—so deep that Cancer natives often have no idea where their overwhelming feelings originate. When the same notions embrace Aquarians, it can be like a lush ocean surrounding unsuspecting Water Bearers, who may *feel* (a difficult word for them) understood (a very *important* word for them).

When the right combination of energies collides between these two, there can be magic. Aquarians' Fixed nature is less likely to make the first move, and may often be flattered by Cancers' impassioned drive. But Crabs need to be prepared for when the lovemaking finishes. Their Aquarian partners may roll over and open a book on quantum physics because their first love is their own minds!

What Aquarius Needs to Know about Cancer

Cancers have a need for defense that emerges when their feeling of safety is threatened. *Safety* is a broad word, and here it will be defined as whatever Crabs have identified as something they need in order to feel protected. In most cases, Aquarius, the threat to their security is being unloved. They're the natural mothers of the Zodiac and need to express their instinctive nurturing somewhere. Hopefully, all that care will one day be administered to themselves.

Cancers love to baby you and adore the loyalty that results from this pampering. Although you're not interested in being cared for, it's a way for them to feel accepted as a part of your life. What you perceive as control is *indeed* just that, but it's designed to make a connection with you, not to hurt you. Understand that your Cancer doesn't care about the homeless or the antiwar rally; they care about *you.* It would be nice for you to work on getting used to these feelings.

What Cancer Needs to Know about Aquarius

Aquarians don't really understand the concept of nurturing. After all, Cancer, it's a product of feeling, and most feelings get processed in the *minds* of Water Bearers—which are like computers. It's not that they don't express emotions—it's just that they have a different way of showing they care. Your Aquarian could perceive your interference as control, and they abhor any form of it (except their own). They all look for a place to relate objectively, without compassion getting in the way. So don't take it personally when you say "I love you," and they respond with: "Well, you 'love' chocolate, too. It doesn't mean anything."

LoveScope

Happy Cancers are funny Cancers . . . actually, they're hilarious. When they're in a good mood, they find a way to lighten up a room using that lunar humor that even the most stoic person can't resist. Happy Aquarians feel unrestrained by the daily "shoulds" that plague them and feel free to soar to mental heights, envisioning ending hunger, finding homes for all living things, and sharing the planet with vigilance and respect.

When each of these two understands the basic nature of the other, the possibility of happiness doesn't require that steep of a climb. They both must be willing to grow. Cancers must learn that self-love is the greatest gift they can give because when they love themselves, they need very little from others in order to feel it. Aquarians must learn that emotions are a valid part of human existence, and one of the greatest gifts they can offer is to share their feelings. Stranger unions have succeeded. This one, admittedly, could be difficult, but a fulfilling outcome is very possible.

Cancer + Pisces

LoveScope: 8.1

The Basic Relationship

Water signs have an interesting reality that's fluid and filled with a certain emotional magic that can move anyone they encounter to many different personal experiences. Cancer is Cardinal (assertive), and Pisces is Mutable (adaptable). Not much conflict exists here, except that those born under Mutable signs are often made up of two very different parts, and insecurity (a Cancer trait) will make that duality feel a bit disconcerting.

Pisceans love an underdog, and Cancers are the mothers of the Zodiac. There isn't much distinction here, *except* that not all underdogs are easy to mother. Cancers may have a difficult time with Pisceans' rather open and unscreened approach to helping anyone in need. Crabs are a bit more discriminating because they sense people's motives and assess their worthiness first. Fish are close to their mothers, as are Cancers. The difference is that Cancers can reject theirs

(probably because they're too much alike), and Pisces can't say no to them.

What may be most difficult here is the Cancers' inability to feel in control of their Pisces partners. The mutability of Pisceans means that if they're disapproved of in one area, they simply create another scenario in which to play things out. Crabs can't always follow Pisceans' emotions, which says a lot about the depth of Fish. One day they're suffering on behalf of someone they care about, and the next they're cold and detached from everything and everyone.

The Passion Zone

It's a hot mixture here because these are two of the most imaginative signs of the Zodiac coming together to create one heck of a fantasy world: Pisceans can become whatever Cancers imagine. It's almost too easy for these two in the lovemaking arena, where the only tough part is encouraging each other to leave the bedroom and go back to work. These two can hang out for a long time with a passion meter that's off the charts.

What Cancer Needs to Know about Pisces

Pisceans are open to anything that comes their way, which is why they're the sign that's most prone to drug or alcohol addictions. When dealing with Fish, Cancer, you're dealing with a list of energies that depends on which people they last had contact with. It's always a surprise to live with a Pisces, as you never really know who's going to be there. Deep, distraught, happy, and playful—the range of emotions for Pisceans is enormous . . . and often without visible cause. You can tell whom they've been talking to by the way they act right after, even if it was just a casual conversation. They're the sponges of the Zodiac, and it's important for you to accept that they aren't in charge.

Your Pisces friend takes on issues you can't imagine dealing with. Be kind and supportive by reminding them to let go of what they absorbed each day. Suggest that they take a long bath—or better yet, share one with them.

What Pisces Needs to Know about Cancer

Crabs are a bit more protected because of their hard shell and natural caution. At their worst, they try to control in order to get the acknowledgment they need. Cancers can all too easily find themselves in the dark, misty places where you reside, Pisces; and before they know it, they can become engulfed in a strange reality that's not comfortable or safe.

Remember that your Cancer friend likes to make a difference in your life, but since you're always feeling change, you may overlook their contribution. Set an alarm if you have to, but be sure to take a moment to appreciate the care your Crab is trying to provide.

LoveScope

These two could make an incredible difference in each other's lives if they avoid the land mines. Pisceans, when healthy, won't turn to drugs or alcohol; rather, they'll embrace a spirituality that guides them in psychic ways. They're caring and perceptive and present a brighter reflection of what's going on around them than any other sign. Cancers need a certain amount of safety. When their Pisces friends remind them that life can be good and should be created in any way they want, then relationship magic is assured.

Cancers can take a protective lead with their Pisces partners without being overly controlling. Crabs should remember that there are many different realities and remind themselves that Fish probably have a repertoire of realities that exceeds most people's personal limits.

Together these signs can make the world a safer place for each other. It helps to keep in mind that when things get murky and either partner starts to feel codependent, there's nothing like a separate vacation—or maybe even just a solo bath would do the trick. Never

fear, because there's an enormous supply of mutual interests that will keep things mentally stimulating, while fostering a deep understanding. These two can have a ball together for a long, long time.

WHAT MAKES CANCERS AWESOME?

- Their incredible humor
- The depth of their love
- Their vivid imaginations
- The magic in their hearts
- Their compassion
- The profound help they give
- The sensitivity they embody
- Their round, watery eyes
- Their "Where did *that* come from?" wisdom
- Their understanding of the children in all of us
- Their deep loyalty and devotion

Leo + Leo

LoveScope: 8.8

The Basic Relationship

Leos are misunderstood by almost everyone except other Leos. After all, the kings of the jungle can spot the other rulers pretty quickly, as it's easy to recognize their feigned humility and ploys for attention. Lions can clearly discern when their own tactics are being pulled off by other Lions, who somehow always seem to know that they've been found out. Unlike many people of other Zodiac signs—who spout off about how they don't like others of the same sign—most Leos like other Leos. They light up knowing that someone else has the potential to blatantly speak out about how much attention this sign needs.

Typically, Leos were wounded by their fathers and wonder if they're really worthy of anything. They'll watch others like hawks to see if they're accepted by them. If the reception goes well, then these people are invited to bask in the royal sunlight.

Because the recognition between two Leos is almost instant, they tend to move a bit faster toward each other than most couples with

the same signs (even though they're Fixed). When they meet, there's an immediate appreciation in seeing the mechanism that works so well for them in another person—for example, the bright, shining smile; attitude of confidence; or inner protectiveness found in most Lions or Lionesses.

The Passion Zone

Two Fire signs focusing on themselves can be a passion magnet. The lust will exist in the beginning of their romance, but sooner or later they'll start fighting because one messed up the other's hair. These two do share a considerable initial attraction, but when both need lots of attention, the question becomes "Who gets it first?" Leo natives know how to talk to each other, but they're so aware of their own motives that over time this bedroom thing could get just a little boring.

What Leo Needs to Know about Leo

The easiest way to cause problems with Leos is to ignore or criticize them without allowing a chance for explanation. It's no shock that you'll tend to be self-centered; both of you will be used to wanting—and *getting*—the approval of others, which is what makes you comfortable. But if each partner has the desire to be seen, then someone has to put the mirror down first . . . and that's a tough thing to do. It's even more difficult if the reward for doing so isn't immediately repaid by acknowledgment of the gesture.

If offended, you often take your typically optimistic rays of light and abruptly tuck them away, leaving the local weather looking a bit overcast. When *both* of you hide your sunlight, the days begin to look pretty dark. And then because your mode is Fixed, you can remain in those cloudy conditions for extended periods of time. Your worst qualities come out through pride and self-absorption, because when you're feeling wounded, you tend not to see your part in the misunderstanding.

With other signs, it's easy to make amends after a disagreement, but with you, "Leo the Dramatic," apologies are almost unheard of, even though both of you will expect one. If problems don't fester too long, it's relatively easy to reach out to your partner. When they're allowed to linger, however, you tend to justify your position by thinking of your Leo partner as bad, which only serves to legitimize your own anger. It's tough when both of you are hurt because you want the other person to see you as right, and that's definitely not going to happen very quickly. This is one of those relationships that will likely be boisterously loud and dramatic.

LoveScope

Awareness is the key in any relationship, and if Leos are willing to expand theirs to include the feelings of their partners, then they'll truly have a kingdom of wealth. They can show their love and devotion by doing something as simple as picking the lint off one another's sweaters to demonstrate an understanding of the importance of image, or by *sharing* the mirror (and thus a warm reflection back).

The gifts in this relationship are never boring and always noticeable. It's never dull and rarely quiet, but generally overflows with love. Love reigns supreme for Leos, and they *know* loyalty. Their connection can last a long time because each knows the other's needs so well.

The only thing they have to watch out for is their own dependence on external approval. This is Leos' weak spot, but it's easily remedied through self-awareness and encouragement. Overall, these two make a lovely team, but they need to be sure there's balance between them.

HOW TO KEEP THE LEO YOU LOVE

- Protect, love, and pamper their hair.

- Let them take the credit for things even if the only way they could have known the answer was from you.

- Make sure their birthday celebrations begin the week they remind you it's approaching and last a week after they stop mentioning it.

- When you bring up things you like about them, speak with profound authority.

- Let them overhear you raving about them to someone else.

- Treat them like a diva, no matter what their gender is.

- Whenever they ask your opinion about what they're wearing, remember to always answer with, "I love it; it looks great on you."

- Never share their bathroom . . . use the shed if you have to.

- Live as if this is true: what's theirs is theirs, and what's yours is theirs, too.

Leo + Virgo

LoveScope: 7.8

The Basic Relationship

When the Lion meets the Virgin, they both become entranced. Leos are unconsciously intrigued by people who believe they know how things are supposed to be, and Virgos have *plenty* of opinions.

Virgos are polite at first, showing proper humility to the grand Leos, who feel empowered by their partners' gentle displays. Virgos are impressed by this, which keeps their inner criticisms at a much lower volume than normal. They're also attracted to Leos' strength and recognize that these Lions need a certain amount of tending to— something Virgos are remarkably good at doing.

Leos have within them a strong desire to be accepted, but Virgos don't give out their stamp of approval very easily. That sets up Leos' first issue to tackle, and all Fire signs love a challenge. Lions are child-like, love grand displays, and delight in being waited on; Virgins are very adultlike, prefer simplicity over drama, and enjoy serving . . .

up to a point. This relationship starts out great, and can remain that way as long as Leos are prepared for the changes that will inevitably occur.

The Passion Zone

While Leos may be ready to demonstrate to Virgins how great they are in bed, Virgos are more likely noticing things like the unnecessary amounts of hair Lions have on their shoulders or in their ears. This example is an accurate indication of their relationship's foundation. Leos are passionate creatures, and Virgos are subtle in their emotional expression—but surprisingly, the pure, proper Virgins are capable of unleashing a primal sexuality that can shock their unsuspecting partners. Of course, if they've made it to the bedroom, Leos have already passed muster according to the hundreds of personal rules that Virgos keep in their playbooks.

What Virgo Needs to Know about Leo

Leos love to be pampered, Virgo. Offering your king or queen of the jungle their morning coffee, serving them breakfast in bed, and making sure not to make too much noise if they're still sleeping are all part of your nature and contribution. Leos have a tendency to get comfortable with this scenario and will soon be taking it for granted. It's best that you know this now so you can save your "special" behaviors (such as servitude) for momentous events like birthdays. Leos are truly sensitive to criticism, and although they don't show it on the outside, *your* criticisms of them sting.

What Leo Needs to Know about Virgo

All that pampering from your Virgo partner will be fabulous for a while, Leo, but then that *other* part of them will emerge. Subtly, your

Virgin will start correcting your words or suggesting better ways for you to dress. "Why not try dark socks with those shoes?" they might advise. Eventually, as things start to become more familiar, they may change from subtle to direct and begin nagging.

This is the primary symptom of Virgins' need to be alone. They're the loners of the Zodiac, and if they don't get their quality time by themselves, they'll start to criticize you. It's important for you to recognize that your partner finds comfort in being needed, but it's *imperative* that you don't look like you expect their care.

LoveScope

When honest and aware, these two can have a grand time together. Leos understand Virgos' need to isolate themselves from time to time, and make it a point to see that they have plenty of time to be by themselves. Virgins see that their Lions need to feel accepted and loved; and they realize that their own incisive, critical minds might serve everyone better if they offered encouragement rather than nagging.

Support is the key here. Leos need to embrace their mates, understand them, and pave the way for them to feel protected. Virgos need to value their partners without cynicism. Together, when healthy, this couple runs a happy household that supports them both. They must commit to their own development, and then they'll reap the rewards.

An important note: The commitment here is provisional, but if conditions are met, these two will share a lot of time together. However, if expectations aren't lived up to, Virgos are the most likely to jump ship first.

Leo + Libra

LoveScope: 8.7

The Basic Relationship

Leo and Libra are separated by one sign on the Zodiac wheel. That means that they'll have compatible elements (Fire and Air, in this case). Leo is Fixed Fire, implying stubbornness combined with a passionate flame, and Libra is Cardinal Air, which indicates that the sign can be aggressive and outgoing. There's instant chemistry between these two: Libras like a certain confidence in their partners, and Leos enjoy the charm and beauty of the Libra demeanor.

Libras are represented by the Scales, which, as I've mentioned, is the only inanimate object in the Zodiac and symbolizes their ability to be completely fair. The Lions, however, may see this impartiality as being completely *cold.*

Both of these signs have their focus on the outside world as a way to monitor their own progress. Leos do it from an insecure place, and with Libras it originates in competition. Libras want to be the best in all areas having to do with relationships. Their desire is to be the most charming, to be the most liked, and to be seen as the fairest. Neither sign likes to go too deep into murky emotions, so each can count on the other to be buoyant and light.

The Passion Zone

This initial attraction may be of the rare, breathtaking type that happens only once or twice in a lifetime. Leos love Libras' refinement because it looks good on their arm, like an adornment—anything that makes Leos proud is what they'll want to "own." Libras adore the dance of flirting and Lions love the attention, so these two are an instant hit, but there's more. . . .

Both love looking good and being envied, and the higher the "beauty-o-meter," the more rewarding things will be later in bed. Just remember that Libras are passionate, but they prefer to keep things light and airy. When the sex is over, they like to read a book or watch a good TV program. Any disappointed grunts won't be acceptable. Leos have already passed the Libra beauty test if these two are in bed together, so they should be appreciative.

What Leo Needs to Know about Libra

Libras' worst traits include the fear of being committed and that icy feeling those Scales leave you with in their quest for balance. They love the pursuit of relationships, so even when they get into one, they'll still want to continue the chase—and it's usually not with you, Leo. It's nothing personal—they just need the fuel that hunting feeds them. They also require alone time, and will find you completely annoying if you hang around them all day. Be sure to have a place to put your attention on that doesn't involve your Libra partner. They scream "suffocation" faster than any other sign of the Zodiac, but will have no clue when *they're* doing the smothering.

What Libra Needs to Know about Leo

Leos are deeply tied to your approval, Libra, which gives you a lot of power *over* them but not much respect *for* them. You like your partners strong and impervious to your meaner moments, but be advised: Just when you think you know what your Lion is going to do, they'll take their sunshine and leave you. It's fast and furious, and often without warning—so check in with them and make sure you're treating them fairly. It could save you from having to say "I'm sorry" later. Your Leo will *become* your image of them, so try changing what you see if you want them to have a different demeanor.

LoveScope

Libras and Leos are natural together. There's a lot of magic to tap into with these two. Libras love strength and beauty, and Leos enjoy being those things. Those ruled by the Scales find the good in everyone, but it's easier when their mates are conscious Leos who know how to hold strong and be independent at the right times. If Lions understand that the more conviction they place behind something, the more likely Libras are to challenge it, then there will be fewer hurt feelings and more awareness. This will mean that Libras trust their partners enough to test them.

There's no doubt that this will be an extremely active relationship—not a single dull moment will dare to hang around. These two should remember that cooling off is a good thing, and communication with outside friends won't hurt either. There's a formula for success for this couple: Leos must stay positive in their conversations, and Libras need to be sure to let their Lions know that, of *all* their friends, *they* are the closest and dearest to their hearts.

These guys just "get" each other. This is often a heaven-made match that, when positive, lasts forever—but it will feel like an eternity when it's negative.

HOW TO LOSE THE LEO YOU LOVE

- Mess up their hair.

- Retell their joke and then take credit for it.

- Remark: "Nobody makes a meal like . . ." and reference someone else.

- Say things like "This isn't about you" several times throughout the day.

- Offer sarcastic standing ovations for overdramatized stories.

- Buy them a hat two sizes too small so they have to say, "This isn't big enough."

- Remind them that the house isn't getting smaller; no, their head is getting bigger.

Leo + Scorpio

LoveScope: 7.2

The Basic Relationship

Leo is Fixed Fire, and Scorpio is Fixed Water; and in astrological terms they form an angle that can present some difficulties. Leos love public admiration and are dramatic, while Scorpios prefer privacy and are brooding and pensive.

There's a strong magnetism between them. Leos are intrigued by the strength that Scorpios get from deep within their psyches, and Scorpions love the shining brightness that Lions can exude—especially after a long day spent analyzing their own inner cauldron of emotion.

Scorpios trust no one; Leos trust everyone. Fixed signs enjoy their own realities; they like how they've designed their world and feel comfortable in it. Coaxing them out isn't an easy task, but if Scorpions are strong within themselves (that is, strong enough to put their own beliefs aside to look at another person's perspective), they have a better chance of broadening their own experience and deepening their self-awareness—and that's an attractive quality.

The Passion Zone

It's pretty steamy when Fire and Water get together, but it takes a while to see past all the games. If these two manage to make it to the bedroom, it will be hot and fun . . . although the journey there could be tough.

Not many signs can remain in the depths of emotional passion for quite as long as Scorpions. It's the same energy that allows them to obsess about their loves, past and present. Leos love the romantic waters that exist within Scorpios, but over time will want a grander display of affection. Scorpions aren't demonstrative, whereas Lions are, and this could be a point of contention between them.

What Leo Needs to Know about Scorpio

Scorpios are deep, looking below the surface of everything, Leo. They'll scan your psyche to find the skeletons in your closet. They survived as children by creating a safe haven from a particularly dangerous world. Scorpios require depth and love in order to invite you to their inner world of fears so that you can help them burn that insecurity away. Their worst qualities come from the assumption that everyone is as aware and introspective as they are, which leads to disappointment ensuing when they realize that this isn't true.

Scorpios will never forget to call you. Therefore, if you forget a commitment you've made to *them,* they'll be sure it was a deliberate slight and form an immediate judgment that's rock solid and extremely hard to let go of. They don't trust easily and are constantly setting up tests to evaluate your loyalty. You must also understand that Scorpions have a secret life and need a certain amount of personal time to explore it. Staying open and understanding your partner's other reality will lead to a deepening of the connection between the two of you, and a bond that will last forever.

What Scorpio Needs to Know about Leo

Leos don't look down. That is, they don't spend a lot of time in introspection. Any deeper meaning that you attribute to their behavior is placed there by you, Scorpio. Lions don't want to go into the deep crevices of their inner psyches; it's too scary. Don't assume that they've done any real amount of looking inward, at least not compared to the kind of self-examination you do. It's not that they don't care—it's that they really don't know how to go about it.

You *can* teach them how to fearlessly get an accurate reading of their own motives—and don't take it personally if they kick and scream throughout the whole process. Leos need a great deal of adoration and are willing to go out into the world to get it. That means jealousy must be dealt with, and trust must be built.

LoveScope

If these two make it over the hump of their differences, there's an amazing relationship that can develop. Both signs have a complementary business savvy. Leos like being the shining star, and Scorpios love hiding in the recesses. Scorpions are more loyal than most and can use their detective skills to curb any problems before they become too big. That's the best part of being Fixed like glue: it takes time to bond, but it's permanent once it's set. When they agree to be connected, few couples will be as ferociously loyal as Scorpios and Leos.

Both signs want to know that their partners put them first and aren't going anywhere. It's a beautiful sentiment, and one that can open them up to amazing possibilities. Leos' optimism and Scorpios' pessimism make them strange bedfellows, but these qualities could contain enough passionate differences to keep the magic alive for a long time.

Leo + Sagittarius

LoveScope: 8.2

The Basic Relationship

When two Fire signs combine, the sparks are always going to fly—we're talking sparks of passion, anger, *and* insight. The Leo-Sagittarius combination is *that* combustible. Sagittarius is Mutable and Leo is Fixed, so there's comfort in knowing that the Archers are adaptable to the often-stubborn personalities of Lions.

Sags are wanderers or gypsies spreading insights and light into the dark caverns of others' lives. They have imaginative minds and see life in terms of surreal dreams of castles, knights, and maidens. Leos aren't strangers to fantasy—or royalty—and can easily accommodate Archers' visions as long as *they're* still seen as the kings (or queens). This isn't a problem for Sags; they want players for their play, and Leos have drama down to a fine art. When these two first meet, there's an instant recognition of those strong flames that burn beneath the surface. Sagittarians are chatty and boastful, and Leos are stable and self-centered. It's a good mix.

The Passion Zone

Two Fire signs can certainly make heat in bed, but these two seem to mesh together a little better than either does with an Aries partner. Sagittarians love a royal fantasy, and Leos delight in being the star of any play that has a throne in it. These two have fun, and indeed they should!

What Sagittarius Needs to Know about Leo

Leos can carry with them a certain elegance—a *regality,* if you will, Sag. They have an air of sophistication and pride. At a party, don't be surprised if your Leo decides to take all the credit for your recent decorative collaboration and just happens to leave your role out of their story. They're Fixed, so they don't change their minds quickly or take action unless they're sure of the consequences. Just understand that this behavior supports you in the art of humility—so that *you* can feel what it's like to have someone stealing all the credit (something you do shamelessly). It also gives you a reflection of how unattractive it is to not share recognition. If you speak of your disappointment with your Leo, they'll probably never omit your name again.

What Leo Needs to Know about Sagittarius

Sagittarians are people lovers and enjoy great diversity. Leo, you'll find no threat in this because you know that you're important in your Archer's life. Sagittarians aren't so interested in the world's view of them, but they do care about their impact *on* the world. Sometimes when they're being antsy and irritable, they'll start shooting jabs at their friends by making personal comments out loud in a room full of people. Sagittarians may simply see this as an honest game of telling the truth, but if their remarks damage your—or other people's—image, then they're sending a message loud and clear: "I'm unhappy, and I don't know how to get out." That would be a great time to have a private and loving chat with them.

LoveScope

It's not hard to make this relationship work. It starts with just a bit of understanding and a lot of willingness on both people's parts to be responsible for their own lives. Sags especially have to watch their insensitivities and impatience. When these two put their own needs aside long enough to recognize that there are other people in this world with their own realities, things will go much smoother.

With two Fire signs in the mix, this relationship will be loud and filled with shouting—both in anger and joy. Leos can hold their Sags up high with reassuring support, and Archers should motivate their Lions by reminding them how great they really are. The true magic of this relationship is that they both really *do* believe in each other, and with good reason. There's too much fun to be had between them to give up. Fire is about inspiration, and if these two are spiritually inclined, they can move mountains with their faith and motivation. Growth is inevitable.

Leo + Capricorn

LoveScope: 6.3

The Basic Relationship

There are some interesting metaphors when looking at the relationship between the Goat and the Lion. Leos are childlike, but they're learning to be adults; Capricorns are adults learning to be children. It's easy to assume that this union should instantly work, but like all things that are worth having, it will take a bit of effort. There are a lot of psychological dynamics that will creep in: Leos are looking for an *inner* father because theirs was weak or unavailable. Capricorns embody the external father because they had to raise themselves from an early age. Lions place their self-worth in the hands of other people and are, by nature, optimists. Capricorns get their confidence from what they do and are pragmatists. Leos love applause; Capricorns don't. Leos *expect* things to get done; Capricorns *do* them.

There's a rhythm here that's crystal clear. These two can really make something happen if they're both willing to look beyond what they've believed up to this moment and accept that there just might be a better approach to life than the way they've been doing it.

The Passion Zone

Even people with the most basic understanding of astrology have probably figured out by now that these two are an unlikely pairing. Their elements are off (Fire and Earth), making for awkwardness when they're together. But one of the things you probably *haven't* learned yet is that these two share deep passions, and when they open up to each other, it can be a wild ride on a roller coaster of love! By the way, Leos like their worlds to be rocked, especially if they're having fun in the process (and *especially* if they're in control of the experience). They also like to be ravished . . . and have the perfect partners for this behavior in their Goats!

What Leo Needs to Know about Capricorn

Capricorns want control and can be cold and calculating in the way they get it. Most of their command is gained by being useful, which is something they'll need to feel. Leo, if you're too independent or expectant, they'll simply leave. Goats want an honest reason to hang out with you, and one that's productive. Whatever you do, just don't try to flatter them; they're way too practical to reduce themselves to such frivolities. Be sure to look at life through their eyes and understand that they evaluate everything in terms of its purpose or usefulness. You may need to nudge your Capricorn into a more playful position. Remember that they've never been supported in just amusing themselves for the fun of it.

What Capricorn Needs to Know about Leo

At their worst, Leos are completely self-absorbed and require you to reflect their greatness back to them, regardless of how you feel. Remember, Capricorn, that Leos are trying to build an inner father— one that resembles the complete support you seem to provide so easily. It does take some practice, and the often-reactive Lions may end up leaving in a huff when you don't play the rescuing game. They tend to become demanding and unappreciative, and that could send *you* over the edge as well. It's fine to give, but you usually don't like to if someone orders you to do so.

LoveScope

The big lesson for both of these strong signs is that they must put their beliefs aside long enough to experience another possibility of relating. Capricorns need to be needed, and Leos want a lot of attention; in a way, there's a great balance here. Capricorns like to stay on a job until it's done, and in this case, the relationship *is* their job. Leos like having someone around who can give to them in the way they're used to being provided for—so there's a good "sticky" factor here.

Leos teach Capricorns how to lighten up and play (the true Cap goal), and Goats can show Lions how to grow up a bit and take some responsibility for anything they need. These two are both good at what they do. In fact, when Leos put their minds to it, they can become the most proficient in their field; and Capricorns have the ability to sway corporations to see a much better way of doing things.

Leos can also show their partners how to take the need for purpose out of everything and just let simple preference account for something. That alone would make this union worth every ounce of angst. With some effort, these two can find solid footing in their relationship as they learn from some of their important differences. Leos have to bring in a love of functionality and understand that their Capricorns require this to prosper. Capricorns grow younger as they get older, and with Leos' need to mature, this could be one of the best matches out there.

Leo + Aquarius

LoveScope: 4.2

The Basic Relationship

Aquarius is Air, and Leo is Fire; and you don't need a doctorate to understand how those two elements feed each other. But as compatible as their motives are, their *modes* tend to compete (both are Fixed, therefore stubborn), causing this to be one of the more difficult relationships to make work.

Leos have long gotten the rap for being egomaniacs, but that's not exactly the truth. It's Leos' *lack* of ego that sends them looking for acceptance, and they'll do whatever it takes to win it. Aquarians, conversely, come off as unconcerned by approval, or the absence of it. They'll often choose to align themselves with something least likely to win acclaim—of the mainstream kind, anyway. Loosely put, if it will shock, Water Bearers will identify with it. This characteristic doesn't mean they have *strong* egos; the real motive that underlies their identity shift is their self-doubting insecurity, which they hide

by their rebellion from the norm. So *neither* Leos nor Aquarians have inflated egos, and that can get in the way of their union.

The Passion Zone

Fixed Fire and Fixed Air both need to learn to give in more often, but if these two find a mutual point of interest between them, then passion can be found as they spar over their different perspectives. Lions love to feel like the rulers of the jungle, and Water Bearers will extinguish that fantasy with a quick decree that all rulers are passé. Between the two of them lies a play of power that would make any dictator cringe!

What Aquarius Needs to Know about Leo

Leos require a certain amount of acknowledgment. You tend to withhold trivial displays of approval because you see them as point-less, Aquarius, but it's important to your Lion that you recognize their significance. They'll follow your lead when it comes to the causes you rally behind. Be sure to show your gratitude; they'll remain loyal a lot longer.

What Leo Needs to Know about Aquarius

Aquarians are riddled with doubt, Leo. They don't always show it, but it's apparent when they get vehemently for or against someone or something. The louder they protest, the more likely it is that they're feeling insecure and could use your words of encouragement. They may act like they don't need or want it, but they *do,* and it will make a world of difference.

LoveScope

Leos radiate expansive warmth and kindness, and Aquarians exude selfless idealism. Bringing a Leo and an Aquarius together forms a union of two people who know they can make a difference in the world—and, consequently, in each other's lives. They often feel that they've found a missing part of themselves.

Neither sign tolerates dismissal, but there is much mutual disregard. One of them is going to *roar,* which will cause the other to disappear. (It's not too hard to figure out who will probably do what.) If this relationship sinks to its lowest form—disinterest, not hate—then a sad separation is inevitable. It will take time to end, but with Fixed signs, once it's over it's usually done for good. Leos will dismiss their Aquarian partners as cold and selfish, and Water Bearers are likely to have already moved on to another plane of reality. Misunderstandings that aren't discussed will just fester, so communication is a key to making this relationship work.

When these two are in harmony, there's an abundance of magic available. Each gives the security and reinforcements that the other thrives on—and all it takes is a little flexibility.

Both are noble in their commitment to causes. Aquarians love Leos' generosity and see its effect on the people around them. Leos admire Aquarians' humanitarian hearts and desire to make a difference. Each can get some nice applause just hanging out with the other. These two forge a connection that's hard to explain yet impenetrable by ordinary mortals. Once they decide to stick it out, it's a done deal!

At this point, the relationship won't take a lot of work, so they may want to make an effort to reclaim those parts of themselves that they see in their partners, which will make them feel whole. Aquarians *seem* confident and clear but are really shrouded in doubt. Leos *appear* insecure and without identity but are actually quite optimistic. These dynamics are like parts of a composition that, when played together, complete the symphony.

Leo + Pisces

LoveScope: 8.1

The Basic Relationship

Leos have strong, catlike instincts that sense good subjects (like Pisces) for their royalty, and Pisceans have an alienlike psychic ability that perceives strength and protection (found in Leo). Pisceans take direction when they feel that the person giving it has their best interests in mind. It's not a flaw in their character; rather, it allows them to know that their external lives are taken care of so they can focus on their mystical inner exploration. Leos melt at adoration, as long as it's sincere, and Fish have a genuine ability to cherish with an open heart and true ease.

Although this is a relationship that requires effort—given that these two signs are vastly different—it can produce some great rewards with the right amount of work. Lions tend to make themselves the center of the universe, and Pisceans tend to merge with this universe to the point of invisibility. They're certainly not threats to Leos, so they're quickly granted entrance into the "kingdom." That's where the training for both begins.

The Passion Zone

The magic that Leos feel when they're with someone who can follow their own fantasies is immeasurable. For Pisceans to find someone who's confident enough to take them outside of their everyday lives is exhilarating.

Fish and Lions create improbable passion that's envied by many. Leos like things hot; their partners prefer them wet and cool. When immersed in sexual desire, Pisceans will know exactly what it takes to give Leos pleasure, which fully enhances the Lions' experience and appreciation of their Fish.

What Pisces Needs to Know about Leo

It's baffling to you, Pisces, that Leos are so demanding, but you have to face the fact that it's just what they do best . . . *demand!* Really, though, Lions love having someone share their reality, and they can go to any store and find the perfect gift that will make their Pisces melt. It's a fun friendship or love affair as long as it's reciprocated. However, finding something in common might be a challenge.

What Leo Needs to Know about Pisces

Leo, you'll quickly learn that Pisceans live in a world of their own—outside of the Leonine kingdom. It's probably quite a blow to your pride that your mate isn't inviting you into their sphere. That would be tough for Fish because they live in an inner realm that only they have grown up with, which was created solely in the watery depths of this complex sign.

Trouble can start to brew if your Pisces has a drug or alcohol addiction, something that's common to this sign. It's a form of escapism, and as a Leo, you hate that kind of weakness. If Pisceans are pressured too hard, they'll withdraw even further, and eventually disappear into their inner world; or worse, they may let their inner piranha loose and show their vicious, seemingly heartless side.

Depression isn't uncommon either. Pisceans absorb the pain of others—or any strong emotion they're subjected to at the moment. They must have a place to consciously release these accumulated feelings, and one way for them to do so is to meditate or go inward. The problem arises when you want to play but your mate is absorbed in a place you can't visit. The watery world of Fish may be too much for you, especially if *you* start getting depressed. At its worst, the relationship may end sorely, but hopefully without violence.

LoveScope

The thing that makes difficult relationships more powerful than easy ones is their ability to strengthen the inner psyche of each person involved. In this case, Pisceans teach Leos that there's a lot more to life than being seen by others, and they also show them how to be compassionate—not because someone was nice to *them,* but because kindness was simply there to give. Lions show Fish that being a martyr serves no one and is a form of selfishness greater than simple narcissism. Feeling someone else's pain is a great gift, but only if it motivates both parties to create a better life.

There's no point in seeing pain in others unless it's used to recognize one's own. Pisceans must keep in mind that Leos won't understand their quirky needs all the time, but that will help the Fish become stronger and feel less victimized. Leos should remember that simply because they don't experience life through the eyes of a Pisces doesn't make their reality any less valid. It's a lesson in trusting that the other person is really living in a way that serves the self, and as a result, everyone else. The happier Leos are, the more they get to reflect joy onto everyone they meet.

Pisceans and Leos can make things happen in a magical way, but a willingness to grow must come from within each. Unexpectedly, these two do rather well together. Fish feel at home in the Lions' kingdom, and even though they don't really understand their Pisces partners, Leos tend to enjoy the comfort they have when they're together. Each has great reasons to stay, but ironically, neither will hesitate to leave when the going gets tough. It has something to do with that Water-Fire combination.

WHAT MAKES LEOS AWESOME?

- The sunlight they share
- Their contagious laugh
- Their boundless optimism
- Their hair—or, more appropriately, their "manes"
- The way they puff out their chests when they're proud
- Their embrace, which reminds you that everything is going to be all right
- Their chivalry
- The way they make molehills seem like mountains
- Their outrageous generosity

Virgo + Virgo

LoveScope: 5.0

The Basic Relationship

As I've already mentioned, Virgos are the loners of the Zodiac and actually prefer solitude to the company of others. They like people and want to socialize, but have reservations about relationships because of the anticipation of being disappointed. It's part of that perfection ideology deep within them.

So why bother with a relationship if both people are loners? There's no simple answer. Perhaps Virgos' strong inner critics need a bond in order for them to become "outer" critics. In other words, their partners can become the reflection of what's going on inside of them. When these two enter into a relationship, it's understood that they're both striving for some form of perfection in a flawed world. They understand the sting of criticism, but simultaneously recognize that it's used to correct what isn't right. There are many rules in Virgo relationships, and no sign honors rules (once they're established) like this one.

This is a Mutable, or dualistic, sign; and it's quite normal for each partner to act out its specific characteristics, including ones that are at opposite ends of the spectrum of Virgo behavior. The two aspects here are the Virgin and the . . . well, *un*-Virgin. You'll often see one as social—someone who loves to go out in the world—while the other prefers solitude and privacy. In a way, it works out perfectly.

The Passion Zone

Virgos can be quite surprising partners when it comes to a passionate relationship. The pure, proper Virgins, when the conditions are perfect, unleash a primal sexuality that will shock almost anyone—except other Virgos. There's a psychic connection that exists between them that's uncanny. Both understand that what they do in private stays there, so there's a fair amount of "cutting loose." Each Virgin recognizes the honor within the other, and they both know how to get past their partners' Do Not Enter signs. Neither likes to waste time playing around *after* sex, so when the fun is over, the work can resume. One will be changing the sheets while the other vacuums.

What Virgo Needs to Know about Virgo

Too much of a good thing can prove to be rather banal if each of you only honors the needs of the other. This is a service sign—Mother Teresa was a Virgo—and those it rules tend to put a lot of attention on their mates. This problem is somewhat complex. It's like having to figure out the dynamics of four distinct parts. As I said earlier, one of you will act like the Virgin, causing the other to become the un-Virgin—and these roles can flip at any time.

It sounds strange, but you'll notice it if you look at the rapport between you two on any particular day. You may be attentive and servile, while your partner is critical and seeks alone time. Later, you might become boisterous and animated where they're now acting shy and withdrawn. There's an inevitable push-pull that exists in all

relationships, but it's more readily defined when the signs are the same.

The worst part of Virgos is your tendency to be martyrs—when you feel that great sacrifices must be made in order for you to have what you really want. If you watch each other closely, you'll recognize the symptoms. Cutting remarks that you said to your partner in jest will usually initiate this behavior. Later, complaining emerges, which sounds serious and almost irresolvable, and that's followed by withdrawal. This is when solitude is needed, and if that isn't possible or it gets interrupted, there's a good chance your partner will soon be walking down that road toward martyrdom.

That's the dark hole for your Virgo—where they're unappreciated and can't seem to find a way out of their commitments. Most of these negative feelings will be aimed at you, the unaffected partner, but since all is fair in love, it won't be long before you're in that same emotional place.

LoveScope

The higher level of Virgos is when they're supportive, clear, helpful, and therapeutic. Giving themselves to their partners is one of the greatest gestures that can be made, and they must enter a relationship knowing there's work ahead—and be willing to do it. Their mercurial energies help them figure out solutions to problems easily, and together they'll quickly find those that benefit them both. There's also an innate understanding of love and the gentle gift of giving that can make quite a difference.

Conscious Virgos know that they become cranky when they aren't taking care of themselves and quickly remedy the situation without complaining. Together, these two can bring honor to a relationship and understanding to each other. They can be protective, assuring, and encouraging . . . and vigilant in finding the truth and sticking with it. Of all the Mutable signs, Virgo is the most consistent and committed, and when that's multiplied by two, the results can be magic. This combination gets a score of 5—smack-dab in the middle of the 10-point scale.

HOW TO KEEP THE VIRGO YOU LOVE

- Accept the fact that they love animals way more than they do you.

- Take a shower moments before you make contact with them.

- Never use their straw to share a drink.

- Always carry a small bottle of hand sanitizer.

- Buy extra towels so they can be washed after each use.

- Shop at health-food stores.

- Go somewhere without them sometimes.

- Only hang up your own clothes.

- Get your own medicine cabinet and bathroom.

- Don't ever get sick.

Virgo + Libra

LoveScope: 3.9

The Basic Relationship

These two signs have quite a bit in common. Libras and Virgos love refined beauty, like to keep things fair and balanced, and take pride in their appearance. Their inherent difference lies beneath the observable layers, so please pay close attention: Libras are social creatures who like to see the good in all things; Virgos are loners and would rather find flaws.

Let's imagine that this couple is about to purchase a piece of art, and examine how the process evolves. Libras see the whole picture and the overall way color is balanced. They then discern whether it matches their current decor and make a decision. (*Note:* If Libras begin discussing the pros and cons of the painting, that means they've decided *not* to buy it—although they may not know it yet.)

The first thing Virgos will do is look at the price, which they'll never think is fair. Then their eyes will notice each individual color and the brushstrokes used to create the piece. They'll also consider the fingerprints on the glass and if the painting was treated respectfully or carelessly. Once their focus is free from human distractions, Virgos then decide if it matches the integrity of its potential home in size and content. If all the conditions are met, Virgins will make the purchase, but only after pointing out every flaw and making it clear that the price should be reduced.

The Passion Zone

Virgos are surprising yet subtle in their lovemaking. Libras' sexuality is light and airy—for most Air signs, sex is more of a release from the mental strains of the world than a physical thing.

Libras want the extra luxuries that enhance the mood: incense, wine, music, and so on. Virgos are willing to accommodate these indulgences—and even enjoy them—but such enhancements are of no practical use to them. They're much more willing to enjoy these bedroom "tools" if their partners are responsible for providing them—and just as long as they don't have to worry about keeping track of them.

What Virgo Needs to Know about Libra

Libras love to keep an air of sophistication, just like you do, Virgo. But they also like all the knickknacks that could drive you crazy. For Libras, the big picture is about creating beauty, although you may only see it as clutter. Libras are also known for wanting control of their environment; while they appreciate your eye for cleanliness, they won't likely endorse anyone's taste but their own.

They'll also want to show off their goods at a party, and you may just have to find other accommodations while they're entertaining. It's common for Libras to say "black" if you say "white," and knowing this, you can easily resort to using logic—and manipulation—to get them to see things your way without being a nag.

What Libra Needs to Know about Virgo

Virgos would prefer to stay in their own space, with only occasional visits to social environments. They'll also use criticism as a cry for help, so be aware of this, Libra. What they really need is to just be left alone to relax, knowing that the world they give so much care to can actually fend for itself for a while.

They won't easily understand why you spend money on the things you do. They're not big into high-end fashion and don't care about where to get the hippest outfit. They love organization, especially when they're appreciated for the order they create.

On the other hand, Virgos are devastated by criticism, particularly from someone they care about, like a partner. Your sign is symbolized by the inanimate Scales, and you tend to proclaim your perspectives with icy neutrality, which is a tone that's easily confused with being critical. The more careful you are to word your sharp perceptions in a positive way, the better they'll be received.

LoveScope

This relationship can flourish with the proper balance between these two signs. But here's the rub: Libras and Virgos know what's proper, but that's not always exciting. Libras do love social functions and should find plenty of time for them outside of the home, thereby allowing Virgins the alone time they seek. Libras prefer beauty, but nagging isn't beautiful. Virgos need quiet, but parties aren't quiet. With a dose of awareness and perspective, these two can bring to each other a balance that fills them with what they desire, without much sacrifice.

Virgo + Scorpio

LoveScope: 8.7

The Basic Relationship

As I've said before, there's an automatic advantage to a relationship when each sign is the second one over from the other on the Zodiac calendar (they're separated by Libra). This means that their elements are compatible (Earth and Water) and their intrigues are high enough to be exciting.

Both Virgos and Scorpios are deep in their own ways. Virgos aren't afraid to walk into any situation and give it some order. Scorpios are willing to approach any circumstance and totally dissect it. Their initial orientation is different, however. Virgos start from a place of giving—of wanting to make the situation more perfect and be of service. With that in mind, they're ready to do anything it takes to achieve their goal. Scorpios' motives are to dig below the surface to see if there's danger underneath.

When these two come together, there's karmic recognition. They instinctively know that there will be good that comes from knowing

each other. Scorpios trust few signs, but their suspicion of Virgos is usually short-lived—and with good reason. Virgins have an enormous integrity that's palpable to Scorpios. Conversely, Virgos instantly understand that their Scorpions aren't harmful, just scared; and once Virgos know what's wrong, they know exactly how to help.

The Passion Zone

Virgos have two parts to them: the Virgin and the un-Virgin, and these characteristics are rarely seen simultaneously. "Scorpio" is often considered synonymous with *passion,* and there's good reason for that. Not many signs can remain in the depths of emotions for quite as long as Scorpions can. It's the same energy that allows them to obsess over a love they once had or their current romantic interest. The trick for these two is timing (which is usually right for Scorpios and almost never so for Virgos).

What Scorpio Needs to Know about Virgo

Perhaps the hardest Virgo behavior for you to understand, Scorpio, is their need for solitude. You like being alone, but want to feel the safety of being close to friends, also. Virgos do need the time to be completely by themselves, and it's important to accept that.

The second-worst trait of Virgos (at least to you) is their righteousness—that sense of acting like they're in the arms of propriety at all times. The problem is that they usually *are* right, and it can be infuriating for you, but don't fret. What you must remember is that irreproachable behavior is a cover for their fear of being criticized. You can help by seeing through their demeanor and protecting them.

What Virgo Needs to Know about Scorpio

Scorpios, at their worst, have a brooding skepticism of everyone. It's something they're essentially born with, and it seems to get profoundly stronger as they get more deeply involved with you, Virgo. What you can expect is a feeling of suspicion that begins to surround them, and they'll try to make you mad in order to shed this distrustful routine. To Scorpios, others appear to be the most honest when they're angry. So, if in the heat of the moment you don't reveal anything "new" to them, then you pass the test.

LoveScope

What's fun about this relationship is the attention to detail that each person brings. Virgos will listen attentively and then give sound and proper advice toward a working solution. Scorpios will listen, too, but they pay attention to deeper issues and then advise you on the likely source of your discontent. Both signs, being feminine in nature, are nurturers—but each comes from a different place when they give it.

When Scorpios finally trust someone, a loyalty ensues that goes beyond time and place. They're strong and emotionally supportive, which helps remove the critic within their Virgin friend with a strong dose of perceptive inspiration. Virgos will go to the ends of the earth for their partners as well, offering a clean, encouraging environment and a willingness to do just about anything to help them get on their feet.

When neither needs support, they'll find humor in the weirdest things because it's part of the way they bond. Virgos love making fun of everyday flaws most people tend not to be conscious of, and Scorpios go for anything that makes them laugh at another person's imperfections—not because they're cruel, but because they learn volumes when they realize that other people have secrets, too. These two, if they stick with it, will find an enormous allegiance growing between them. This is love that's built on real friendship and trust.

HOW TO LOSE THE VIRGO YOU LOVE

- When they're talking, point to your mouth as if you're trying to tell them that there's something stuck between their teeth.

- Use *their* towel to dry off after taking a shower.

- Tell them you don't believe in deodorant or germs.

- Suggest that you two should move in together.

- Pass gas or belch.

- Drink milk straight from the carton.

- Treat your athlete's foot with a spray . . . and use lots of it.

- Ask for seconds during dinner.

- Offer them a sip from your can of soda.

Virgo + Sagittarius

LoveScope: 2.5

The Basic Relationship

Comparing two Mutable, or adaptable, signs is really an exploration into the relationship between four people. Mutable signs have two sides to them: Virgo has the Virgin and the un-Virgin, and Sagittarius has the wizard of enchantment and the pauper of entrapment. If that isn't enough to complicate the relationship (and that's dealing with what's *similar* between them), we can compare their elements or basic motives: Virgos are practical Earth, while Sagittarians are impractical Fire—true opposites in the Zodiac. Sagittarians like to flirt, exaggerate, play, wander, and philosophize; Virgos like to be alone, minimize, create order, and think.

Virgos will analyze the heck out of anything, and Sags give them plenty of opportunities for scrutiny. Archers spout off theories and beliefs that are often bigger than life, and then Virgins have a great time separating fact from fiction. Just that exchange alone is worth

hours of connection. Virgos are logical and unemotional, but by Sagittarians' standards, they appear depressed. Sags are filled with hope and bravado, but to Virgos, they appear egocentric and evangelistic.

When they're together, these two can look like oil and vinegar— with Sagittarians being the oil. It requires numerous shake-ups for them to blend into a flavorful combination that's connected, but never permanently. Over time, and without a lot of effort from either, these two will continue to seek their respective (and natural) states of being.

The Passion Zone

The passion between these two is not as far-fetched as you might believe. Sagittarians love to inspire, and by all accounts, have no problem psychically retrieving Virgos' true desires and then fulfilling them in intimate moments.

There's also the matter of Virgos' rules about how things are done. This is instant death to the Sagittarian passion, but it also offers itself as a challenge that Archers can't resist. Overall, it's an intriguing connection—but, honestly, there's usually little to sustain it over time.

What Virgo Needs to Know about Sagittarius

The worst trait of Sagittarians is their lack of desire to perform life's mundane tasks. This is a sign that resents having to do mere mortal jobs, especially if *you* do them so much better, Virgo. The issue here isn't laziness; it's ego identity. Sagittarians identify with what they're doing and whom they're inspiring, and in their world there isn't much motivation in taking out the trash. Still, it needs to be done, and you'll get a lot more work out of your Sag if you play your empathy card. They love knowing that they aren't walking the trash can to the street alone.

What Sagittarius Needs to Know about Virgo

Unfortunately, Sag, Virgos are the most self-critical of all signs. They're very aware of imperfections in the physical world (after all, this is an Earth sign). Virgos care greatly about things like haircuts, matching clothes, proper English, and other proprieties. They'll definitely care about "things," and you won't have the slightest idea why. Just remember that order helps them feel like they're in control. Also, don't forget that the more upset Virgins get, the more nagging they do, so give them some time to themselves.

LoveScope

If both of these signs understand that love sometimes means walking in someone else's shoes, they'll avoid a lot of problems. Virgos are great support people, but they need acknowledgment for what they do and confirmation that those they're helping are changing their bad habits. Sags are true companions—and inspirations to all their friends—but they're afraid to take their truest dreams and see them become reality, so they'll often use their partners as the excuse for why they can't go out into the world.

When these two understand that their needs are different and that they both have a tendency toward blame, a lot of hurt can be prevented. Virgos know that not everyone cares about a perfect house or inner rules to govern their lives, but those things still mean something to *them* and should exist in *their* lives (although not necessarily in everyone else's).

Sagittarians must remember that their dream of taking a spiritual ideal to the masses is Virgos' worst nightmare (after all, Mother Teresa just did her own work and didn't try to turn herself into a religion), but it's exciting to *them* and is something that should be pursued. No one outside of ourselves is responsible for our losses or successes, and if both partners in this relationship remain aware of this, they can offer twice the support (remember there are *two* of each of them) of any other sign. Virgos can demonstrate humility to Sagittarians, and

Archers are able to teach expansion to Virgins. There can be bliss here; it will just require mixing in a certain amount love, a dash of commitment, and a pinch of respect, plus a whole lot of shaking!

Virgo + Capricorn

LoveScope: 9.2

The Basic Relationship

The Virgo-Capricorn couple has a definite edge over other Zodiac combinations. They can relate to each other through things that exist outside of the relationship. Both are Earth signs and are familiar—*quite* familiar, in fact—with the material world and how to approach it. Virgos sort and file, and Capricorns build and provide. It's a perfect match of productivity as long as there's an understanding of inherent differences.

Both signs are loners of sorts. Capricorns don't mind meaningful connections—nor do Virgos—and Virgins need to know that there will be some alone time in the schedule. Goats don't mind solitude either, but they prefer to be available in order to control the situations *and* people in their lives due to their Cardinal nature. Overall, there's a very smooth chemistry between these two; it's only in their exaggerated idiosyncrasies that there tend to be problems.

The Passion Zone

This couple's theme song is Olivia Newton-John's hit "Physical." Both have extreme carnal desires and can really let loose when they feel intimate, and luckily sex isn't a trivial matter for either of them—yet it's also not always at the top of their to-do lists. For Capricorns, it must serve a purpose. Whether it's procreation or intimacy, there has to be a reason to make love. For Virgos, there must be sincerity and dedication—once they commit, it's usually for life . . . and this is also true for Caps.

Capricorns are impressed by Virgos' sense of duty, and vice versa. Sex eventually will become a utilitarian function undertaken for pragmatic reasons: propagation, relaxation, control, and so on.

What Virgo Needs to Know about Capricorn

Capricorns are doers and providers. They have a serious way of looking at the world and often believe that since *they* did it the hard way, that's always the best approach. Of course, Virgo, you'll usually win every battle because you'll be fighting with facts, but if your Capricorn feels out of control, they'll shut you out . . . and it will suddenly seem like they built a wall of granite right in front of you. They have the ability to look at you (*through* you, actually) as if you're a complete stranger, and if they get to that degree of anger, tread softly for a while. Be diplomatic in your criticism; and never, *ever* correct them in public.

What Capricorn Needs to Know about Virgo

Virgos resort to complaining when they feel unappreciated, which is really a call for help and support. But if you blow your chance to make a connection, Cap, and redirect this building energy, then the grumbling will escalate to martyr mode. That's when Virgos begin to sound horribly self-indulgent, caring only for themselves and moaning endlessly—albeit accurately—about the ills around them. Ironically, it's good for them to boot everyone out of the picture long enough to find their center; the complaints are just irritants used to clear the area. And they *will* find their focus if you can let them alone long enough without pestering them with questions like "Are you done yet?"

LoveScope

When two signs take responsibility for what they're giving and receiving in a relationship, the union has a strong chance of survival—both Virgos and Capricorns are fit for this task. They understand the nature of the material world and just what's needed to make it work successfully. Both signs want to feel useful and need a certain amount of freedom to obtain their goals, which are usually compatible.

Virgins and Goats are starting with a strong foundation and naturally understand one another's idiosyncrasies. The effort put into this relationship should be aimed at developing a style of setting goals and then meeting them. The feelings of function and purpose are then fulfilled, and Earth signs *love* knowing they're productive.

Virgo + Aquarius

LoveScope: 4.3

The Basic Relationship

There are many things that Virgos have in common with Aquarians, including their appreciation for order and dislike of people. Well, that may sound harsh, but if they're given the choice of living alone or having a roommate, they'd both pick living alone. Virgos are impeccable about their environment (I didn't say neat; I said *impeccable*). There's a feeling that goes with their homes that reflects systematic organization. The order may *look* like chaos if they're the messy Virgo types, but they'll know where everything is at any given moment. They need a certain routine or consistency to their day, and without it they feel unbalanced or uneasy.

Aquarians need structure, too, but for different reasons. They keep pictures in their heads about how things should be, and it bugs them if their environment isn't a perfect reflection of that image.

Together, these two understand the need for order and respect each other's ability to achieve it.

246

Virgos, being Mutable, will yield to the Fixed sign of Aquarius, and probably meet the standards set forth by Water Bearers. This partnership forms with both parties knowing something about routine and ritual, but they have many differences. Virgos can be gentle and selfless, and at other times moody and critical. Aquarians have a tendency to be abrupt and self-absorbed, but also cold and disapproving. Virgins like the eccentric qualities of Water Bearers; and Aquarius enjoy their partners' tender, honest caregiving.

The Passion Zone

Virgos fluctuate between pure and wild, while also being picky. They can wait a long time for the right person—actually, the *perfect* person—and Aquarians could be just who they're looking for. Water Bearers' avant-garde, imaginative style could sweep Virgos right off their feet with a different acrobatic style of lovemaking each night.

Virgins love stimulation and surprise, and Water Bearers can easily fill that bill. Aquarians are crazy about the gentleness of Virgos, and they feel safe with the easy way their partners accept the unpredictable styles that they bring to the bedroom. These two can add a degree of kinkiness to the physical mix without skipping a beat.

What Aquarius Needs to Know about Virgo

Virgos have an instinctive urge to care for you, Aquarius—almost to the point of martyrdom. *You* may not like to deal with the trivial details, but Virgos love them, so be encouraging rather than dismissive when it comes to their need to organize the minutiae. Virgos require time for themselves—as do you—but they also want to know that you have an eye on them. That is, they need to know that they make a difference, and you may wish to remind yourself to speak of their virtues more often.

What Virgo Needs to Know about Aquarius

Aquarians love the big picture. They may not like the cat living in the house, but would be the first to put money in the local animal shelter's donation box. It may seem contradictory to you, Virgo, but the truth is that Aquarians have a broader view of life. You'll likely never have that outlook. Although you both share minds full of *shoulds* and *oughts,* Water Bearers are way more sensitive to criticism than they like to admit. You see, they're stable and fixed, and don't easily detach from their loops of thought. Be careful when criticizing them because they'll just dismiss you as a complainer if you do it before connecting with them first.

LoveScope

These two are alike in so many ways that it seems funny when they don't understand each other. It's true that both hate criticism and love order, but they react to those things for very different reasons.

Aquarians are interested in the global concerns or the bigger picture. They'll often support the rights of a group but deny those of the individual. They've been known to shine a bright light of hope ahead and cast a darker shadow behind them. For example, notice the double message in the statement "Those who don't believe in democracy should be locked up." This is where there can be a problem in this relationship. Water Bearers' minds are often singularly focused and have a hard time seeing both sides of an issue.

The problem with Virgos is almost exactly the opposite. They tend to see *too many* sides to the same problem. Together, they can help each other; but, unfortunately, they also tend to find mutual criticisms that could eventually wear down the fiber that keeps them connected.

Virgo + Pisces

LoveScope: 3.6

The Basic Relationship

Opposite signs on the Zodiac wheel each tend to have one skill that the other specifically lacks. In this case, Virgos have an eye for specifics, while Pisceans grasp the big picture. One notices the trees, and the other observes the entire forest. Pisceans won't worry about matching the paint on the wall to a specific color in the carpet; if they like something, it "goes" in the room. Some call that eclectic, and Virgos may dub it unconventional, messy, or just poor taste.

Fish refuse to discriminate. They don't see the amount of money their partners have, the clothes they wear, or the color of their skin; they only know how it feels to be around their mates. Virgos are cognizant of everything and make choices based on preference. They'll notice mismatched socks, dirty nails, or socioeconomic background. It all matters to them because in the physical reality (where Virgos focus) everything has a place.

Of course, all those predilections wouldn't stop Virgos from help-ing someone in need, but they are indicators of how open Virgos are to letting others in. Pisceans are almost totally opposite; they're helpers, too, but their method is to completely open themselves up to others. The details of a person's life don't matter to them. People's faces could be plastered on WANTED posters in every post office, and Fish would still completely embrace them, only acknowledging that they're in a bad situation and could use some assistance. The biggest difference between Pisceans and Virgos is discrimination, and it's a *big* difference that matters in a *big* way to Virgins.

The Passion Zone

I've said it before, and I'll probably say it again: Virgos, when inspired, will unleash a primal sexuality that will shock most unsus-pecting signs. Pisceans are Water and can merge into a deep pool of intimacy, often sweeping Virgos into a magical world of simmering passions. Nothing shocks Fish, which is one of their most delicious traits. They get between the sheets and say, "Come on in, the water's fine." Remember that neatness counts to Virgins, so their partners *must* take a shower before and after. There's no room for dirt in the bedroom . . . unless it's in a magazine!

What Virgo Needs to Know about Pisces

Pisceans' darker side emerges when they start acting like the suf-ferer. That term isn't as negative as it sounds, but it does point to a part of them that's prone to brooding when they've absorbed heart-ache and pain from the world around them. And, Virgo, you may find them pulling away in a moping manner with self-medication of some kind in hand. For them, that can be food, alcohol, or drugs; it's what-ever makes them relax. Although it may seem escapist—and could put your sense of propriety on alert—sometimes it's okay to just let Fish find their own way out of this state.

What Pisces Needs to Know about Virgo

Virgos' darker side is martyrlike. They see the pain in you, Pisces, and may sacrifice their own needs to offer you comfort. It's not so different from what you might do, except Virgos will keep their boundaries intact. Virgins never really lose their identity when helping; rather, they accumulate a mental list of all that's being done for the people they're assisting—and this isn't a negative thing unless it's unconscious. That's when they'll start their infamous nagging and criticizing, which you must realize is a call for a break from others. Virgins may seem stuck in an endless loop of fussing and nitpicking, so be sure to encourage them to seek some time alone. Of course, that means you'll have to assure them that you can keep up with the chores.

LoveScope

Yes, these two can create a web of frustration and suffering that could last for years. The more Virgos venture into the realm of self-righteousness, the more Pisceans go into the suffering zone.

But there are a few things each of these Mutable signs can do to transform their coexistence into something remarkable. These issues will take some work and the willingness to be self-aware, but they can be tackled. Virgos have to recognize that water will take on the shape of its container, and one way to communicate with Fish who may be lost in an ocean of feelings is to create safe boundaries that allow them to find their way to their own center. Virgos' discriminating eyes can help their Pisces weed out the emotions that don't belong to them and offer a time-out period to mentally release the accumulations of the day. It's important that Pisceans take responsibility for the fact that they change based on the people around them and are prone to psychic absorption. Whether they feel like it or not, Fish should take the time to be alone.

Virgos have to assume responsibility for creating limits as to when to help and when to remove their attention. They also need solitude to ponder their lives and feel the purity around them. Fish can help

Virgins by offering their enormous compassion for the way they tire-lessly support the disadvantaged. These two have a dynamic connec-tion, but it will take enormous effort to overcome their natural states.

WHAT MAKES VIRGOS AWESOME?

- Their dry, hilarious humor
- Their innate capacity to know exactly what you need
- Their natural ability to heal
- Their organized and detail-oriented minds
- Their knack with numbers
- Their capacity to live simply
- Their editing abilities
- Their honesty
- Their integrity

$\mathcal{Libra} + \mathcal{Libra}$

LoveScope: 2.4

The Basic Relationship

When two Libras come together as a couple, the end result is all about staying in balance. They particularly like having people in their lives who match their skills at the relationship game. For these two, it's all about the *R* word: *relationship.* They're Cardinal (aggressive) and Air (mind oriented), so they appreciate challenges—although they may complain about them as they plow through every resolution.

Libras love the pursuit, but they don't always like to *catch* their prey. They'd rather tantalize and seduce, using their remarkable charm and dimpled smiles. However, other Libras are privy to that game and not so easily persuaded by these tactics.

The Passion Zone

Sex for most Air signs is more of a respite from the mental strains of the world than it is a physical thing. With two Libras, all the components will be in place: both find each other attractive, like to keep it light, and want to figure out a way to make their partners more attached than they are. This mutual mirroring makes for occasional fun but has the effect of causing the relationship to dwindle rapidly. These two need to work hard at keeping the mystique alive, which isn't easy when they're balancing individuality with the need for partnership on delicate Scales.

What Libra Needs to Know about Libra

You're notorious for seeing both sides of any situation, so when you meet another Libra, the game is in full swing and the outcome is up for grabs. You love to be courted with fancy restaurants and good movies, and you instantly understand your own inherent instinct to be alone once the social engagements are over. There's both comfort and *dis*comfort (it's *always* balanced with Libras) in this relationship because there's a fair amount of anticipation—but this is offset by a substantial lack of intrigue. Boredom is a curse for any Air sign.

The worst part of Libras in relationships with Libras is their knee-jerk reaction to claim the other side of any argument. For example, if one says, "We should turn left," then the other will insist, "No, *right* is the correct direction." The hard part is that they don't know what their true positions are on any topic. Libras could be conservatives arguing liberal points simply because their partners are doing the opposite. This couple will become like a set of twins who have chosen to mirror each other. Luckily, neither enjoys the feeling of confined commitment, for as much as both dream about marriage and entering into a long-term partnership, the actual *act* scares them silly.

There's a dynamic that's common to Libras—since they have this knack for taking the opposite side of any discussion—where they'll tend to trade roles. One of them seems strong and aggressive, while the other looks weak and submissive; then they'll switch so the one who *was* acting fragile suddenly becomes courageous, and vice versa. It's the ultimate push-pull game of relating and can grow wearisome for both. This is the result of identifying with each other but refusing to assume any risks or responsibilities. If there's no emotional connection to act as the glue, both partners could drift off in their own separate directions—thereby dissolving the union without either person noticing.

LoveScope

It's no fun to watch a natural and easy connection disappear without knowing why or what could have been done to make it better. Sometimes realizing that the relationship is threatened from the start can create the motivation to make it work better. At best, these two have an understanding of each other's motivations, and rather than responding in the typical "reject the other person's position at all costs" manner, conscious Libras could attempt to look at their own stance—and at the very least ask themselves whether or not it's what they really believe. It's not that Libras can't commit; it's that it means giving up all the other choices they're used to having.

Together, at their best, these two bring a beautiful reflection of each other into the relationship. Libras' greatest gift is their ability to see the good in others. As a couple, they can bypass the social niceties and go straight for direct honesty—not just the truth about each other, but about themselves and their own desires.

HOW TO KEEP THE LIBRA YOU LOVE

- Buy them subscriptions to the top fashion magazines.

- Watch your language.

- Change into something snazzy after work . . . and then again for bedtime.

- When they ask for your honest opinion, give it to them—they probably won't use it, but it makes them feel fair-minded.

- Take them out to dinner with people they know so that they can show off their new clothes.

- Don't agree with them too quickly—they'll take the other side. Pose thoughtful questions that they have to answer.

- Act like you don't notice them flirting.

- Expect them to take the other person's side when you tell them about an argument you had.

- Never insist on going shopping with them.

- Don't compete with their taste—they'll always win.

Libra + Scorpio

LoveScope: 3.7

The Basic Relationship

It pays to take note that Scorpio is the sign directly after Libra on the Zodiac wheel. That usually means that the signs have something to teach each other. To put it quite simply, Libras look at what's good about someone, and Scorpios look for what's bad—and this happens not by choice but by instinct. Libras have to feel good about people because Air signs aren't instinctively skilled at going too deep. It makes them feel safe to know that their partners can take care of the skeletons in their *own* closets, or at least arrange them neatly so they'll look good at their dinner parties.

Scorpios' instinct is to mistrust. They spend much of their lives looking at the deep recesses in every corner of their own psyches for evidence they can use to defend themselves when their minds bring them before the judge in their inner courtroom. As a result, they don't know whether Libras' light charm is a cover for flaws or if they're

simply oblivious. Libras look at Scorpions' world as tormented and difficult, but that's not what they find most distasteful. To them, it looks like Scorpios are *insisting* on being in that mess and could snap out of their conspiracy-oriented mind-sets with a simple change of focus.

They're right, on the one hand: Scorpios *could* ignore their own suspicions, but it would be equally hard to get Libras to open up to theirs. They need to be able to trust people, and Scorpios must doubt everyone—so why would these two even attempt a relationship? The truth is that Libras love causes, and there's none bigger than to get Scorpios to see that there's good in life, even with their scary cauldron of suspicion—and Scorpios welcome that challenge.

The Passion Zone

Everyone enjoys making love, and the intimacy for these two can be riveting. Their issues aren't about being compatible between the sheets, because there they have a great connection. The problem is *afterward.* As I've said before, "Scorpio" is often used synonymously with *passion.* Not many signs can remain in the depths of emotions for quite as long as Scorpios. It's the same energy that allows them to obsess about a love they once had or their current romance. But *obsession* is a naughty word to Libras, who, once satisfied, can reach for the closest fashion magazine or start to plan their next dinner party.

What Scorpio Needs to Know about Libra

Despite a nice exterior, Libras have a mean streak. You don't really mind that, Scorpio. In fact, when they're in this mood, it will likely be when they tell you what they truly believe in (a reassuring secret for you). What *you* need to know is that your infatuation with them is something they deeply want, despite the fact that they constantly run from it. Now, that isn't permission for you to become their favorite stalker, but remembering this will help you through the times when they have to push you away and go to their ivory tower (which can last a couple of weeks). This is tricky because the word can't get out that you know they like your attraction to them. They must rebel against everything, so they'd probably deny it. Ironically, this is how they keep things honest!

What Libra Needs to Know about Scorpio

When Scorpios are angry, they're really just hurt. If you remember that, Libra, you'll be fine in this relationship. It won't help to cover up their anger with a nice party—and if you *think* it's working, then they've just buried their feelings *temporarily* (this last word is very important). Eventually—and this is the scary part—they'll catch you doing something that will give them the perfect opportunity to let it all come out . . . and when it does, this release will have some serious horsepower behind it. It's best to brave the monsoon while it's still sprinkling.

LoveScope

These two don't have a great foundation, which means that they'll have to work harder than other combinations to attain a mutually supportive relationship. It's not that it can't last; it just can't be satisfying for both without some intention. Libras love variety, and Scorpios choose to fixate on one thing at a time. Libras brush through people with an airy lightness that can conjure envy in even the most brooding, self-focused signs. Certainly, there's a great deal of learning that can occur between them.

Libras' love of beauty can be painful if it's obvious that they won't reach beyond the superficial. Without even trying, they can make their partners believe that life's problems will dissolve with the help of the proper plastic surgeon. Scorpios must learn that their fixation, or worry, changes nothing. Both signs can take their partners' skills and use them to deepen their own experience, but it will require changing what they truly believe. If they're up to the task, this union could be amazing.

HOW TO LOSE THE LIBRA YOU LOVE

- Reveal that you're in love with them.

- Ask them to pick the restaurant.

- Let them know you're going to a party, but don't tell them it's for a five-year-old.

- Remark that with the right surgeon, they could almost make it in Hollywood.

- Hide their Pilates video.

- State that your favorite show is professional wrestling.

- Show them that one of their feet is bigger than the other.

- Mention that you want children.

- Tell them you filmed them snoring, and it was cute.

- Paint their special room as a gift.

Libra + Sagittarius

LoveScope: 7.8

The Basic Relationship

Libra and Sagittarius are separated by one sign on the great Zodiac wheel, which means that their elements (in this case, Air and Fire)—and, therefore, their personalities—work well together. They appreciate each other, especially for their shared ability to elicit grins—both signs *love* to see others smile. For Sagittarians, it's because they've inspired people with a story or a spiritual revelation; and for Libras, it means that they've charmed them.

There's instant chemistry when Sags meet Libras. Grandiose language pours out of Archers' mouths, and Libras are amused—although they don't believe a word of it. Libras will never let on that they disregarded most of the conversation's content and focused on the entertainment value. The happy Sags don't care; they know that Libras will be in the palms of their hands in no time.

That's right . . . Sags are flirts, too; and if they see a *hint* of interest, they'll fan those flames until they become a forest fire. Libras are, of

course, too proper to engage in overt displays of affection, but they secretly love it when *others* do. These two connect with each other instantly and learn something of value. Archers could use some guidance in the area of social niceties—that is, how to appropriately show their interest in someone—and no one has more expertise with this than Libras. Conversely, Libras really *want* to cut loose, but must learn from Sags how to quit wondering what others are thinking about *them*. If nothing else, this union is fun for both.

The Passion Zone

Sagittarians understand the rules of flirting and, as long as they apply a delicate technique, should be able to seduce their airy Libra partners. Most of the foreplay will embody some spiritual ideal. Air and Fire signs have what it takes to create plenty of sparks. Much of the sexuality in this relationship is mythic in nature, as both parties feel some connection to "higher" parts of themselves when they're together.

What Libra Needs to Know about Sagittarius

Neither you, Libra, nor your Sag will want to spend much time regretting your behavior. Both of you have an ability to tint the way you see situations to let yourselves off the hook. If Sagittarians think they've done wrong, they'll simply try something else in a bigger way so they don't have to stop and belabor the point. Alternatively, they'll blame whomever they hurt. They seek their revenge with harsh gossip and tall tales of their own victimized status. Sags don't take criticism easily, so if you've got a problem with something your Archer has done, then *you've* got a problem. When Sagittarians withdraw their love, life can seem hopeless.

What Sagittarius Needs to Know about Libra

Libras play both sides of the fence at all times. If they said something to hurt your feelings, Sag, they know how to easily convince you that *you* were in the wrong. If you two start aiming judgmental barbs at each other, you're likely to see the mean side of Venus (Libra), and then the angry side of Jupiter (your ruling planet, Sagittarius) will come out as well. Most of the time the difficulties will leave as quickly as they appeared, but if there's a stalemate, things could get pretty icy. Libras will retreat and continue to play their social role, showing the outer world that nothing is wrong at home. Life will seem very banal when your Libra withdraws their love from you.

LoveScope

William Tell was an archer who was ordered to shoot an apple from his son's head, which he did brilliantly. That sums up the precision that's typical of all Sagittarians: when the pressure is on, their focus is amazing.

Libras are leaders; Sagittarians are adapters. When these two are in sync, they're in a rhythm that can accomplish anything. Their problems are dissolved when both make an honest commitment to understand the self, and then allow their partners to understand the people in their lives.

Sags long for the kind of support that recognizes their true strength of spirit. They don't want to have to work at proving anything, but need their partners to feel the power within themselves. That's what being inspired is all about. Libras have a natural tendency to see the good in everyone, but it's harder for them if they're in a committed relationship. They need to understand that a romantic involvement doesn't mean cutting out the rest of their lives, but rather that it means allowing another's energy to contribute to the sum of their existence.

Sagittarians don't have to be wounded to be heard. Libras like their people strong and directed. They will correct their partners' social

clumsiness with gentle discrimination, but Archers must be willing to call upon the healer within them and trust that they'll be guided on a path that isn't filled with pain. Sags bring Libras the gift of magic, and in return receive the gift of refinement. These two have a good chance of making miracles together as long as they allow each other the breathing room they both really need.

Libra + Capricorn

LoveScope: 4.5

The Basic Relationship

Libra and Capricorn are both aggressive energies on the Zodiac wheel, and this means that they don't wait for what they desire to be delivered. Libras want a relationship and the feeling of communion with others. Capricorns just need to build, whether it's a family, career, or house (as long as it's bigger than what they started out with). Upon first meeting, Libras might not like Capricorns' sense of style or the stoic belief system ingrained in this rather tough, traditionalist sign. Goats certainly won't appreciate Libras' fluffy superficiality and party mentality, but there *is* an attraction here. Libras secretly love the safety inherent in the sobriety of Capricorns, who love to have Libras' light and smiling energy around to help break the monotony of their daily routine. There's chemistry here and, in essence, the makings of a good relationship . . . provided that each sign respects the other's need for independence (that is, *control*).

The Passion Zone

Capricorns are passionate in a very physical and purposeful way, which doesn't mean that they have quick and meaningless sex. It is, however, in the realm of Libras' experience to simply enjoy sex for the sake of what it is, and nothing more. Each will likely perceive that longed-for "something" in the other. Libras see stability and security, and Capricorns observe grace (and there's nothing like a little carnal knowledge to help us feel that we're at least able to touch what we long for).

What Capricorn Needs to Know about Libra

This may come as a shock to you, Cap, but Libras can be a bit superficial. They're capable of being nice to people they may not like or mean to those they love, and vice versa. It doesn't matter what the relationship is, as long as they feel fair. Also, you're a very possessive sign, so you must understand that Libras need to flirt and connect with a wide range of people. The more they're allowed to do so, the better they feel about coming home to your arms. So try to relax and give them plenty of open range to safely romp; they'll rarely do more than just flirt. Capricorns who get frustrated by Libras' constant search for beauty are encouraged to scream "Not fair!" It doesn't matter what the crime is; an accusation of being unjust is close to the worst insult for those ruled by the Scales.

What Libra Needs to Know about Capricorn

Capricorns' worst trait may be blind ambition or the belief that if *they* had to do it the hard way, so should everyone else. Libra, if you don't understand that their childhood was serious business for them, you could easily dismiss their current motives . . . and you *don't* ever want to reject Capricorns' purpose as frivolous. They take great pride in providing for you, and in *not* using their relationships to get ahead.

You'd have little or no problem calling upon *your* relationships—at least, not at first—but that's part of your makeup. It would be smart to talk to Goats about your accomplishments in terms of what you did to achieve them, not who helped you. They'll simply leave if there's no promise of a future. You've now had fair warning.

LoveScope

Both Libras and Capricorns are independent, yet they have certain things they need from their mates. Libras want the feeling of a new relationship—all the time—and Capricorns have a desire to be useful. If these two can give each other what they need just by being themselves, then this combination has a chance. Their LoveScope score is slightly low, but it's high enough to create a wonderful foundation if they both choose to build on it. Capricorns may be too traditional for Libras, who need to follow the latest trends, but the chemistry between these two could override everything else.

Libra + Aquarius

LoveScope: 8.3

The Basic Relationship

Combine two fresh, breezy Air signs and you'll have a union marked by mutual understanding right off the bat. The theme for this relationship is simple: "Don't fence me in." These two have a natural inclination to discuss any problems to the point of clarity, but an outsider listening in would wonder what in the world they're always *talking* about. Libra is a Cardinal sign known for the ability to be charming and coolheaded. Aquarius is Fixed, known for the ability to be calm and detached. These two can discuss anything, as long as Libras sense that Water Bearers are being fair (an important word for Libras). Fairness is something Aquarians are known to mistrust. After all, they're in an *un*fair and unjust world, and no one gets on their soapbox about this more than Aquarians.

The Passion Zone

There's a great deal of ease here. Libras' bright smile instantly attracts Aquarians and can easily tame at least part of that wild Water Bearer mind. When connected physically, these two mental signs feel the magic of the body. Libras can put all worries and concerns aside, and Aquarians can watch their visions of world peace melt away into meaninglessness when they're in their Libras' arms.

When lovemaking is over, it's back to work as usual—only it's just a little quieter than it was a few minutes before. Sex is a release for Air signs, who store lots of things in their heads and don't recognize their own physical needs for long periods of time.

What Aquarius Needs to Know about Libra

Libras are represented by the only inanimate object of the Zodiac, the Scales. You, Aquarius, are a Water Bearer, implying that it's the *act* of bearing water—and not the person—that matters. If you two get into a situation where there's no trust between you (as is typical with Air signs), the results could find you *calculating* the relationship rather than *feeling* it, thus creating a cold day in "loveland." When hurt or angered, Libras may take action that they deem fair and just, but which might make you quite angry.

What Libra Needs to Know about Aquarius

Aquarians hate to feel misunderstood or betrayed, Libra, and it may take them months, or even *years,* to overcome a slight from another (remember their energy is Fixed). At worst, the relationship just ends—no words or contact, just done. That can frustrate your desire for connection—or at least for a fair resolution—but there will be no opportunity for renegotiation. So do what you can to foster understanding.

LoveScope

When there's understanding, anyone can get along—and there's the potential for lots of love between two Air signs. Each "gets" the other's need for space, change, and communication. Their temperaments are different (Cardinal and Fixed), so they may have to learn to work around those variances. It's not hard with Air, since they both have a natural tendency not to take things too personally and accept that disagreements are what make things interesting. Too much similarity and you have just a friend; too little and you have a stranger. When in harmony, these two can be trusting friends for life who are tantalizing enough to keep things passionate and who have the vision to avoid serious long-term conflicts. A smile from Libras and a brush of acceptance from Aquarians can make a hurtful situation turn completely around. After all, Air signs have great minds . . . and short memories.

Libra + Pisces

LoveScope: 6.1

The Basic Relationship

The combo platter that is Libra and Pisces is a strange mix. Much of this relationship's success will depend on the strengths that exist among other components within their natal charts. Pisceans change more than people of any other sign, often gathering their identities and feelings from whomever they've been hanging out with. Libras and Pisceans both see the good in everyone, but have different motivations.

Libras love social interaction, including picking someone's brain just so they can have a conversation. It's a social thing . . . and a mental thing. They can't *feel* what others are feeling, but they understand and can offer good advice. When the dialogue is finished, however, they're off to do their own thing, hardly affected by the encounter at all.

Pisceans, on the other hand, perceive *everything* about those around them—and don't require actually talking to people for that

to happen. For them, there's very little distinction between them and others, and they're oblivious to the fact that they're changing just by being in proximity to others' energies. It's a boundary problem: Fish have a hard time knowing where their own boundaries are . . . or anyone else's, for that matter. Unlike Libras, Pisceans will hold the energy of every encounter until they consciously release it—through meditation, a hot bath, or some other ritual.

If there are complications, Libras will find solutions to them rather quickly and with a distinctly refined style. Since the Pisces world is often nebulous, it's not an easy thing to just bust through, often leaving Libras frustrated—or at the very least, dumbfounded.

When these two first meet, there's real magic, like something out of an Arthurian legend. The watery Piscean world is desirable and holds a secret portal that anyone would have trouble *not* falling into. Libras see the delicate beauty in those gorgeous Pisces eyes (beauty is a Libra requirement), and know that this isn't going to be an ordinary relationship.

The Passion Zone

While those ruled by the Scales are logical about sex, there's little that logic can explain about their passion toward Pisceans. Both signs are easily seduced by the beauty of their partners, although Fish are more apt to allow Libras to fawn over them. These two create a lot of steam given the right conditions, although it's Pisceans who have to watch out for attachment. Libras have to be careful of being hot then cold, or intimate then superficial (those Scales can swing back and forth pretty quickly).

What Libra Needs to Know about Pisces

Pisces is a complex sign that might require some study, Libra. It ranges in expression from cruel and self-absorbed to completely giving and compassionate. Pisceans are not so unlike you—who shift on the grand Scales from one extreme to the other—and the difference is their motive. Fish don't have as strong a center; they merge with, and often lose themselves in, people or situations. They always seem to land on their feet, although they may have altered forms countless times—depending on who they've been with through the process.

Fish can sink into deep wells of depression, or drink their way into not feeling a thing . . . and this could last for months. They can scare your Venusian delicacies, so learn to lighten up if their socks don't match, and try to see it as endearing rather than irritating. Pisceans will never judge a book by its cover, no matter how much you implore them to try.

What Pisces Needs to Know about Libra

Libras are trying to find their inner balance and constantly looking at both sides of a situation to find the truth. It's difficult for them to understand both your depth and lack of boundaries, Pisces, which could make them turn aggressive and cold. They may appear to enjoy your shared nightly ritual of eating, listening to music, and watching a movie . . . but make no mistake—they *will* need to isolate themselves to find their center again. It wouldn't hurt for you to try doing the same thing on your own simultaneously—this Libra time-out can serve you as well.

LoveScope

When all the fantasies are allowed to die out and the pictures in their heads are ready to be reframed, these two are prepared for a real relationship.

Both Libras and Pisceans suffer from a certain kind of idealism. It doesn't really matter why; it just matters that they both accept that fact—at least a little. In order for them to get *real,* they must accept what makes them *un*real. If Pisceans would just concede that they're easily swayed by others' energies—that they'll likely become a victim or a martyr if they don't clear their energies regularly—*and* that they let people in too easily, then they have a chance of releasing those behaviors and accepting the risk of loving someone without all the distractions they so masterfully create. If Libras would admit that they have a fear of real commitment, an image in their heads of the perfect mate, and a need for time alone *while* throwing a party, then they could also start an honest relationship, with all the lessons available for them to learn.

Libras and Pisceans can make a relationship work, but the first step should be for Fish to establish boundaries and for Libras to lose some.

WHAT MAKES LIBRAS AWESOME?

- Their complete objectivity when it's needed
- Their ability to see the good in anyone
- Their eye for beauty
- Their sense of fairness
- Their gift of making you feel good about yourself
- Their refined ability to make a judgment call
- Their smile
- Their willingness to listen

Scorpio + Scorpio

LoveScope: 5.8

The Basic Relationship

Whenever two people of the same sign get together, there's an opportunity for immediate understanding. The superficial stuff isn't necessary because the "getting to know you" issues seem to be resolved before they even begin, especially with two piercingly intuitive Scorpios. Those born under the sign of the Scorpion are the investigators of the Zodiac, and they read below the surface masterfully—which is what makes them such good therapists.

When they first meet, there's instant recognition. They may nod heads and smirk with knowing, but there won't likely be any overt signals (these two are off the charts with subtle nuances). Once the gestures confirm that there's mutual interest here—and then it's verified by gut feelings—Scorpios will actually allow themselves to feel excited. And once there's excitement, there *will* be obsession . . . there *has* to be.

Obsession isn't a bad thing for Scorpions; in fact, it's needed. Fixations drive them to seek understanding about what this "thing" is that's now taken their bodies and minds captive so they can't make a move without thinking of it. It's a sign of power to Scorpios, and since both are now feeling it, they're likely to discover a direct portal to understanding—and therefore a quicker conclusion to their story.

Being understood is wonderful, but the inherent need to leave some mysteries intact is even more important for Scorpios. These two risk losing that individual unknowability when they come together. At the same time, Scorpios instantly understand how to offer safety to their partners, which is something that's hard for them to do themselves. It's pretty easy, though, with someone of the same sign.

The Passion Zone

As I've previously mentioned, Scorpio is synonymous with passion. Those born under this sign love the sexual "dark side," and can often take things to extremes. They rarely engage happily in anything that doesn't involve strong emotions and power, and will often look for ways to deepen the experience of their carnal connection. Since Scorpions feel safe in the presence of others who aren't afraid of their own intense desires, these two can take things as deep as they desire to go. But, as in all relationships, a polarity must exist, and it may happen that one partner is acting shy and the other is being aggressive. It's a state that can change, but it will likely define itself early in the relationship and remain that way for some time.

What Scorpio Needs to Know about Scorpio

The ugly part of you, Scorpio, isn't your lack of trust—which is usually formidable—but what you do as a result. Because you're inherently insecure, you can become suspicious, making you quite good at snooping. Most of you are masters at hiding your deepest thoughts and rarely leave a trail behind. For as deep as you go, it's surprising how few of you keep journals or diaries (and if you did, it wouldn't say much to incriminate you unless you were *hoping* for someone to read it).

The big thing for the two of you to remember is that each *thinks* things that aren't being communicated, and this can lead to a lot of assumptions—*wrong* ones. So if you want to know something, just ask. If your partner doesn't tell you the complete truth, you won't be held accountable for complications that may result.

LoveScope

Scorpios' best attribute is intense loyalty. When two hook up and make a commitment to the relationship, magic can happen. Few signs are as concerned about integrity, honesty, and truth as Scorpio is. Whenever there are people who are willing to look this deeply within themselves, there's a chance for growth without blame. The possibility of these two sticking it out and creating a strong bond is very likely, with certain cautions. Scorpios like each other, but they must be backed up by a good mix of other planets in their Zodiac charts to experience the intense passion they love.

This partnership will be there for the long haul, since Scorpios are Fixed and unafraid of their partners' more sinister qualities. This lack of fear *could* have a negative effect, too. Scorpios must face their dark side, and they find it through their interactions with others; the greater the differences, the greater the healing. The challenge for two Scorpios is having enough tension between them to satisfy this urge to grow. The answer will lie within each individual's personal desires.

HOW TO KEEP THE SCORPIO YOU LOVE

- Never, ever lie.

- Don't force them out of their brooding; just let them know you're there.

- Lighten up their negative thinking with a joke.

- Make them promise big things during sex, then don't hold them accountable.

- Know that what happens in private always stays there.

- Expect to be tested—it's a sign that they're getting attached.

- Appreciate it when they defend you to others.

- Be ready for anything in bed, and give them a few surprises of your own.

- Remember that there's no such thing as casual sex with them.

- Be direct; they can handle it.

Scorpio + Sagittarius

LoveScope: 4.5

The Basic Relationship

Sagittarius follows Scorpio on the grand Zodiac wheel, which means that these two signs are brought together for a learning experience. Scorpios have their heads down, focusing inward on the deepest, darkest caverns of their inner psyches. Sagittarians have their heads held high in the sky, looking for what's possible beyond the big horizon. They proselytize, flirt, love to talk, and forget everything. Scorpios analyze, shun the world, are critical, and remember each conversation and thought they have . . . and the list of differences goes on and on.

When these two come together as a couple, there's enough magic and mysticism to send Sagittarians into an excited frenzy and Scorpios into one of their moods of intense obsession. Scorpios like the light yet deep feelings they get from Sags, who enjoy the brooding intensity they see in Scorpios. They're both seeking what they fear the most:

Scorpions *hate* the thought of public exposure, and Archers are the most likely sign to blurt out Scorpios' secrets (bad choice, by the way). Also, Sagittarians despise receiving heavy-handed criticisms, which is exactly what the truth-telling Scorpio is known for. In spite of their glaring dissimilarites, these two usually find their initial connection quite exciting.

The Passion Zone

Sagittarians are flirts and see sex as a giant playground where everyone is naked and spinning on the merry-go-round, just waiting to be chosen. Meanwhile, Scorpios have such passion that there's very little that's of interest to them without a certain amount of sexual attraction . . . and they find it interesting when people appear to be free from the heavy burdens of life. They seek someone quite different from them, and the initial meeting with Sagittarians often fits the bill quite nicely. Archers are open to new sexual menus and certainly like to take things as far as they can. Then it's time to move along, leaving their Scorpions with a mixed bag of intrigue and mistrust.

What Scorpio Needs to Know about Sagittarius

Sagittarians carry deeper traumas than they initially portray. They have a wonderful and contagious optimism that inspires and encourages, but it lies on top of a depressed and often wounded person. Naturally, it's easy to root for the jovial side, Scorpio, but be prepared: Sagittarians take things to the extreme, and their melancholy could be overwhelming if you aren't prepared. When they're down, they *need* the encouragement of someone who believes in something bigger, and that's an area you need to work on as well. Remember that depression for Sagittarians is usually temporary and doesn't necessarily reveal a flaw in their character; it's more a reflection of the cyclical process of their growth. Be patient when you find them in this space, and avoid giving pat answers to questions about those feelings they're trying to understand.

What Sagittarius Needs to Know about Scorpio

Scorpios will remember everything bad that you've ever done to them, Sag. It's part of their personality to look for what hurts. Sometimes they don't let you know that you've harmed them until some random moment when you accidentally trip a switch that causes them to unleash a barrage of verbal attacks, bringing up every slight you were ever guilty of. They expect loyalty (you'll get your share from them and more) and don't tolerate feeling betrayed or embarrassed, even if you explain it as temporary insanity (or having one too many drinks).

Scorpios have a habit of assuming everyone functions from complete awareness, and even things you do *un*consciously tell them about you and your true nature. In fact, they're known to provoke anger just to hear your uncensored honesty.

Scorpios are jealous creatures, and you like to flirt. That's probably all that needs to be said about that . . . but do use common sense. It would also be wise for you to honor their deep confessions. It might make for good gossip, but you'd better be able to prove you can keep a secret.

LoveScope

The union of Scorpios and Sagittarians has a strong initial foundation. Intrigue, passion, and appreciation abound at the outset, but as these two deepen their connection, a willingness to stick with it is necessary, because much of what each requires won't be naturally obtained from the other.

Sagittarians are children of Zeus; thus they carry a rather large sense of entitlement. This doesn't completely define who they are, but it's the part of them that loves drawing attention from the outside world. This works in public, since Scorpios like to remain invisible; but it doesn't work very well in their private lives, where Scorpios want to experience a personal and shared depth . . . a place Sagittarians *don't* want to go. Archers need someone to get excited about life and help

them believe that they can soar, but to be cheerleaders or see the glass as half full is against Scorpions' natural tendencies. They call it being realistic, but their mates would call it just downright negative.

If they choose to make a go of it, these two have the potential to know great joy together. Sagittarians can find complete support from loyal Scorpios through thick and thin, and Scorpios will be supported with laughter and hope in every dark chasm they may happen to fall into.

Scorpio + Capricorn

LoveScope: 8.4

The Basic Relationship

Both Capricorns and Scorpios are the survivors of the Zodiac, which makes them an indestructible pair. Capricorns grew up early for one reason or another. Perhaps the family valued a particular work ethic, there were just too many children, or their parents were strict. Scorpios were raised with the feeling that something was wrong with them, or they were the only ones in the household who perceived emotional undertones—and were rejected for it. These two are by far the most serious of the Water and Earth signs.

Scorpions radiate an emotional passion that Goats find fascinating, while Capricorns exude security and a masterful understanding of the physical world—something Scorpios love but would rather not recognize as their partners' main trait. Scorpios are great at knowing what they like and don't like, but tend to focus only on displeasure, which creates an air of negativity. Ironically, like their mates, Capricorns tend

to expect the worst, mostly to avoid disappointment. Since neither are risk takers, they appreciate each other's caution. Sometimes these two can appear to be the most pessimistic couple, yet the complete safety and power that exists between them is palpable.

The Passion Zone

Capricorns are passionate, which is one of the Zodiac's greatest secrets. They understand how to move the earth and rock their partners' worlds. Make no mistake about it, this couple can have some serious between-the-sheets action, although they're not opposed to the floor or any other venue within a five-mile radius when they're in the mood. Perhaps it's more accurate to say *if* they're in the mood, because Scorpions take a while to develop trust. Goats, meanwhile, will need some time to figure out if there's a purpose to the union.

What Scorpio Needs to Know about Capricorn

Capricorns expect very little from their partners, Scorpio, and as a result, they're willing to do most of the work, which gives them a form of control. They don't expose much of themselves and have little regard for anything that seems to be without purpose—and emotions may fall into that category. In battle, there will be little communication except through innuendo and the cold shoulder. To keep the peace, Goats will set aside their negative judgments to avoid criticizing you, but if you push them to anger, it *will* get scary. They can look right through you as if you're not even there—like you've never even met.

What Capricorn Needs to Know about Scorpio

Scorpios don't like to feel out of control and will dig in their heels in an attempt to gain some of it back. They'll test you with a series of personal questions that may seem harmless at first, but your answers won't be forgotten, Capricorn. Their agenda is to look as deeply into their partners as possible so there won't be any surprises. If they feel that you're pushing or trying to control them, they'll rebel. Scorpions have a stinger that's plenty willing to strike you more than once. This piercing blow usually takes the form of scathing verbal attacks and will feel like a volcano has just erupted. Don't push your Scorpio too hard; rather, consider the words *gently coax*.

LoveScope

These two are deep; there's no doubt about it. Capricorns are more matter-of-fact, and Scorpios are pretty black and white. Between them, there's the possibility of complete respect, but they'll have to prove themselves to each other . . . more than once. Both have tests for their partners and are insanely jealous, but ultimately extreme in their loyalty. Once the initial proving grounds are covered, these two can enjoy complete care and safety with each other—in what has otherwise felt like an unsafe world all of their lives.

Scorpios aren't the most tender of the Water signs, but do offer more dedicated support—provided that their partners take responsibility for their own well-being. Capricorns must learn to realize and accept that part of companionship is sharing, and they need to let others help or at least be involved in what they're building. When healthy and aligned, these two can find growth that couldn't easily be taught. What started as a hard, unsafe world turns into a place where they can share and play. That's a big deal, especially since both were born to be so serious.

HOW TO LOSE THE SCORPIO YOU LOVE

- Tell them that you're considering the virtues of abstinence.

- Quickly hang up the phone when they enter the room.

- Tell them a story . . . then tell it again in an hour with different details.

- Look them in the eyes and sincerely say, "I know all about it."

- Mention that you hate the color black.

- Hide the handcuffs.

- Leave a letter from an ex around for them to see.

- When you're done using the computer, clear your browser history, even if you weren't on the Internet.

Scorpio + Aquarius

LoveScope: 3.5

The Basic Relationship

Adjustments must be made anytime two Fixed signs link up. Scorpios live in the underworld, reading into the deeper meaning of every nuance in others. They use their keen observational abilities to track what people are doing and why, which is what makes them great therapists. But it could also be their most annoying feature to someone who doesn't want to be watched so closely. Aquarians live in their minds; they formulate a picture or ideal and then live by that vision. Water Bearers love groups for what they represent and are annoyed by individuals. When these two signs get together, there's the perfect amount of tension to stir their pot of passion, although differences must be approached carefully to avoid conflict. The structure of this particular relationship is unique.

Air and Water approach life very differently. It would never even occur to Aquarians (Air) that their perspective is anything but correct.

They may have formulated this idea from personal experience or an ingrained belief system, but if they believe something, they're willing to defend it to the end. Scorpios (Water) see their view as the correct one as well. They conceive ideas from their feelings, and logic doesn't even enter into the picture. Both signs *know* that their positions are right, and this creates an immediate hurdle.

The Passion Zone

Water and Air signs have a natural fascination with each other, which adds vigor to private moments. Scorpios can become drunk with sexual desire and see their airy god or goddess as a prize that must be won.

The only way Aquarians will be wooed by their admirers is mentally. Since their minds hold preconceptions about what they want, that may be easier said than done. The shortest route to the Aquarian libido is through admiration of them—they *love* that idea. If these two do find their way to the bedroom, they'll have a good time together, if the mood isn't ruined by high expectations.

What Aquarius Needs to Know about Scorpio

Scorpios don't interpret the world the same way you do, and it's their right not to. You have a way about you, Aquarius, which reeks of righteous arrogance, and you're willing to defend your thoughts and ideas at all costs. Scorpions trust a deep instinct—one that doesn't easily translate into a mental construct. You may want to just take their word for something they're experiencing, and you should try hard not to condescend. There are many ways to interpret the world, and all of them are correct.

What Scorpio Needs to Know about Aquarius

Scorpio, Aquarians fear attachment . . . period. They march to the beat of a different drummer and would prefer to remain an ideal in someone's mind rather than being made into a tangible partner. They love the idea of their relationships being "different"—in looks, communication styles, and so forth. This separation feeds that part of them that needs to live outside the rules. If you're too needy with them, it destroys their image of what you two are as a couple. You can make a difference with your Water Bearer by letting them rebel until it bores them. They'll come back to the nest that you've built together.

LoveScope

Given the right help from a compatible moon or Venus, these two could be loyal and respectful allies for life. Scorpios value authenticity even if their mates' version of it seems cold and detached. As long as Scorpions can trust and rely on Water Bearers' intentions, there can be a long-term alliance. People born under both of these signs have great business savvy and can use it to their advantage. Scorpions know how to read the pulse of markets, and Aquarians know what the world needs—although they're usually way ahead of their time.

If these two signs manage to make it in a relationship, whether of business or romance, it's a sure bet that both of them are strong and independent enough to keep things fresh—but they must avoid the pitfalls of their signs. Aquarians should notice how their partners judge anything that comes from an emotional or feeling place. Water Bearers like logic, but it prevents them from discovering an entire side of life that should be *felt*. On the other hand, Scorpios must learn how to judge the *mental* side of life. They see it as detached, robotic, and without warmth; but they need to realize that it can support them—especially when objectivity is necessary. These two have something to give each other, but they'll first need to recognize their own weaknesses in certain areas, which may be the biggest challenge of all.

Scorpio + Pisces

LoveScope: 9.1

The Basic Relationship

A relationship made up of two Water signs makes jumping into the deep end easy. Pisceans and Scorpios cause the phrase "getting to know each other" to be obsolete. The great thing about two people of this motive coming together is their ability to nurture, feel, and understand. The challenge with them, on the other hand, is that they can stagnate and become overindulgent while remaining under-stimulated.

Scorpios and Pisceans have a particularly strong psychic connection. Neither will need to utter a word to have a complete conversation. An entire world exists between them that—from an outsider's perspective—is quite remarkable. If they're attracted to each other from the start, that alliance will grow even stronger. They'll send telepathic signals as efficiently as e-mails.

What Scorpios like best about Pisceans is how unfazed the Fish are by them. Scorpios *expect* a negative response to their intensity, and it's refreshing that their Pisces friends handle it with unfamiliar ease.

Pisces is Mutable, so those of this sign have a chance of hiding their feelings from Scorpio investigators—but the truth is, nothing between these two is really *hidden.* When they meet, there will be an immediate knowing that comes over them. Even if this recognition isn't positive, at least they grasp right away whether they should opt to continue.

The Passion Zone

Scorpios and Aquarians experience such a heartfelt connection that "merging" begins almost instantly when these two agree to get intimate. Scorpions think they have their Fish "in the bag" from the start, but the truth is that Pisceans never really let *anyone* own them completely. They have a profound ability to merge, create magic, and then re-create it somewhere else—but the difference between Pisces and other Mutable signs (Gemini, Sagittarius, and Virgo) is that they know how to *re*connect as if they never left.

Scorpios love feeling that their partners can be seriously intense in the bedroom, enacting any fantasy they have with ease. The danger for these two is not being able to leave the bedroom energy *in* the bedroom. Unlike other signs that can make love and get on with their day, this couple tends to let feelings linger for hours afterward. There's nothing wrong with that, but it's the initial indicator of the depth of these two's merging.

What Scorpio Needs to Know about Pisces

Pisceans have a mean streak that can be even more insane than the one that rages in *you,* Scorpio. They're Water, so it's hard to know exactly what sets them off, but here are a few hints: *don't* talk about their mothers, accuse them of making a terrible mistake (even if they

did), or tell them that they drink too much (which they might). Fish tend to use mind-altering substances more than other signs do, probably because they can handle it—after all, they live with one foot in another world. They see *this* plane of existence as a dream that reflects back to them what they're feeling. Don't be surprised if you hear them say, "I made it rain," because they just might have (in their minds).

What Pisces Needs to Know about Scorpio

Scorpios have a few obsessions that no one can talk them out of. The nature of these infatuations will greatly depend on various factors, but can include jealousy, drugs, sex, and rage. Pisces, Scorpios are extremely self-critical, which makes them even more sensitive to censure from others—something you're good at directing at them (after all, you are the sign opposite Virgo on the Zodiac wheel). Your remarks are often facts based on observations and can be quite stinging. Be sure to mind your words and, rather than criticize, offer helpful suggestions—it could save you from a confrontation later.

LoveScope

The higher side of Water is its ability to support without conditions. These two have an incredible ability to assist each other in whatever needs arise. When conscious, Pisceans are remarkable healers, with compassion that wells from deep within. Scorpios need to be reminded to be more understanding of themselves, and their Fish companions communicate this kind of love beautifully.

Scorpions are fearless therapists and can act as the perfect guides for their Pisces mates when they lose their way. Water is a world of imagination and fantasies, and rarely have two signs been more able to meet their dreams with such conviction. Once they've set their course, these two will move like a raging river, and nothing can stop their path. Scorpios and Pisceans can create magic and bring extraordinary visions to life—all they have to do is desire them.

WHAT MAKES SCORPIOS AWESOME?

- Their undying loyalty and ability to keep secrets
- Their depth of understanding about most emotional issues
- How they see below the surface of situations
- The quick and often accurate assessments they make
- Their strength in facing fears
- Their incredible memory
- Their passion
- Their hypnotic gaze
- Their tenacity

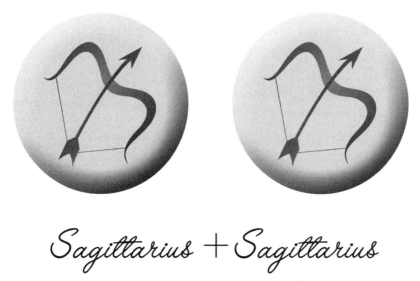

Sagittarius + Sagittarius

LoveScope: 4.6

The Basic Relationship

There's an ease when two sun signs get together. On the one hand, it makes relating easier; on the other, it's harder for partners who have so much in common to get things past each other. Getting away with something is almost second nature to Sagittarians. After all, they're ruled by Jupiter, and being children of the largest planet in the solar system gains them some privileges—which they take full advantage of on a daily basis.

Sagittarians can be compared to marinara sauce: zesty, robust, better tasting the next day, mild (or too strong), and suitable for formal or casual occasions. What's likable about Sags is their vivacious optimism; what's *not* is their big mouths. When they're involved with another Archer, it can be a big party or a visit with the walking wounded where they try to one-up each other with their scar count.

Overall, these two have a great initial spark and can maintain it simply by virtue of their mutual need to be free. They do require some amount of pressure or resistance to push against, which is why many of them see their mates as holding them back. It's possible that when they get together, one of them will act out "the player" and the other will take the part of "the played."

The Passion Zone

Sagittarians are fiery and fast. They're passionate, but to them sex must be a spiritual experience that leaves them in awe. These two can indeed give that to each other, but if both are seeking inspiration while simultaneously being expected to give it, the encounter can be flat. Neither may ultimately feel satisfied, forcing them to soon move on in search of their next awe-inspiring relationships.

What Sagittarius Needs to Know about Sagittarius

Sag, you have a dualistic nature: one side of you is free and gypsy-like, and the other is burdened and wounded. Each part will need its time to express itself. Now imagine what happens if both of you are acting out your hurt selves—the competition to be the *most* wounded will soon ensue. You will become too blind to each other's needs because you're both too busy insisting that your own aren't being met. So try to notice if there's a competition emerging between you, and opt out of it if there is. *Now.* It's better for you to let Fire run its course than to fan its flames.

The Sagittarian archetype demands that you must have some area in your life where you're misunderstood. Sometimes it will be your job and others times your friendships, but it *will* be something that you can push against to prove to yourself that you can do anything. One of you will likely play that role for the other, but avoid a scenario where *both* are in it. That trap would be just too hard to climb out of in the short or long term.

Last, you're known to have egos the size of Jupiter, so it's important to quit trying to outdo each other. There will be plenty of opportunities

to validate yourselves in healthy ways—perhaps through a job or making something for the house—but keep the volume turned down on competition.

LoveScope

At best, these two share the magic of Jupiter, which brings them an existence that's often lush and filled with wonder. The not-so-pleasant parts of their journey can contribute to that delight as well—it's all part of living a life of extremes. The thing about two Sagittarians being together is that when they choose to be fully present and take responsibility for their own happiness, it becomes truly contagious.

Sagittarians' homes may have hundreds of books piled in a seemingly chaotic arrangement throughout the hallways. There might be a boat in the yard, travel maps scattered about, or sporting goods in the garage; or it could look like the inside of a great big school yard—and there may even be a podium sitting in the living room. Think *big*. Everything around their place is grandiose, including the house itself. There's an instant appreciation for the quest that burns inside both of them, as well as for the difficulty in being able to fully embrace that adventure.

For all the fun these two do have, there's a huge risk of boredom in this connection, which is really only about seeking to satisfy that eternal mission outside themselves. They'll just continue to pursue it and never find it until the search turns within . . . then the magic will really happen.

HOW TO KEEP THE SAGITTARIUS YOU LOVE

- Role-play as if it's for real.

- Believe them when they tell you about their godly past lives.

- Do something for them every once in a while because they "shouldn't have to."

- Look interested on the days they need to show you what they know.

- Buy them airline tickets.

- Tell them that you know they're overqualified.

- Be the designated driver once a week.

- Support them in boycotting reality TV shows.

- Remind them of their magic, and encourage them to use it to make a better life.

- Let them in on a secret so they can make others promise not to tell.

Sagittarius + Capricorn

LoveScope: 5.1

The Basic Relationship

Astrological folklore says that adjacent signs have something to teach each other. What could Capricorns have to teach Sagittarians? After all, Archers are light, playful, immature, flirtatious, hard to pin down, full of tall tales, excessive, and proselytizing. Stoic Capricorns will never waste words, are extremely mature and serious, believe in hard work, and sometimes require arm-twisting to get them to tell a complete story.

It's not that Sagittarians don't know how to be mature, but there's certainly a contrast when they're up against the earthy Goats. Folklore aside, Capricorns often *do* need to lighten up, and Sags can be the perfect prescription, provided that they can hide some of their infamous need for extremes—at least until after the first date.

There are many issues that they'll disagree about, and money will be a big one since Capricorns are realistic to a degree that Sagittarians aren't. (It also doesn't help that Sags have WHO CARES? stamped across their wallets.)

The Passion Zone

As I've said previously, Capricorns are passionate and understand how to move the earth and rock worlds. They're Cardinal Earth, so they'll take a while to figure out if there's a purpose to their relationships. Sags, being Fire, are also extremely emotional, but as with all signs of this element, the problem is in *sustaining* that passion for any length of time. Capricorns know how to bring things to a slow simmer, then a boil, and then a simmer again. It's intense, seductive, and powerful, prompting the question, "Will their passions overcome their differences?"

What Sagittarius Needs to Know about Capricorn

Capricorns, guided by Saturn, have a different inner drummer than you do, Sag. They believe that hard work and dedication are the paths to freedom (admit it, you don't like to wait for *anything*). You must realize that actions speak louder than words for Goats, who have little tolerance for lengthy explanations of why things didn't get done. Capricorns, at their worst, can be cold—not the icy cold of Aquarians, but a grounded, in-your-face cold—with a stone-faced expression of utter dismissal. The big issue here is one of respect. Your Capricorn will do anything for you, but they'll need to feel that it was not in vain and that their support is appreciated.

What Capricorn Needs to Know about Sagittarius

At first, it's easy for you to delight in Sagittarians' playfulness, Cap. In fact, it's important for you to see that it's possible to have fun *and* still have a productive life. But Archers tend toward excess,

and because the nature of Fire is often self-centered, they may not realize that their over-the-top way of living could be harmful to both of you. They can be critical and dismissive of lifestyles different from their own and will just want to leave if they feel pinned down. Try to see if you can make sense of their frustrations. Once you understand the fire within them, you can help show them how to use it to their advantage.

LoveScope

We can learn from every single person who enters our lives. Sagittarians and Capricorns both understand this concept, but need a little encouragement to really absorb it as truth. Sags are meant to travel and express their philosophies, but when they meet Capricorns, they feel the underlying pressure to do more than just *talk* about something . . . they have to *walk* their talk if they're going to get any respect from Goats.

Conversely, Capricorns must see how an all-work-and-no-play attitude can squelch the spirit of the very child they're trying to nurture within themselves. These two are wholly different, with contrasting goals, and could prosper greatly from the lessons each has to offer. When healthy, they can take each other to remarkable places. Just in being who they are, they point the finger toward happiness for their partners. This relationship is worth the big effort, but whether they're up to the challenge will determine their ultimate success as a couple.

Sagittarius + Aquarius

LoveScope: 9.4

The Basic Relationship

Chemistry 101 taught us that there's an increased reaction whenever Fire and Air combine—one feeds the other. Sagittarius is a Fire sign, and those born under it are hard to contain and unpredictable. Aquarius is an Air sign, and Water Bearers are strong-minded and focused. When the two come into contact, it's like a spark in a room full of concentrated oxygen!

Their differences are easy to spot: Sagittarians are chatty and cheerful around others, always on the move, and perpetual learners. Aquarians are quiet and may not even notice people when they walk in a room, have no problem staying put in familiar surroundings, and seem to think they already know all there is to know. When these two signs are together, the similarities will become apparent, too: both love their freedom, have strong convictions, and abhor the rules of others.

Sagittarians fuel the twinkle in Aquarians' eyes and remind them that there's a real world outside the Water Bearer mind where actual,

sentient creatures dwell. Aquarians inspire Archers to reach for the stars in order to make a real difference on the planet. Both bring a natural empathy to the relationship and have a quirky mutual tolerance. Sags' Mutable Fire means that they're often seeking new adventures. Aquarians' Fixed Air prefers to watch the world from their fence post. They delight in each other's wit, and it's actually a requirement that their partners have good minds.

The Passion Zone

We've already had our chemistry review and know that combining Fire and Air results in more heat. The temperature can get pretty high when these two get together. Sagittarians have mastered the art of flirting and instinctively know that in order to connect intimately with Aquarians, they have to connect with their minds.

Most of the couple's foreplay will embody a spiritual ideal. Aquarians will lament the plight of the world, and Sagittarians will offer Jupiter-sized hopes for healing it. Before they know it, they've looked into each other's eyes and, well, combustion quickly follows. Water Bearers love the spirituality that comes naturally with Archers, and Sags adore the appreciation that Aquarians dole out . . . even if it's rare.

What Sagittarius Needs to Know about Aquarius

To say that Aquarians live in their heads is an understatement, and it will serve you to understand this, Sag. Water Bearers spend their lives thinking, reviewing, thinking some more, and questioning everything they do. They identify very closely with their own ideals—they *are* what they think. So if you ridicule their vision, you're essentially mocking *them*. Aquarians' focus is on humanitarian causes as a way to allow all that brain activity to serve a broader purpose. Their world is a mental one, and it's real to them. Remember this: don't tell them to "snap out of it." You'll avoid pushing them farther away.

Aquarians sense that they're ahead of their time, and consequently feel ostracized. You can be their haven from that cold reality by understanding their world from the inside out. They aren't jealous, per se, but they do hold clear ideals about love and fidelity. Your propensity to flirt may challenge these standards.

What Aquarius Needs to Know about Sagittarius

Sagittarians' children-of-God spirit feels trapped in a mortal body, and it's hard for them to remain inspired when this mundane world demands mundane tasks. Aquarius, you can help your Sag counter this "ordinary" hell by reminding them that *you* see their magic—and, if possible, find a way to fit it into your system.

Although your Sagittarius may love to flirt, it's not serious and certainly not a threat to your relationship. They need to feel the winds of freedom beneath them . . . not because they'll fly away, but just so they know that they *can.* Don't reveal any secrets to them unless it's okay that they tell their 3, or 40, best friends.

LoveScope

These two stand a remarkable chance of making things work. Sagittarians have a dream of inspiring the world, and Aquarians live to heal it. When they're on the same team, it's hard to imagine how much they can accomplish. Archers know how to tease Aquarians in a way that amuses them—and anyone who can bring the slightest frivolities out in Aquarians is well on their way to a long-term connection with them.

Each sign cherishes freedom and knows how to bestow it upon the other. Aquarians must learn to trust their Sagittarians, who must be willing to be more sensitive and attentive to their Aquarians . . . then long-term harmony can be found.

HOW TO LOSE THE SAGITTARIUS YOU LOVE

- Tell them there's no such thing as magic.

- Ask them to take out the trash.

- Act like you're falling asleep when they start to tell you about their spiritual experience.

- Tell them you're taking them on a trip, then decide you'd rather watch a Travel Channel marathon with them instead.

- Swear them to secrecy.

- Tell them you're an atheist.

Sagittarius + Pisces

LoveScope: 4.8

The Basic Relationship

Both Pisceans and Sagittarians are Mutable, which means that this is one of those relationships where each partner has two sides to them—so there are really four personalities involved. They both have aspects that express hope and despair, depending on their states of mind. This combination can be elating or depressing, so their success will depend on how they support each other—and themselves—through the inevitable ups and downs.

At first glance, Sagittarians are drawn in by those Piscean eyes, which are like watery, uncharted worlds they can explore. Pisceans get hooked by Sags' carefree optimism, along with their ability to talk to anyone about anything. Fire and Water don't usually sound like a good mix, yet there's an intrigue here that nudges them together. Both are dreamers; they just have different ways of pursuing their goals.

Fish get easily pulled off course when they see into the hearts of those around them, and they can't allow themselves to win exclusively at the cost of others. It's not that Archers would *deliberately* run over anyone in their path, but the chances of it happening are higher because their eyes are on their goal, not on what's right in front of them.

The Passion Zone

Pisceans merge and become one with their partners, enjoying variety in expressing their sexuality. Rarely are they put off during intimacy, unless their mates are too fiery or fast . . . and Sagittarians are both fiery *and* fast. Passion for these two must be an adventure. Fish don't bat an eye as Archers inform them of their status as children of Zeus and that they should be treated as such. Pisceans, at least when intimate, happily comply, and Sags will love it.

What Sagittarius Needs to Know about Pisces

Although they have the reputation of being kind and receptive, Fish do have a side that can bite (think about piranhas). This characteristic emerges when their support of *you*, Sag, isn't balanced by your support of *them*. Pisceans will tolerate your insensitive, almost narcissistic nature for a while, but at some point they'll rebel and leave you hanging without anyone to reflect back just how great a person you are.

So be kind to your Fish, and let them know how deeply you appreciate them when they give you what you need to feel even better about yourself. Being a Water sign makes Pisceans more prone to retreat into drugs or other forms of escapism. You're drawn to do the same, so when you see this addictive behavior beginning to unfold, remember that it's very important to stay strong.

What Pisces Needs to Know about Sagittarius

Sagittarians tend to blame others as a defense against their fears of not being good enough. It's important for you to know this because you're prone to *accepting* the blame of others, Pisces. It's easy for you to offer your sympathetic heart to someone in pain, but be careful that you aren't the only one putting supportive energies out there in the relationship. Make sure there's a reciprocal reaction coming from your Sagittarius. They'd love it if you spent the rest of your life holding an emotional space for them, but be sure that you get what *you* need, and that they don't drain your energy.

LoveScope

At best, these two will share the love of their spiritual quests. Pisceans live with one foot in the metaphysical realm, which is much more encompassing than any single religion. They're open to many aspects of faith that others can't see. Sagittarians exist in the domain of the abstract and theoretical: seeking, sharing, and exploring the truth. When these two can remember that their spiritual goals are the most important, they can support each other and let go of those day-to-day problems that are the reality of any relationship.

Mutable signs can be childlike, constantly waging an inner battle between the parts of them that are the responsible grown-ups and the playful inner children. Pisceans offer Sagittarians a desperately desired refuge from their difficult journeys, and Sags can be the navigators for their Pisces—both will be able to find safe passage through rough waters with the help of their mates. The highest expressions of Archers and Fish can combine in this relationship to overcome any of their lesser traits, keeping things fresh and manageable.

WHAT MAKES SAGITTARIANS AWESOME?

- Their jovial demeanor and contagious enthusiasm
- Their eclectic and vast knowledge
- Their fantastic teaching abilities
- Their knack for knowing how to celebrate
- Their boldness in learning new things
- Their interest in diverse cultures
- Their lush imagination and the magical ways they explore it
- Their willingness to delve into philosophies different from their own
- Their ability to inspire others

Capricorn + Capricorn

LoveScope: 6.9

The Basic Relationship

What's interesting and unique about Capricorns is that they grow up very early so they can deal with family issues. They may have had to learn how to handle a controlling mom or a demanding dad, stand in as a parent for their siblings, or fend for themselves. Whatever the scenario, Goats are built to survive despite any adverse conditions.

When two Caps meet, they know that they can completely rely on each other because, if nothing else, they're just plain trustworthy. Mottoes like "A person's word is their honor" or "A handshake is as good as a contract" are ingrained in them.

Capricorns want nothing for free and respect those same values in everyone around them. When two of them partner up, there's an automatic authority. The only problem is figuring out *who* takes the lead.

The Passion Zone

Capricorns are bubbling over with passion, although few recognize that at first. They also really know how to drive their partners crazy between the sheets. Purpose is crucial to every aspect of their lives, so if a couple is at the intimacy stage, it's likely they've decided to build a relationship or family—or opted to have joint mutual funds and checking accounts. If they don't intend to get seriously involved, they'll most likely have "fun" set as the relationship's purpose . . . along with romantic rendezvous scheduled in their daily planners.

What Capricorn Needs to Know about Capricorn

When you aren't particularly conscious, you desire control and are cold and calculating in your motivations. When two of you are involved in a relationship, a breakdown in communication can look like a stone wall, and you'll both probably hold out for long periods before it begins to erode. Yours is a possessive sign, and since you believe in hard work and discipline, competition that exceeds the boundaries of imagination could creep into the relationship. At worst you two can be ruthless and easily cut off any sign of emotional attachment . . . with anyone.

Capricorns have no problem with frugality, and you can get miserly when there's an undercurrent of fear running through you. You like power, but must earn it. If you become blinded by your own need for control, ruthless ambition can easily replace love. At that point it's best if those close to you step out of the way until you're back in an emotional space that's safe enough to feel again. Just remember that you're used to being alone and are here to learn cooperation, playfulness, and trust.

LoveScope

When they're healthy, Capricorns can create anything they want. Their relationship likely started off based on respect, which is a component of love that's often underestimated. Both need to learn to play more and safely express their emotional sides.

Goats are *doers,* and beyond anything else, they can provide support for their partners that's way beyond their wildest expectations. Together they can encourage each other in trusting in their abilities to manifest whatever they might need, regardless of circumstances. The biggest lesson they can both learn, and *teach,* is that they're lovable regardless of what they do. "Doing" is Capricorns' way of feeling self-worth because they survived by doing *everything;* in the past, it was essential to their survival. It's hard for them to let go of their identification with action because it's what they think has kept them alive to this point. It might just take another Goat to grab them by the hand and drag them to the park to enjoy the view.

When this couple puts their heads together, there's little they can't accomplish. Capricorns can endure just about anything, and this relationship is no exception—but it can be about a lot more than endurance.

HOW TO KEEP THE CAPRICORN YOU LOVE

- Buy them vintage clothing.
- Pay for everything with the cash you saved from your second job.
- Collect coupons.
- Take an interest in used cars.
- Create traditions with them.
- Create a need that only they can fulfill.
- Make a list of goals you can check off.
- Have fun *only* after a particular list has been checked off.
- Remember that a day of rest means you can finish the things you didn't get to yesterday.
- Don't complain about working too hard and expect to get sympathy.

Capricorn + Aquarius

LoveScope: 5.6

The Basic Relationship

Life can be interesting when a rebel and a traditionalist get together to form a partnership of any kind. Just by their very natures, there's an inherent push-pull between these two signs. Aquarians shun all externally imposed systems and tend to always move toward the unusual instead of the ordinary; Capricorns embrace structure and those tried-and-true things in life they can count on. There's potential chemistry here for many reasons. Goats are often attracted to the rule-breaking Water Bearers and can find them to be a refreshing change from the day-to-day grind. Aquarians are secretly stimulated by anyone who can masterfully manipulate the material world, something Caps are known for. Participating in cultural traditions is typically repugnant to Water Bearers, but they *love* the freedom it can create.

It would be cruel to wait until the end of the chapter just to mention that these two have a very tough road ahead. It's certainly not impossible, although it all depends on how ready these two are to have their lives stretched open to new possibilities!

The Passion Zone

Capricorns are often underestimated in the arena of sexual passion—a quality they actually posses in droves because Earth signs are so sensual. They often see Aquarians as attractive because of their ethereal looks and avant-garde approach to the world.

There are conditions that both signs must have met before intimacy can proceed. Goats will need a purpose to the relationship. Sex is an obvious one, but they'll ask what the meaning of it is with *this* person. Aquarians will need the union to fit into their ideal picture. They require certain formulas to be adhered to that can't be altered. Both signs could have a lot of fun here if these conditions are satisfied, but much will depend on the positions of the moon and Venus in their charts.

What Capricorn Needs to Know about Aquarius

Aquarius may actually grow tired of your routines, Cap. Not because *you* are routine, but rather because their sign is that of the inventor. If a stimulating idea isn't crossing their minds every other day, that won't be enough. Unhappy Aquarians can put the chill on you like the North Pole. It's also likely that, when disillusioned, they'll withdraw into their mental world and remove all cords of connection to you.

Even though they're a Fixed sign, Aquarians don't like to wait for anything. Their minds are in constant motion, and when they strike gold with an idea, they don't want to take your methodical route—they want to turn the world upside down. It's best to step aside and see if they ask for help; otherwise, you'll likely just be in the way.

What Aquarius Needs to Know about Capricorn

Capricorns won't tolerate betrayal or humiliation. Their form of anger can be as calculating and mean as yours, Aquarius. They rule the earthly realm, and one of their strongest expressions of anger will be to take back the possessions that they once shared with you. Saturn governs Capricorns, and therefore Goats won't be moved by manipulation or control; if you cross the line, the results could be explosive.

If you maintain a respectful connection to your Capricorn, they'll do anything you ask—but they won't tolerate your dismissal of the traits that are a part of them. You need to appreciate that they won't be taking any shortcuts and will move at their own pace.

LoveScope

When these two signs are in harmony, they can create magic together. Imagine the heights of creativity Aquarians could scale if they felt safe and supported by their responsible Capricorns. Water Bearers' inventions would likely serve in a way that makes life easier for humanity, which would feed their capacity to support humankind and Capricorns' need for a purpose.

This relationship isn't an easy one because these two come from such different worlds, but if they *do* choose to be connected and are willing to embrace the learning that's bound to happen, they could have a grand time bringing about change in the world.

HOW TO LOSE THE CAPRICORN YOU LOVE

- Extol the virtues of unemployment.
- Explain how you plan on lavishly spending your inheritance.
- Tell them they're acting childish.
- Use a computer program to do your taxes.
- Ask them to pull over and give money to the homeless veteran.
- Break tradition and go gambling for the holidays.
- Borrow money from them.

Capricorn + Pisces

LoveScope: 8.2

The Basic Relationship

Fish and Goats may seem to come from two entirely different worlds and have nothing in common, but their similarities might actually surprise you. Capricorns must have a purpose in their lives—something that allows them to set a goal and achieve it. They work hard and expect little for free. Pisceans have no problem with work, but do have a difficult time setting purposeful objectives. This is mostly due to the fact that their intentions change depending on who they're around or what emotions are enveloping them.

Pisceans appear to need some looking after, although they do astonishingly well on their own. They can't help but have a bleeding heart for the downtrodden and unlovable and are touched by things that would leave most Capricorns—and most everyone else—unmoved.

It's the nature of Mutable Water to take the shape of whatever contains it. Fish are mergers, and they mold with the people who are in close proximity to them (including a person sitting next to them on the subway). Although it's not typical of Capricorns' style, some find the heart-centered openness of Pisceans charming and in need of true support—and they'll offer it in ways that only Saturn-ruled people can. But a word of caution has to be issued here because Capricorns get used to having control, and their nature is to take a mile for every inch they're given.

The Passion Zone

Capricorns have lots of hidden passion, but it may take a while for them to figure out if they want to take this relationship to its next, more intimate step. Pisceans are a little quirky sexually. They're not necessarily kinky, but that's definitely not ruled out; it all depends on who they're with. They have a sense of safety when in the hands of the kings and queens of the Earth element, a kind of inner peace that allows them to relax on a deep level.

Caps love the softness of Mutable Fish and find their vulnerability irresistible as long as it's genuine and not manipulative. The sexual world between these two is indeed different and might require a passport. Just remember that Pisceans are creative and Capricorns are fearless, and that makes a super combination behind closed doors.

What Pisces Needs to Know about Capricorn

Capricorns can be ruthless. The inevitable turn in the relationship will come when they're fed up with you playing the victimized, fragile Fish, Pisces. This is, of course, only if you've indulged yourself in the infamous Piscean martyr drama zone. Goats hate victims; after all, they had to pull themselves up by the bootstraps to survive early in life—if they can do it, anybody can. Also, if they start to enjoy you too much, they may begin to close down for a bit. Capricorns don't like feeling vulnerable. There's nothing you can do here except to remain steady and strong . . . they'll return.

What Capricorn Needs to Know about Pisces

Pisceans can be much tougher than they appear. They may actually find themselves in the middle of deep emotional distress, which they picked up from someone at work—or even from you, Cap—without realizing it. One of the best ways for them to reclaim their own energy is through anger. Getting upset is an antidote that's common for Fish because it snaps them out of their Neptunian dreamworld and into a more sober place. Speaking of sobriety, or lack thereof, it wouldn't be unusual for Pisceans to be comfortable with the overuse of drugs or alcohol, but those aren't the only ways for them to "medicate." Try to see where your Pisces is experiencing addiction—it could be television, music, or almost anything. You might be able to correlate stress levels with an increase in vices.

LoveScope

Capricorns can build anything, including a psychological boat that will gladly carry their Pisces through turbulent waters. With understanding, Caps gladly take Pisceans under their wings and offer the protection and security necessary for Fish to prosper. Pisceans know how to dissolve those harsh Capricorn walls with some spiritual discussion or even a home-cooked meal (although Pisceans' forte isn't usually in the kitchen).

There's chemistry here, especially if Fish remember that Capricorns started old and are learning how to be young, and Goats keep in mind that Pisceans are old souls who also have a true innocence inherent to their nature. In essence, they each have what the other is looking for just by being who they are. When it's working, this relationship is creative, inventive, and magical. There's a real capacity to build a unique and long-lasting union here without major effort.

WHAT MAKES CAPRICORNS AWESOME?

- They can survive anywhere.
- They're responsible at a very early age, and this continues throughout life.
- They respect systems and the order of things.
- They're amazing providers.
- They can organize individuals into a group.
- They know where they're going and what it takes to get there.
- They learn from history.
- They don't need anyone except themselves, but can include others in their lives.

Aquarius + Aquarius

LoveScope: 5.2

The Basic Relationship

Aquarians *are* peculiar, and they know it. They pride themselves on individuality, something that's prevalent in their makeup. If ever there were a sign that takes satisfaction in beating its own drum, it would be Aquarius. There's an instant knowing that occurs when two quirky people meet—a sense that they've found a kindred spirit. It's a comfortable experience, and they'll both feel reassured when they're in the company of someone else who translates the world in the same mental way—everything will make sense.

Water Bearers are known to be overzealous about many things, including friendship, which means just as much to them when they're lovers—if not more. To them, "friends" mean something that transcends everyday romantic relationships; it's about not *needing* others, but still being there for them.

Two Aquarians may take a while to get to know each other—as Fixed signs often do—but it also might be a surprisingly short time before they're living together and acting like . . . a *couple.* Well, not exactly like a couple. They may become more like very separate roommates—perhaps even less connected than when they were dating casually—but there's such comfort here in knowing someone else sees who they are and is fine with that. It really doesn't fit into the conventional definitions of *relationship.*

The Passion Zone

Aquarians like to break the rules. They particularly love to push against standards regarding romance. Most of us think of intimacy as something ruled by the heart—not these two. For them it's a product of the mind. Foreplay for Aquarians often doesn't get much better than hot talk about the origins of the Babylonian empire. Being able to express larger concepts to someone who can actually converse *with* them is sheer ecstasy. Who cares if they ever physically touch?

What Aquarius Needs to Know about Aquarius

You need to know that you're capable of casting dark shadows onto your family, Aquarius. You can become so convinced of your ideals that you're often blinded by the impracticality of your own goals. For example, say you believe that relationships should be a partnership born of equal and shared responsibilities (you may become the voice of hope and inspiration for many people outside your family!). As you manage your campaign for equality, you may find that—for reasons of practicality—you must ask your spouse to cook, clean, watch the kids, run errands, and so on . . . all in the name of *your* work. If your partner complains, it's not beneath you to ostracize them and even become cruel in your punishment of them for impeding your grander vision of the world—even if it *is* in direct contradiction to their own situation. So, Aquarius, your shadowy side here is worth trying to shed light on.

LoveScope

The house of two Aquarians might be a huge Victorian decorated with art from Warhol, Monet, da Vinci, the Etruscans, and early *Mad* magazines. Considering who's living there, the combination makes exquisite sense. There may even be a bear rug and two nude wood nymphs made of bronze above the entrance to the foyer. It won't be a surprise if coming from upstairs is the sound of clanging pots and pans or the clucking of chickens (anything is possible in an Aquarian household). One thing that will surely be present is happiness flowing throughout this particular household. The eccentric Aquarians have found their peace with each other's brand of otherworldly existence and discovered the highest expression of their love, which could be a special combination of quantum physics and an old episode of *I Love Lucy*. Quirky? Yep. Eccentric? Of course. Love? Without a doubt.

This LoveScope rating is lower than expected because there may not be enough differences between these Aquarians to stimulate the need to rebel against a norm. There's plenty to get together and rally against in the outside world, though, so they'll need to team up and take to heart what their partners bring to their lives.

HOW TO KEEP THE AQUARIUS YOU LOVE

- Love their campaign—whatever it is.

- Challenge their ideas with proof from ground-breaking sources.

- Believe in their power to create change.

- Plan on a life that embodies the opposite of what the world embraces.

- Realize that to them foreplay is following their line of thinking.

- Be graceful when you lose arguments—and you *will* lose.

- Put things back where they belong.

- Start loving art films now.

- Know the histories of some classical composers.

- Learn their rules, which are implied but not written —they *will* have them.

Aquarius + Pisces

LoveScope: 4.6

The Basic Relationship

Just the sound of "the Fish and the Water Bearer" together seems like a match, but there are a few particulars to keep in mind. These two can work if there's inherent compatibility in their charts. Just know that Pisceans have emotional viewpoints about the world and Aquarians use their minds. Pisceans would give the shirts off their backs to a homeless person, and Aquarians would devise a plan to have factories donate all their hand-me-downs to a shelter.

There's naïveté about Pisceans that intrigues Water Bearers, who love playing just left of center—and no one is more off center than Fish. Pisceans are attracted to the strength that seems natural in Aquarians, even if it can sometimes be hurtful. Aquarians don't like the idea of jumping into the chaos of love. They want to test to see if their partners can merge with their minds. Both signs have their quirks, and that alone gives them a head start in opening the doors of trust.

The Passion Zone

This arena could go either way. Water Bearers surrender to no one unless, and until, certain tests are passed. If they like someone, they may actually do everything in their power to appear *un*interested to see if this person *really* likes them. Pisceans' capacity for understanding would allow this to go on for quite some time. They might shed a few tears of hurt, but never so intrusively as to make their partners feel guilty . . . they instinctively know that would shove them away. On the other hand, once Water Bearers feel that they have companions who don't want to own them and who support their idealistic vision, they can take their partners on a physical journey that makes the wait worthwhile. The ironic twist here is realizing *who* was actually made to wait. Aquarians will be caught off guard, but they'll be delighted by the lush and magical passion that awaits them with Fish. It's a rare and connected intensity.

What Pisces Needs to Know about Aquarius

Aquarians are very much concerned with how things look in relation to how they *pictured* them. It's the result of living with a mind where everything has its place. It may not look like it to *your* untrained eye, Pisces, but they have strategically placed that priceless vase at the perfect angle on the shelf. There's a good chance that they measured its proper distance from the wall, so if you have to look at it, do so with the utmost caution—and by all means put it back the exact way you found it.

On a more serious note, Water Bearers don't like the experience of more emotion than their minds can control, and dislike—no, *hate*—the betrayal of friendship. Aquarius is a Fixed sign, and those born under it are willing to stay in uncomfortable situations for a long time. You could become ostracized by their cold winds if they tire of picking up after your messy nature.

What Aquarius Needs to Know about Pisces

It would be easy to misunderstand the heartfelt way Pisceans gave away the savings account to the neighbors because they missed their mortgage payment. You, Aquarius, *have* boundaries, but as you'll soon learn, your Pisces doesn't. Fish are very connected to their mothers for better or worse, and you'd be wise to leave this topic alone . . . especially if you don't have anything nice to say about that connection. There is a good chance Pisceans endured some very serious mom issues, and they could use a little understanding from you here.

LoveScope

Imagine idealistic Aquarians looking into those deep, watery, Piscean eyes and recognizing the wisdom of a million years looking back at them. That's the potential here. Rebellious Aquarians meet the old-soul Pisceans, and they both see friends who can understand them after what seems like a lifetime of solitude. When self-awareness is intact, these last two signs of the Zodiac can find peace and passion with each other that's often hard to recognize in our fast-paced, hedonistic society. Pisceans are a refreshing spring of awareness to Water Bearers, and Aquarians are the brilliant magicians that Fish so love to be with.

It takes some work for them to accept that another reality can be so different from their own, but it's well worth the effort when these two misfits remember that their combined strengths are exponentially superior to their individual ones.

The relationship might *not* work, however, because Pisceans are all about compassion for the individual, whereas Aquarians concern themselves with considerations of the group. Fish will invite that homeless lady to the house, and while Aquarians might hold a swanky fund-raiser for the less fortunate, they'd never press palms with a real vagrant. See the difference? The low score on this relationship is due to the likelihood of disregard and hurt that could exist.

HOW TO LOSE THE AQUARIUS YOU LOVE

- Tell them you saw their hairstyle in last year's fashion magazine.

- Rather than having a holiday dinner at home, suggest going to an expensive restaurant.

- Compile a list of rules for living together.

- Argue that the poor just need to work harder.

- Disagree with them.

- Tell them that you love that they're not cutting-edge.

- Break their GPS.

WHAT MAKES AQUARIANS AWESOME?

- Their brilliant and inventive minds

- Their desire to help the underdog

- Their ability to wake us up to standards that need to be changed

- Their willingness to hear a different drummer

- Their visionary approach to life

- Their tenacity in holding on to what they believe to be true

Pisces + Pisces

LoveScope: 3.2

The Basic Relationship

The Pisces relationship is much like watching two drops of water sitting on a leaf, barely touching until a soft breeze pushes them together. It doesn't take much of a gust to engage these two with the greater whole, because that's what Pisceans do so well. Mutable Water signs are extremely fluid, and they bring a barrage of characteristics into a relationship. Every person Pisceans have ever been around for any length of time is still in their psyches, and that includes parents (especially their mothers), siblings, lovers, teachers, and friends. Their relationship will be the collective sum of both partners' experiences. It's never certain who's coming together in this union, but if the chemistry is there, the connection is sure to be an interesting one.

The Passion Zone

Pisceans are mergers. They become one with their partners and definitely enjoy a variety of expressions of their sexuality. Just remember that they're ruled by the sweet, spiritual Neptune and its ocean. This planet dissolves boundaries and opens others to the magic of its watery world.

As sexual partners, Pisceans are in danger of merging too completely. It isn't a problem if they're aware of their tendencies to do this, but most aren't, so by the time they *do* notice, they can't even tie their own shoes without wondering how it will affect their partners. At this point it's a little too late. Outside of these negative repercussions being thrown in their faces, there's the consolation that Pisceans have a fun "kink" factor. When two are thrown together, it might be wise for at least one to hide the latex and leather!

What Pisces Needs to Know about Pisces

Pisces, without any doubt, is the most complicated of the Zodiac signs. Your ability to be without a center can be overwhelming to most others. You often like to live without rules and function simply from instinct rather than logic. You're Mutable and can be easily influenced by those around you—often without even knowing it—and are Neptune ruled, so you may find that you have a tendency to escape into drugs, alcohol, spirituality, or television.

You're religious beings, but at your worst will hide behind a holy wall and only let in people or information that fits your chosen beliefs. There are no boundaries in your world, so you'll pick something to believe in as a container to hold you. You often have no real attachment to a specific ideal, so if you've become committed to one, you're often protecting yourself from the influences of other people. This relationship can turn into one that's filled with blame and control (depending on the nature of the other planets in your natal charts), but you have the ability to use your inherent compassion to make it work out.

LoveScope

After everything that's been said about these two, they can still have a sweet relationship built on mutual caring and understanding. Pisceans love deeply and are quite loyal to the important people in their lives. They're also sympathetic and wouldn't hurt a fly. Mix two people together of a sign that's brimming with feelings, and the outcome is a resilient and extremely compassionate couple. Sure, these friends might look like the outcasts from a circus, but neither will care. Pisceans should help their partners avoid drama, or at the very least curb the tendency to deeply feel close friends' pain without helping them find an outlet to release it. They have incredibly strong defenses and can scare the meanest bully away, but don't be fooled; inside they're humanity's biggest fans. This relationship should certainly be given a try if they fully support each other in recognizing the deeper parts of themselves . . . but it may be easier to remain friends and leave the relating to a different mix.

HOW TO KEEP THE PISCES YOU LOVE

- Don't make fun of their mother.
- Plan on feeling merged for hours at a time.
- Don't nag them about their addictions.
- Anything goes in the bedroom, so go for *anything*.
- Keep cold remedies on hand.
- Encourage them to take lots of baths to wash away others' emotions they've absorbed.
- Know that sickness is related to stress and worry.
- Don't flinch when they go from tender to treacherous. The graceful side will cycle back around.
- Expect their friends to be weirdos.
- Remember that they can handle depression better than most.

HOW TO LOSE THE PISCES YOU LOVE

- Ask them to be the designated driver.
- Make fun of their friends.
- Suggest that their thoughts don't create reality.
- Just "happen" to have on hand whatever vice they're giving up.
- Hide their antidepressant medication.

WHAT MAKES PISCEANS AWESOME?

- Their lush inner world
- Their ability to see others' hearts and completely ignore the bodies that house them
- Their compassion and depth of feeling
- Their ability to understand your emotional side
- Their simple honesty in the midst of a complex reality
- Their ability to maneuver in a culture that typically hates emotional people

Afterword

911 for Your Sign

When in Meltdown

There will come a time when each sign has a serious problem in a relationship. Maybe you've gone from a simple disagreement into a battle zone where the entire future of your love is threatened. Perhaps it started with something simple, but now it's escalated and your partner is even talking about leaving.

What should you do when you're in one of those 911 moments of love? Well, what follows is your emergency plan. Use it by looking up your own sign and choosing to change your behavior; then take full responsibility for the breakdown that's happening right now. It's just like Cher in the classic film *Moonstruck,* where she slapped Nicolas Cage across the kisser and screamed, "Snap out of it!"

You want the truth about your sign in battle? . . . Well, get ready for it!

Aries

You have to be careful here, Aries. You don't know when to stop because you become blind about winning. What you'll do is go on the campaign trail. You'll probably call everyone you know and tell them what a jerk your partner is. What you're doing is marking your territory; that's right—friends are basically being told up front whom they must side with . . . and you do this shamelessly. Again, for you it's all about winning, not about saving the relationship.

If you want it to last, you must know when to stop. Pull away and go for a walk. Don't get into your antagonistic, "Let me prove you wrong" state of mind. The biggest problem is your inability to *not* claim the win. At some point in this game, you must realize that it's more important to save what you have with your mate than be right. Do you really want to win the fight but lose your love?

Remove your energy from the battleground until you and your partner cool off. When the charged emotions pass, extend the olive branch by letting them know you've put down your weapons. Remember, you're the type who won't care what you're doing to anyone else if it means winning. If you have kids, you *must* think of them.

Taurus

If you're in a serous meltdown, you've likely dug in your heels. You've planted yourself in an immovable, fixed position and don't realize just how stubborn you appear. Most partners will threaten to leave in order to shake you up. If they do, take it seriously.

You've likely taken on the role of dictator, with a list of demands that aren't negotiable. This isn't the time to win your claims. Open the lines of communication so that you can see where the breakdown has occurred. You'll only stop this by first telling yourself that you are not in serious danger.

Let me repeat that: you are *not* in serious danger. You may feel unsafe because you think what you want isn't going to be considered. Stop now! Take a breath and make yourself say these words: "Things are not as bad as they seem."

Now, make the first move by letting your partner know that you've changed positions and are willing to hear their point of view. You can even announce, "Perhaps I've been too rigid," and your partner will faint from shock, because they know you're traditionally so adamant about coming out on top. Budge a bit, and don't forget about Hitler, who was also a Taurus. Don't be like *him*; be fluid enough to shift and patient enough to allow your mate to see that you'll wait until communication can be established again.

Gemini

You're a Twin, so two possibilities exist here: (1) you're stuck in your negative thinking, or (2) you got busted being positive . . . with someone else.

It's time for you to take some responsibility for your erratic and often-negative reasoning. You don't hear yourself, but you complain a lot, and it tends to make you sound like a victim—and that's about as attractive as when you get completely drunk.

Every now and then it's nice to spread a little cheer and add some silliness to the mix—even if it's your partner who's having the bad time. Sure, things can always be better, but *they* don't want to hear about it. They're doing what they can to keep their heads above water, too.

Also, you're not allowed to dump all these gripes at home and then go out and be Mr. or Ms. Positive with everyone else in the world. It's a known fact that you need extra stimuli, but if things are really bad at home, it's time to step up.

Be ready to take responsibility for blaming everyone else. You're good at that—now just own it.

Cancer

You have pinchers for a reason. You have the ability to change the tone of any relationship, and your partner is probably fed up because they can't take your abusive control. Cancer, you don't realize it, but you determine the mood of any and all situations. Now you're in doom-and-gloom mode, which is overbearing because you aren't getting your way and don't care who's getting tortured by your flood of emotional disappointments.

It's up to you to find your own security, pull yourself up, and let your partner know that you may have overstepped your bounds . . . and then *apologize.* You may actually know what's right for everyone, but sometimes it's best to let people find out for themselves. Also, there are moments when people just don't want to coddle you and

say nice things. The day doesn't *always* revolve around you, and having your every move watched can be invasive and bothersome.

If you're breaking down right now, zip up your needs and try to let the situation settle down without any tears or dramatic overtures. Be strong and willing to apologize, and mean what you say. There's no time to be a mom, dad, or little kid. Right now you need to be sober and honest.

Leo

Clearly, the problem is that you're self-centered and won't admit it. Your partner is letting you know that they feel invisible and unappreciated—and have likely had enough. If you're trying to defend your position, stop it. It's time to think of *them* right now, no matter how much you *think* you already do that.

You can't be trusted to stop putting yourself in the middle of every situation, so make sure you have your full attention on your mate and what they're going through. Maybe it's time to acknowledge how supportive they've been of you and quit thinking of all you've done for them. You must tell your partner you appreciate them. Stop assuming that the intentions behind everything done to you are hurtful.

There's just no getting around the fact that you're a drama king or queen, but put all your energy into making your partner feel loved today.

Virgo

Let's face it, Virgo, you've probably crossed over into the bitch zone a little too much. You've nitpicked your partner to death and gotten into that place where nothing can make you happy and everything is wrong. The more your mate did to make you feel better, the more you criticized.

Your precious alone time needs to be put on hold while you start realizing how righteous your attitude is. It's one thing to be right, but it's another to reopen the dialogue for discussion. Rather than spending your time thinking about how wrong your partner is, start using your brilliant mind to find where they've actually been supportive of you—albeit not perfectly, but caring nonetheless.

Most times you don't realize how entitled you sound. The truth is that you're probably just doing something guiltily and don't want to be caught. Telling yourself the truth is more than halfway to fixing the problem. You can keep your special room, but if you want to save this relationship, you'd better start turning down the nag and revving up the caregiver.

Libra

The community loves you, and the neighbors think you're sweet. Even your kid's teacher adores you. All that niceness unbalanced your scale, and you went home and became a little bit too mean to those closest to you. You know that you start acting ornery when you've had to be nice all day long. And yes, you don't *believe* you're upset, because you've trained everyone to put up with your tirades and to see the world the way you think it should be.

Well, you are the only sign on the Zodiac wheel whose symbol is inanimate, which means you can be icy cold—that's right . . . you can be insensitive and judgmental.

If you're having a breakdown, there's a good possibility that you're dumping your one-sided Libra judgment on your partner. You *think* you're being fair when you're just trying to be right, so stop it. It's time to recall why you love your mate in the first place. Remember, you're very skilled at seeing the good in people—start now.

Scorpio

You're paranoid and let it build up. Now you believe your own thoughts and just attacked your partner with all of them, full tilt. You remember every wrong you've ever experienced and found your

perfect opportunity to let it all come out, which is horrible. It's unfair of you to keep things pent up, and then when your partner hurts your feelings, decide that they deserve your full wrath.

You burn them good and then feel guilty and want to apologize because you realize that they didn't deserve that kind of rage. Now they're probably too hurt for that concession. You know you've gone too far and can't just repent once you've let the bomb go off.

Take a good look at this behavior and make some decisions about it. You may be able to have a sobering talk with your loved one but can't approach the conversation too remorsefully. You must sound rational.

Sagittarius

Hey, Sag, I've got news for you: there are other people in the world, and when you're in a breakdown, it's time you realize that if you gallop away, there's little chance you'll be able to come back. The problem is that you spend way too much time forgetting that there's someone else in the relationship. They have feelings and actions, too; and they might be unrelated to you. You continually forget to recognize the importance of every other life around you.

Although you mean well and would be upset to know you were actually hurting someone else, you do tend to filter life through your experience. It's hard for you to understand that some people don't know how to laugh at their plight.

Do what you're best at by bringing your magic to the relationship. Offer a spin on the problem that changes gloom to optimism and hope; only this time, you'd better speak from your heart.

Capricorn

You've clearly put your emotional wall up, as you so often do, and become a cold and calculating individual. Your partner wants you to hire someone to mow the lawn and another to paint the house, but you're too bent on believing that you know the right way to do everything. Feeling needed is what you love, but that's just a hidden form of control. It's time to realize that you've become that parent you used to hate.

Although you pride yourself on being the responsible one in the relationship, or have a reputation for being cheap that you're trying to uphold, break tradition and offer an olive branch to your partner that shows them that some rules can be forgotten. Be generous, open your heart and your wallet, and show the person you love that nothing is worth losing them.

Aquarius

Everything your partner said (or screamed) is probably true. You tend to pout and live your life in slavish devotion to rules that rival those of any dictator. It's never fair living with you. You fight for freedom around the world, but want to imprison the people in your life who don't agree with you.

Despite not believing in dictatorships, you rule with an iron fist. If you want to heal your relationship, make your lips form the words "I was wrong." And you better say it *to* your partner. Apologize even if you don't understand why you're saying you're sorry—and it would help if you wiped that smirk off your face first. You're acknowledging that other people have hearts, even if you don't feel your own.

Pisces

You're likely reading this because you've slipped into self-pity and self-abuse. You feel tortured. If it's true, what are you still doing in this relationship? You probably feel that suffering leads to salvation. Stop it!

You may have drowned yourself in "medication," which includes prescription drugs, alcohol, television, or magazines. Quit letting your partner hurt you and sniveling around, acting weak, when you're capable of incredible strength.

Own your addiction if you have one, and seek help. You're a slippery one and tend to see little problem with lying because there's truth in everything. That's actually only the case in philosophy class, but now it's your turn to give your partner something to believe in.

How to Say "I'm Sorry" to Your Partner

Aries: "I'm waving the white flag: I'm sorry."

Taurus: "I've reconsidered, and I'll trust you until I have reason not to."

Gemini: "I'm not afraid to carry my share of the responsibilities."

Cancer: "I've been selfish. You know what's best when it comes to your life and ours."

Leo: "I'm sorry I treated you like someone who's unimportant. You're very important to me."

Virgo: "You're perfect just as you are. I'll work on the complaining."

Libra: "I was being unfair and didn't show compassion."

Scorpio: "I have trust issues, but they shouldn't be your problem. I'm sorry. I'll rein in my paranoia."

Sagittarius: "I'm sorry I get too self-absorbed. Let me hear what you have to say."

Capricorn: "I've become what I didn't like as a child. I'm sorry. I have to relearn my definition of caring and am open to your input."

Aquarius: "I'm genuinely interested in your opinion and will allow it to be different from mine."

Pisces: "I'm strong, and I'll start acting like it."

Acknowledgments

I would like to thank . . .

. . . Mom and Dad—Virgo and Cancer—who fed me love and money during the dark 11th hour of writing this book. Louise Hay, Libra, whose love has supported millions and who cared enough to see me in that vast sea. Reid Tracy, Capricorn, whose guidance I trust completely. Shelley and Stacey, Leo and Gemini, the right arms of Louise and Reid, respectively, who represented the voices of reassurance when I needed to approach the altar. The Hay House Radio crew, a team of amazing people who make me laugh and sound good: Summer, Diane, Emily, Steve, Kyle, Joe, and you, too, Sonny! Jill Kramer, chief Virgo editor for Hay House and my compassionately honest voice for extensions—and *no more extensions!* Alex Freemon, Virgo, who always caught my errors (some of them egregious) and presented them to me with grace and kindness! Patrick Gabrysiak, amazingly conscientious Sagittarius copy editor—thank you! Cindy Pearlman, what a find you are! A funny, smart, sassy Aries who possesses an ability with words that I've never seen before. Kelly Crowther, Cancer, who knows how to dot *i's* and cross *t's* better than anyone I know. You were a trouper through this process, Kelly.

To the entire staff at **12Listen.com** and **12Angel.com**: I appreciate you all for unfailingly checking in on me to see how things were going and respecting my crazy cycle. The world will soon know why you're dubbed the best psychics in the world. Thomas Strapp, Libra, of Powersource kept me laughing and the Website running smoothly while I was scribing. His encouragement was priceless during my less enthusiastic days. Michael DeCamillis, Gemini, for unfailing

and guidance. Rev. Keith Ruback, Cancer, author of *Psychic Youth* (**www
.keithruback.com**). I want to be you when I grow up. James Stolzen-
bach, Taurus, the world's most brilliant graphic designer (**www.jamess
tolzenbach.com**). Jeanne, Jen, and Teila (Virgo, Virgo, Leo): love always
wins! Sahvanna, Virgo, loving author of *Sahvanna of the Light,* for flaw-
less encouragement (**www.soulsjourney.net**). Cristof Guerin, Scorpio
(**www.SpiritualHealingByCristof.com**), for keeping me energetically
tuned up (no easy feat) and ready for prosperity. Elizabeth Pendleton,
Leo (**www.elizabethpendleton.com**), for reminding me that passion
will always create. Angela Hartfield, Scorpio (**www.angelahartfield
.com**), for understanding the entire venting process and letting me
demonstrate it. Christopher Matthews, Cancer, for giving nothing
but your complete encouragement. Audra Garcia, Taurus, host of
www.12angel.com, for impeccable angelic guidance. Ethney, Scorpio,
for demonstrating the limitlessness of love; and her amazing family,
Marcos, Logan (go Long Tail Monkeys!), and Vienna.

John Joseph, Libra, who's the world's greatest astrologer and my
best friend who kept me completely sane during the entire process.
My fans (and not the kind used to blow air), who have written loving
words of encouragement and support from the very beginning. We
got our weekly show!

About the Author

A man with a lifelong interest in the inner workings of the mind, **Mark Husson** received his undergraduate degree in psychology and went on to earn his master's in counseling from West Virginia University. It wasn't until a copy of *Linda Goodman's Love Signs* fell into his hands in 1979 that it became clear to him that astrology had the potential to be the fastest and most definitive map of the psyche.

In 1982, that map became the focus of Mark's career when he moved to Denver and met Jungian astrologer John Joseph. The two opened Denver's premier astrological store, the Twelfth House, in 1989, which developed a reputation not only for its psychological approach to astrology, but also for its promotion of the ideal that spirituality is something that's guaranteed regardless of one's beliefs. Thus, the slogan "Inspiring the Human Adventure" became the store's trademark, and a mantra that Mark believes is an integral part of being a good astrologer.

Mark has developed a training program for psychic readers, teaching them advanced tools for working with people and directing themselves to focus on their own personal growth—a philosophy that has made the Twelfth House readers among the most trusted in the world.

Subsequently, Mark launched two critically acclaimed psychic hotlines, **www.12Listen.com** and **www.12Angel.com**, where he makes highly screened, trained psychics from all over the world available by phone 24 hours a day, 7 days a week.

Mark has written the weekly *Power Peek* newsletter that's sent to thousands of subscribers throughout the world since 1998, hosted his own radio show at **HayHouseRadio.com**®, and written two other books: *Mark's Power Peek 2007* and *Mark's Power Peek 2008*.

Notes

Notes

Notes

Notes

Notes

Notes

Notes

Notes

Notes

Notes

Notes

Notes

Notes

Notes

We hope you enjoyed this Hay House book. If you'd like to receive our online catalog featuring additional information on Hay House books and products, or if you'd like to find out more about the Hay Foundation, please contact:

Hay House, Inc.
P.O. Box 5100
Carlsbad, CA 92018-5100

(760) 431-7695 or **(800) 654-5126**
(760) 431-6948 (fax) or **(800) 650-5115 (fax)**
www.hayhouse.com® • **www.hayfoundation.org**

Published and distributed in Australia by: Hay House Australia Pty. Ltd., 18/36 Ralph St., Alexandria NSW 2015 • *Phone:* 612-9669-4299 *Fax:* 612-9669-4144 • www.hayhouse.com.au

Published and distributed in the United Kingdom by: Hay House UK, Ltd., 292B Kensal Rd., London W10 5BE • *Phone:* 44-20-8962-1230 *Fax:* 44-20-8962-1239 • www.hayhouse.co.uk

Published and distributed in the Republic of South Africa by: Hay House SA (Pty), Ltd., P.O. Box 990, Witkoppen 2068 • *Phone/Fax:* 27-11-467-8904 info@hayhouse.co.za • www.hayhouse.co.za

Published in India by: Hay House Publishers India, Muskaan Complex, Plot No. 3, B-2, Vasant Kunj, New Delhi 110 070 • *Phone:* 91-11-4176-1620 *Fax:* 91-11-4176-1630 • www.hayhouse.co.in

Distributed in Canada by: Raincoast, 9050 Shaughnessy St., Vancouver, B.C. V6P 6E5 • *Phone:* (604) 323-7100 • *Fax:* (604) 323-2600 • www.raincoast.com

Take Your Soul on a Vacation

Visit **www.HealYourLife.com®** to regroup, recharge, and reconnect with your own magnificence.Featuring blogs, mind-body-spirit news, and life-changing wisdom from Louise Hay and friends.

Visit **www.HealYourLife.com** today!